SENSE, NONSENSE,
and SUBJECTIVITY

SENSE, NONSENSE, and SUBJECTIVITY

MARKUS GABRIEL

HARVARD UNIVERSITY PRESS
CAMBRIDGE, MASSACHUSETTS
LONDON, ENGLAND
2024

Copyright © 2024 by the President and Fellows of Harvard College
All rights reserved
Printed in the United States of America

First printing

Library of Congress Cataloging-in-Publication Data

Names: Gabriel, Markus, 1980– author.
Title: Sense, nonsense, and subjectivity / Markus Gabriel.
Description: Cambridge, Massachusetts ; London, England : Harvard
University Press, 2024. | Includes bibliographical references and index.
Identifiers: LCCN 2023033152 | ISBN 9780674260283 (cloth)
Subjects: LCSH: Subjectivity. | Sense (Philosophy) | Meaning (Philosophy) |
Knowledge, Theory of.
Classification: LCC BD222 .G33 2024 | DDC 128—dc23/eng/20231107
LC record available at https://lccn.loc.gov/2023033152

To Wolfram Hogrebe, teacher and friend

CONTENTS

Introduction	1
1 Sense	10
Part One: Extending Sense	22
Part Two: Restricting Sense	66
2 Nonsense	84
3 Subjectivity	141
Part One: Subjectivity and Fallibility	148
Part Two: Subjectivity's Place in Nature	175
Part Three: Practical Subjectivity	194
Conclusion	208

Notes *221*
Acknowledgments *271*
Index *273*

SENSE, NONSENSE,
and SUBJECTIVITY

INTRODUCTION

WE ARE SUBJECTS who make knowledge claims. Some of our knowledge claims are successful, others fail. Successful knowledge claims amount to knowledge. In the context of philosophy, where accounts of the structure and scope of knowledge have been formulated for millennia, theories of truth and justification have enabled us to understand how subjects can be in epistemic touch with how things are in the subjects' environment, often called "the external world." These theories thus guide us toward building blocks in the architecture of the good case of knowledge.

While theories of truth, justification, and knowledge as the maximal epistemic achievements abound, negative epistemological phenomena, such as ignorance, delusion, mistakes, confusions, incoherence, and false thought, are much less studied. Yet on closer inspection, they turn out to be inextricably linked to our status as subjects capable of making knowledge claims. Hence, we need a theory of false thought that is anchored in an account of how both true and false thought, knowledge and its variegated counterparts, can be implemented in the actual reality of the socially orchestrated, embodied practices through which we, specifically minded animals, produce objective, shareable knowledge under fallible conditions. In a nutshell, we need to understand the nature of being wrong. Such is the project of the book you are about to read.

SENSE, NONSENSE, AND SUBJECTIVITY

As Aristotle pointed out at the very beginning of his *Metaphysics,* humans are constitutively interested in knowledge. We desire to know.[1] What followed this declaration was his own account of different forms of knowing. The most important form of knowing is what he—like his teacher Plato—called "science" (ἐπιστήμη), which must not be confused with the now popular, yet wrongheaded idea that the scientific methods definitive of the natural sciences are the only ultimate guide to truth and reality.

"Knowledge" or "science," as Plato and Aristotle rightly thought, are titles for our maximal epistemic achievement. They are results of knowledge claims, made and shared by humans, who transcend their mere opinions (δόξαι) concerning how things are by successfully being in contact with a reality largely not of their own making.

Aristotle and Plato realized early on that in successful knowledge claims thought and being seem to merge. What connects thought and being in the achievement of knowledge is a particular form of justification or accountability (a λόγος, as our philosophical ancestors put it). To make a long story short, knowledge or science (ἐπιστήμη) amounts to non-accidentally justified true belief, where a belief is a "taking something to be true" (a δόξα, which comes from δέχεσθαι, to take), and non-accidental justification is what relates the knowing subject to the facts, the truths, it desires to know.[2]

In that sense, knowledge is simple—which does not mean conceptually unanalyzable. It unifies a subject with a largely mind-independent reality at which the subject directs its intention in its desire to know how things are. In light of this line of thought, then, the paradigm of knowledge throughout the centuries became propositional knowledge of the form "*S* knows that *p.*" Here *p* refers to a true proposition, or a fact, while "knows" refers to the subject's non-accidentally justified taking something to be true.

However, as simple and familiar as all of this sounds (at least to contemporary epistemologists, who focus on analyzing the elements of propositional knowledge), the *subject (S)* who makes a knowledge claim, which can both go right (and amount to knowledge) or fail (and amount to some form of not-knowing) is usually left out of the equation. If knowledge is non-accidentally justified true belief, then who is the subject of a knowledge *claim,* and how is the success case of knowledge related to its fallible bearer?

INTRODUCTION

The following investigation positions itself in this blind spot of contemporary epistemology by bringing in a largely forgotten element of the philosophical tradition. While knowledge and truth are simple in the sense that we are familiar with their basic analysis, their counterparts, ignorance, falsity, and their ilk, are mostly ignored. This is ever more striking in a sociopolitical situation in which ignorance, denialism of facts, fake news, digital systems of manipulation, social media, ideology, propaganda, science fiction, conspiracy theories, mythmaking, uncertainty, false judgment, and all sorts of illusion and delusion haunt the public sphere.

To be sure, recently there has been much prominent philosophical and sociological writing on epistemic vices, denialism, ideology, propaganda, agnotology, manipulation, and the post-truth era in politics.[3] And, of course, psychology, behavioral economics, neuroscience, and philosophy have studied illusions, delusions, hallucinations, biases, noise, and other fundamental flaws in thinking, judging, and acting. However, what is still missing is conceptual insight into the connection between the multicolored modes of *being* wrong (the ontology of confusion, mistakes, falsity, etc.) and the theory of embodied, subjective thought without which we cannot fully understand the subject of fallible knowledge claims.[4]

Plato himself put the problem of falsity and error center stage, both in his thinking about knowledge in the *Theaetetus* and in his ontology in the *Sophist,* by wondering how being wrong (ψεῦδος) is possible. For him, the problem of falsity and not-being (μὴ ὄν) are connected, because he realized that our capacity for false thought is tied to the fact that we do not necessarily get reality or being right. While knowledge is a paradigmatic way of getting reality right, making a knowledge claim presupposes the intelligibility of getting it wrong. Getting it right, thus, cannot be a fusion of thinking and being that just happens to take place. Otherwise, we could not think of the successful case of knowing as an achievement. It would be a mere mental event over whose success we have no control and, thus, incompatible with the idea of a *logos* or a method that binds thought and being together, holding us accountable for our strongly held beliefs.

The mental state of knowing is immune to rational revision: it is not fallible. But this does not mean that knowers are generally capable of making successful knowledge claims by way of inspecting their reasons for holding the successful belief. Getting it right leaves room for a possible (second-order) doubt concerning one's mental state, even in cases where

3

it constitutes knowledge. Being wrong, on the other hand, is compatible with a dogmatic attitude: one can be simultaneously wrong and entirely certain that one not only got it right but secured one's knowledge claim by way of the best available method at a given moment in one's epistemic life.[5]

Since the origins of epistemology and ontology, truth, knowledge, and being have become better understood. There has been significant progress in the theory of propositional truth, which has resulted in impressive formal and technical feats that transcend the realm of academic knowledge production. Artificial intelligence is but the latest articulation of our insight into the architecture of logically controlled successful thought and knowledge acquisition.

Remarkably, however, what is missing is an equally sophisticated philosophical account of falsity, ignorance, and other epistemic shortcomings. This book tries to close the gap by offering elements of a theory of false thought. I will argue that the theory of false thought is part and parcel of the theory of subjectivity, i.e., of a systematic answer to the question of who the S is in the formulation of a knowledge claim that connects someone with the facts they desire to know.

Just as the theory of knowledge (epistemology) goes hand in hand with an associated account of truth, the theory of ignorance (agnotology) is inextricably bound to a theory of falsity or being wrong. In this context, I distinguish between *mere falsity* and *being wrong*. Mere falsity is just the counterpart of truth, i.e., not-truth. If we think of truth and falsity as properties of propositions (which is only part of the truth about truth and falsity, as we will see in due course), it is straightforward (though not very informative) to define falsity simply as not-truth. Depending on one's more specific theory of truth, not-truth would, for instance, amount to non-correspondence of sentence and fact, of mind and reality; a form of incoherence; of irresolvable dissent; or just a negation sign in front of a regimented proposition stipulated to be true.[6] Yet, this does not clarify what it is for someone to be wrong. It misses the positive kernel of negative epistemological phenomena, as I call the modes of being wrong.

The positive kernel of negative epistemological phenomena is itself a form of being. The ineliminable subjective factor in the realm of knowledge claims bestows a solidity upon mistakes. Given that subjects desire to know and make knowledge claims, they are in particular states when they fail in their attempt to get hold of details in their largely mind-

INTRODUCTION

independent environment. But these failures are certainly not unreal, let alone inconsequential. Getting it right or being wrong are often matters of survival, which is one of the reasons why we value knowledge as the good case.

The theory of false thought, of being wrong, and of subjectivity I offer with this book is embedded in a larger theoretical framework from which I derive the methods deployed in what follows. For some years now, I have been calling this framework *the ontology of fields of sense,* or FOS for short.[7] FOS's basic tenet is that to exist is to appear in a *field of sense* (a fos, as I will say for short). We never deal with isolated objects, but always only with objects that are parts of a context or a larger domain. To exist, then, is to be in a domain (or multiple domains), to stand out (as the etymology of existence, ek-sistere, suggests) among other objects. Material objects exist as parts of the universe, whereas numbers exist as parts of mathematical structures that are by their very nature non-material. Other objects, such as fictional or imaginary objects, exist in domains or fields of sense that depend for their existence on mental acts. In short, FOS sets out from the thought that there is a plurality of fields of sense, which amount to a form of strong ontological pluralism whose outlines I will reconstruct in Chapter 1 with a focus on the role of sense in the constitution of reality.

If "reality" is our preliminary name for the domain to which our thought is directed when we make knowledge claims (a domain ipso facto containing knowledge claims), one can read the basic tenet of FOS as supporting the claim that in knowing and failing to know, we do not produce or make sense of a senseless reality. If anything, when we enter the existential and epistemic scene, we find sense that is already there. In short, we grasp sense, an idea encapsulated in the (largely dead) metaphor of a con-cept ("con-cipere" means grasping together).

The last major figure in the history of logics and epistemology who put his finger on the haptic dimension of knowing as a kind of contact was Gottlob Frege, to whom we owe the modern conception of sense as a mode of presentation of objects.[8] In Frege's wake, the following pages first argue for and then rely on a form of *realism about sense* that is part of the contemporary philosophical landscape of New Realism.[9] Frege thought that thinking was a way of grasping a sense. Yet, he never clarified the sense in which thinking could be a thinker's activity, as he feared that bringing the subject into the picture would undermine the objectivity of knowledge. He

SENSE, NONSENSE, AND SUBJECTIVITY

was wrong about that. In contradistinction to Frege's own realism about sense and his account of the objectivity of thought, I will argue that our only way to understand falsity is by way of a theory of being wrong. Through being wrong we recognize the signature of the subject in logical space. False thought and subjectivity are, therefore, part of our road to reality.[10]

Again, we can motivate interest in the phenomenon of being wrong by harking back to a moment in Plato's original articulation of the very stage-setting of epistemology and ontology. In a famous simile in the *Theaetetus,* he compares a knowledge claim with someone's attempt to get hold of the right kind of bird in an aviary.

> Because it's possible not to have one's knowledge of that thing, but to have some other piece of knowledge instead of it. That happens when, in trying to catch some piece of knowledge or other, among those that are flying about, one misses, and gets hold of the one instead of the other. It's then that one thinks eleven is twelve, having got hold of the knowledge of eleven that's in one, instead of the knowledge of twelve, as one might get hold of a dove instead of a pigeon.[11]

In our analogy, the right kind of bird (in Plato's simile the pigeon) would be a true thought whereas the wrong kind of bird (a dove) would be a false thought. The position of the subject is one where we are trying to grasp a moving target in a dynamic environment of which we ourselves are a part, in the shape of minded animals.

Throughout the book, I will argue for a *subjectivity assumption,* which has it that to be someone, to be a subject, is to be wrong about something. Getting anything successfully into epistemic view at all can only be realized under conditions of being wrong somewhere in our belief system. To be a fallible thinker means being subject to a constitutive and often wide-ranging ignorance as to which of our beliefs are actually true and which false. To be a subject is to be wrong about some things without ever being in a position to settle once and for all which of our beliefs are non-accidentally true (and thereby constitute knowledge). For this reason, even our factive (epistemically successfully) mental states (paradigmatically knowledge) are embedded in the dynamic unfolding of mental reality

INTRODUCTION

in such a way that they are integrated into our web of beliefs and therefore, in one way or another, tied to false beliefs without the subject ever being in a position to isolate the good cases from the bad ones.

This thesis borders on the obvious if we look at our entire "web of belief," as the saying goes. Yet, in what follows, I will defend a stronger claim according to which there is never a fully isolated episode of a completely individuated subject who simply grasps p and non-accidentally believes it, such that she knows that p on the basis of her utterly clear grasp of p. If we look at the actual implementation of the knowledge claim in the subject's life, we will soon see that her overall justification for the knowledge claim at some point falls short of knowledge. This does not mean that she does not know what she knows, but that her actually implemented mental state is embedded in the confused, temporal, non-propositional and nonsensical field structure to which she, as a real subject, belongs.

Who we are as subjects is thus best characterized in view of the limits of our current individual and shared objective knowledge. Our actual overall mental states are thus fundamentally *confused,* consisting of both true and false thoughts. This does not mean that we do not or even cannot get it right: fallibilism is not a form of skepticism according to which knowledge is impossible due to some subjective factor or other. Rather, fallibilism is an indispensable element in any realistic conception of knowledge acquisition. It belongs to the realm of heuristics, the theory of which would be irresponsibly incomplete if we forgot to provide a reflexive understanding of ourselves as subjects of knowledge claims.

The fallibilistic theory of subjectivity I will offer differs both from infallibilism about knowledge and from skepticism. Infallibilism about knowledge rightly results from the idea that knowledge is our concept of the success case of knowledge claims. To know something is to get it right for the right reasons (i.e., non-accidentally). If a subject actually gets reality right, it does not make sense to think of this particular mental state as potentially wrong. Having said that, the subject's knowledge would not count as an achievement had it not been possible for the subject to get it wrong. This brings in the concept of a fallible knowledge claim that conceptually precedes that of knowledge as the paradigmatically epistemic success case. The bearer of fallibility, in this context, is not the knowledge nor the knowledge claim, but rather the subject whose activity of knowledge acquisition unfolds as part of its mental life. As soon as we think of

7

knowledge and knowledge claims as parts of broader mental lives of subjects, we get the reality of being wrong into view. This does not play into the skeptic's hands. Skepticism in the sense of a set of arguments and paradoxes designed to demonstrate that knowledge is impossible due to some shortcoming or other in the nature of justification cannot be motivated on the basis of the very idea of fallibility alone.[12]

The specific claim about fallibility that runs like a thread through the following investigation is the notion that subjectivity is part of specifically minded animals. In the case of animals capable of explicit knowledge claims that can amount to knowledge, we are dealing with human animals.[13] The mental lives of the animals we are unfolds in the form of subjective consciousness. In the following chapters, the issue of consciousness will be reconstructed in terms of a realist ontology of both sense and nonsense, rather than as a confused topic at the interface of psychology, neuroscience, and speculative (meta-)physics. This leads, by way of the account of being wrong, to a contribution to a fundamental topic in the philosophy of mind at the intersection of ontology and epistemology, i.e., consciousness and its relation to self-consciousness.

Centering on *realism about sense,* Chapter 1 argues that it is a mistake to think of reality as sense-, thought-, and meaningless. No metaphysical or ontological priority should be assigned to a "world without spectators" that existed for eons before the evolution of knowing and acting subjects with a capacity to make their own sensemaking explicit in an otherwise meaningless "cosmic exile."[14]

Chapter 2 focuses on *ontological nonsense.* Ontological nonsense is a form of field confusion that paradigmatically manifests itself in the form of consciousness as an objectively existing illusion. The issue of nonsense will be distinguished from discussions of mere meaninglessness in the wake of Carnap's, Wittgenstein's, and more recent attempts to clarify the relationship between linguistically and semantically meaningful utterances, sentences, propositions, and thoughts.

The temporal unfolding of reality and our subjective, indexical position in this evolution cannot be reduced to our propositional standing as knowers of atemporal, structural facts in which clear-cut objects are embedded. Chapter 2 takes seriously the grounding of propositional thought (governed by parameters of sense) in non-propositional activity and offers

INTRODUCTION

an account of nonsense, confusion, illusion, and mistakes that does not see them from the standpoint of our successful grasp of objects.

Ontological nonsense (which differs from semantic meaninglessness) serves as a mode of accessing the subject's reality, its subjecthood, which is the theme of Chapter 3. This chapter advances a theory of subjectivity as a site of confusion. Nonsense is thereby relegated from the realm of alleged category mistakes or semantic illusion to an ontological category in its own right, one that accounts for the real presence of subjects among their objects. In this way, the subject-object distinction remains a functional device for articulating a theory without succumbing to the temptation of inflating subject and object into a metaphysical dualism of two entities.[15]

Chapter 3 rejects the idea that the core topic of a theory of subjectivity is formed by the subject's or self's reflexive incorrigibility or otherwise epistemically privileged position. Being someone, a particular subject or individual thinker, is to be wrong about indefinitely many things, including facts in which a given object of knowledge is embedded. To know something or to know that something is the case need not involve a complete grasp of the object or the fact in question. Our knowledge claims are and remain fallible due to their integration into our life-form as subjects.

Therefore, the right topic of a theory of subjectivity is not the stunningly empty self-reference of self-consciousness, whereby we seemingly come to grasp our own mere existence as thinkers. On the contrary, the relevant fact about ourselves that accounts for our subjectivity is the highly heterogenous reality of being wrong.

I

SENSE

WE ARE SUBJECTS. Among other things, this means that we experience reality from a shifting perspective or point of view in virtue of being grounded in its temporal unfolding. We are thereby in contact with a reality that in some way or other always differs from the way in which we represent it. This feature, subjectivity, is not limited to conscious visual perception, whose line of sight can be embedded in perspectival models so that we are able to distinguish between the form of our representation and the reality we are able to grasp through and in it.[1] Objects whose properties we process in sense modalities other than sight are equally presented to us from the "human standpoint,"[2] as Immanuel Kant famously put it. Sounds indicate the location and other properties of a source at a distance from us and the chemical senses (smell and taste) do not only inform us opaquely about the chemical properties of objects with which we are in touch. Rather, we like or dislike a taste and a smell, and they present us with features of reality.

Through perception, subjects learn something about both their environment and their position within it. Each sense modality presents objects that are embedded in a larger state of affairs as being a certain way. Insofar as these objects appear to us, they radiate sense as modes of presentation or senses.[3] The notion of senses as ways for objects to be in relation both to subjects and to other objects will be the focus of this chapter.

For objects to radiate senses is for them to be the way they appear to us in our perceptual and epistemic dealings with them. Against this background, just as Frege (to whom we owe the notion of senses as modes of presentation of objects) reminded us, we should not reduce senses as modes of presentation of objects to subjective states that block the objects themselves from sight. They are not merely psychological vehicles of acquaintance with our own subjective states, but modes of being in touch with how things really are. I will call those *objective senses*.

In this chapter I will introduce some of the main concepts of what I call *the ontology of fields of sense,* or FOS for short, with a focus on the role of sense and the senses as modes of grasping reality that are themselves part of it. In this context, I will argue for a type of *realism about sense* according to which *senses* are properties of the things themselves or ways for things to be:[4] objects are presented as being such and so, they never merely are *tout court.*

Having said that, the realm of senses is not exhausted by objective senses. There are also *subjective senses,* by which I mean senses that constitutively involve a subject. As will be argued throughout the book, a subject is a fallible knower, someone whose epistemic capacities (from low-level non-conscious sensory registration to the highest level of self-knowledge) at some point or other always fall short of getting it right. A subject is someone who is wrong about something—even in a scenario where it gets something as right as can be. In Chapter 3 I will flesh this out in terms of a theory of subjectivity according to which fallible thinkers, i.e., subjects of knowledge claims, are constitutively wrong about some things even in scenarios where they get something right. For subjects of knowledge claims grasping reality means being in fallible contact with how things are.

To substantiate these claims, I will set out from the observation that we do not and cannot know of a senseless reality, that is to say, a reality that would not be a certain way that is presentable to thinkers.[5] For the time being, let a "thinker" just be someone who grasps reality.

A *sense modality* is a way of being in fallible contact with reality, and the most general name for such a contact is thinking, i.e., grasping how

SENSE, NONSENSE, AND SUBJECTIVITY

things are in terms of their being a certain way.[6] In light of these elementary considerations, I assume that senses as modes of presentations of objects and ways for them to be are not merely "out there," at least not in general. They are as much "in here," i.e., where we are located as thinkers, as they are "out there," beyond our skin or whatever the outmost surface of our animal bodies might turn out to be. For this reason, in what follows, I will be drawing on a unified conception of sense that embraces both *objective* (strictly speaking Fregean) sense and *subjective* sense, i.e., sense modalities that are tied to the presence of embodied thinkers to whom objects are presented in a certain way. Sense and the senses are intertwined. Subjective sense is sense processed by subjects in such a way that we need to understand the subject's contribution to its content in order to grasp the sense. Objective sense is sense for which this is not the case.

The fact that objects are presented to us from a point of view does not mean that they are exclusively perceived by the senses narrowly construed. Presentation does not only kick in at a level of reality where straightforwardly causal stimuli are non-consciously or consciously processed by certain animals, such as humans. Rather, objects in themselves are the way they are presented to us, which means that their modes of presentation cannot be merely "subjective" projections that come into existence through non-conscious or conscious representation.

We are the paradigmatically thinking animals in that we are capable of grasping our own thought processes and of articulating theories about it. We thereby make senses explicit, many of which are already there regardless of our theoretical activity of grasping them as such in a variety of registers (in linguistic, mathematical, psychological, and other codes). Our involvement in the presentation of reality cannot be reduced to the facticity of our sensory registration in it. Due to the omnipresence of sense, sensory registration cannot be a merely causal affair. In order for it to be a kind of registration of anything at all, objective sense has to be operative on the level at which the actual registration takes place.

Mathematical senses are modes through which the kinds of structures tracked by mathematical thinking are presented to us. Frege's original insight to postulate senses in order to solve the identity riddle ("how can identity statements be both informative and non-contradictory?") is therefore still essential for the notion of sense: To realize that $\cos^2(\varphi) + \sin^2(\varphi) = 1$ is to think of a particular sum as equal to 1 such that we can always replace "1" by the sum and thereby hope to make progress in mathematics. There are transfinitely many ways of thinking of 1, one of them being "$\cos^2(\varphi) + \sin^2(\varphi)$." This thought does not mention subjects who process it, either explicitly or implicitly; its sense is, thus, objective.

In the following examination of the realm of sense, sense should not be misconstrued as the sum total of all senses whose mode of presentation of an object does not mention or implicate subjects, as Frege thought. Not all sense is objective in that respect. On this front, Frege partly got sense wrong. He overgeneralized on his insight into the objectivity of mathematical sense, which led him to postulate a purely subjective realm of representations (*Vorstellungen*) without recognizing that the subjective is part of the content of a type of objective thought directed at it—for instance, in the scientific modes of psychology, sociology, neuroscience, and biology. Moreover, the humanities and social sciences deal with subjective thought or subjectivity, as I will generally say, without thereby somehow being less objective in their epistemic purport. Hence, there is a need to extend sense first beyond the subject and then to reintegrate our conception of ourselves as subjects into an account of reality that does not somehow repel us.

As Tyler Burge's has shown in his seminal book *Origins of Objectivity*, scientific investigation into the nature of perception has clearly demonstrated that reality is presented to us on lower levels of organization in the form of tracking relations to our environment that we do not consciously process.[7] Though non-conscious to a large extent, these modes of presentation are senses too, which is why we can model them in the empirical disciplines dealing with the neurophysiological, psychological, and cognitive details of how we maintain relations with objects in our environment.

We do not merely represent objects in perception, but we represent them as being a certain way, as round, loud, salty, and so forth. It is an old chestnut of the philosophy of perception that we represent things *as* being such and so, a feature that is present already in non-conscious processes that significantly contribute to the overall mental state we find ourselves in at higher layers of conscious reflection. To think of sense as objective should not, therefore, mislead us into imbuing reality with consciousness. Panpsychism—the view that everything is conscious or at least proto-conscious (whatever that means)—is just the type of mistake that occurs when we confuse objective sense with the subjective dimension of sensing and conflate the latter with consciousness or proto-consciousness (whatever that would mean). The fact that reality is thinkable does not mean that it is quite literally waiting to be discovered by self-conscious scientific thinkers who become aware of themselves as conscious.

In the context of theories of perception, the concept of representational content has been forged in order to cover the different cases from low-level sensation to highest-level reflection. What they share is the fact that reality is presented to someone in a particular manner. Usually, we are capable of distinguishing the mode of presentation of features of our environment from that very environment. To the extent to which this is the case for a given representational system, we are justified in attributing *objectivity* to it. So, again, neither does objectivity preclude the presence of subjects nor does the presence of subjects undermine their contact with objective sense.

Starting from this entrenched and broadly correct line of thinking about perception and sensation can be potentially deceptive, though. It easily misleads one into believing that reality first and foremost (or even exclusively) consists of objective structures composed of (mind-independent) objects, such that our non-conscious and conscious representational devices ought to be measured against some associated normative standard of veridicality or other.[8] Following through with this kind of argumentation typically results in more or less sophisticated versions of a correspondence theory of truth according to which some subjective device of representation (be it a mental state, a sentence of a natural language, or what have you) represents an objective structure as being a certain way. If the representation matches the objective structure, it counts as successful, such that we are entitled to attribute truth to it; otherwise, the representation counts at most as a merely subjective state. My account of *realism about sense* here rejects this aspect of the representationalist paradigm and articulates a "contact theory" of a subject's embodied knowledge in a sense similar to that recently proposed by Hubert Dreyfus and Charles Taylor in their *Retrieving Realism*.[9]

In general, *senses* are modes of presentations of objects. The presentations are at the same time properties of the objects, even when they are misleading. Appearances can *be* deceptive. The objects present themselves as being a certain way. Some senses are correlational in that they essentially involve a subject. For instance, perceptual senses are ontological looks essentially correlated with a subject that grasps them in a particular way.[10] This overall idea of senses entails neither that all senses nor that all objects are somehow mind-dependent. We are perfectly able to understand that some objects are mind-independent in a fairly undemanding way: They would have been as we take them to be in true thought, even if we had never directed our thought at them. It takes heavy-duty philosophical argumentation to disprove this basic realist direction of thought.

Thus, we ought to have a grip on the very idea of mind-independent and thereby objective senses without confusing objectivity with mind-independence, for the way in which we think about an object, and the way in which it is presented to perception, thought and intentionality more generally, need not include us as specifically minded animals. Perceiving something as being thus and so or thinking of something as being thus and so need not contain any hint that the object's being the way we rightly take it to be depends on us as specifically minded animals.

In light of this elementary consideration familiar from the Fregean tradition of thinking about senses as modes of presentation, the idea of ontological looks can serve to illustrate the idea that senses are manifest at the *interface* of subject and object.[11] Here, "interface" refers to the line or plane of contact that is generated by the causal interference patterns brought about by the encounter of subject (more on that notion later) and object. An interface precisely need not be subjective. Other than in Hilary Putnam's Dewey Lectures on "Sense, Nonsense, and the Senses," the idea of a line of contact between the subjective and the objective dimensions of sense does not commit one to "a picture that imposes an interface between ourselves and the world."[12]

The fact that a certain object or entire scene looks a certain way when perceived from a certain literal perspective (i.e., appears to a subject) is not just a fact about us, but in varying degrees about the objects that make up the scene. We can think of our position in a perceptual scene as occupying a slot in a relation such that the way the objects look when perceived is there in advance, ready for us to grasp as a sense. The advantage of such a picture of perception is that it allows us not always to construe the subject's contribution to the scene as a distortion of a reality. We turn the already existing relation into an actual correlation by perceiving

SENSE, NONSENSE, AND SUBJECTIVITY

the object.[13] The fact that it has been perceived by S at a given point in space and time is from this point onwards a feature of the object itself that leaves a (usually quite minimal) causal trace in the object. A perceiving, thinking subject is essentially part of any real situation of which we can be conscious and make true or false judgments, and is hence also an object of true or false thought.[14]

While the full content of the perceptual case is always to some extent affected by the specific causal and mental contributions of the perceiver, as she fills in the position of one of the relata, this does not generalize to all forms of intentionality. That $e^{\ln(10)} = 10$ does not bear the mark of subjectivity, and yet it provides a thinker with a relation between two modes of presentation of a mathematical object. That mathematical object can be thought of as the number ten, which in turn can be thought of in transfinitely many different ways. The mathematical object broadcasts objective senses.

In this chapter, I will argue that senses (regardless of whether their content is entirely objective or, in part, subjective) generally are grasped and not produced in virtue of the grasping. This is the thrust of *realism about sense*. Objects broadcast senses; reality is manifest without further ado.[15] Its manifestation includes subjects. Subjects are legitimate parts of reality too; they are as real as it gets without having to be reduced to a layer of non-subjective, non-mental objects (such as neuronal cells or their causal organization). Reducing subjects to an allegedly senseless layer of reality is a form of confusion: it fuses subjects with something they are not and, thus, fails to recognize their presence at a relevant level of reality, namely the one they inhabit. To think of reality as senseless, and of subjective thought as merely subjective representation of an otherwise mind-independent reality, is to be mistaken about subjectivity. Chapters 2 and 3 will deal with this type of reflexive mistake concerning our own status as subjective thinkers who make fallible knowledge claims about reality.

In this context, *reality* is our concept for that to which thought is answerable and therefore, on closer inspection, includes our self-conception as fallible thinkers. That to which thought is answerable without ever being in a position to fully guarantee its epistemic and practical success merely in virtue of directing itself to its target domain is also that which can frustrate thought's objective purport.[16]

SENSE

Thinking about senses as generally produced or even (mentally, neuronally, socially, linguistically, etc.) constructed is a form of being wrong. It confuses senses with our own presence in reality. Here is a particularly intriguing instance of subjectivity. Constructivism about sense is a form of delusion of grandeur that leads to a nihilistic predicament when the subject realizes that as soon as one turns away from reality, it ceases to make sense.

The reality of senses is fundamental. There is no senseless bottom line of meaningless reality—such as a spatiotemporal smear of elementary particles. Reality does not reduce to a bunch of vector fields in n-dimensional spaces with a certain metric, say, whose mathematical architecture represents the behavior of objective, non-mental stuff. Sense is not only prior in the *mental* order of accessing how things are but also prior in the *ontological* order. There is no layer of reality that is metaphysically deeper than sense, which is not to say at all that reality is mind-dependent or that physics does not discover how things would have been, had there been no minds. On the contrary, physics' privileged code of access to the universe is fundamentally mathematical because mathematics is an investigation into far-reaching (at least transfinite) sense-architectures. Physical structures are a subset of mathematical structures, which is why it is utterly misguided to try to divorce the universe from sense and think of it in terms of brutal materiality impinging on our detectors, as it were.

Sense does not exclusively arise at the causal interface of subject and object but also regulates object-object relations. While the subject-object relation must not become the paradigm of ontology (which is the mistake critiqued by Quentin Meillassoux as "correlationism"[17] in the contemporary European debate on realism), the subject-object interface remains part of any respectable epistemological paradigm.[18] Knowing how things are centrally involves our being in touch with a reality not entirely of our own making. At the same time, we cannot account for knowledge without invoking subjectivity.

This runs counter to contemporary philosophical and scientific common sense. Senses are widely regarded as linguistic or mental entities. Extending senses beyond the linguistic, semantic, and mental realms where they seem to have their proper home will therefore strike many as heterodox. It is much easier to convince people that reality (or the world, as it were) is furnished with mind-independent objects that at most

SENSE, NONSENSE, AND SUBJECTIVITY

exhibit lawlike patterns of regularity that can be unearthed by natural-scientific knowledge acquisition than to persuade them that reality as such is manifest to thinkers like us without further ado.

I reject this naturalistic starting point and find that the very distinction between (mind-independent) reality and senses is flawed from the get-go. Just consider that senses have to be part of reality even if we relegate them to the realm of the mental or the linguistic. Mind and language are as real as it gets. Thus, opposing reality and sense falls short of the relevant fact, namely that reality cannot lie on the other side of a metaphysical border neatly separating mind and world.[19] Such an opposition of reality and sense only looks attractive if we wrongly assume that to be real (or even to be) means to be mind-, language-, and theory-independent.

The notion that reality repels senses is a flawed starting point for our philosophical account of how we are able to understand and explain anything at all. The relevant basic grip on reality constitutive of any more or less demanding epistemic attitude (from mere intentional, non-conscious aboutness to higher-level knowledge claims concerning knowledge) cannot be taken into account unless we think of our attitudes as real along the same lines as their target systems. Here, to be real just means to exist, i.e., to appear in a field of sense.[20] A *field of sense* (fos) is a domain of objects such that its population is defined by rules of inclusion and exclusion. These rules of inclusion and exclusion (what can belong to the domain and what cannot) are the senses of the field in question. This is the basic tenet of my work on fos, which this chapter carries further by focusing on sense and the senses as modes of presentation.

The notion that to be or to be real is to appear in a fos can easily be brought into view by the following consideration, which will be a thread running through the entire book. We are evidently capable of knowing that some objects are thus and so regardless of our specific, individual taking them to be thus and so. Thus, we are in possession of a straightforward notion of objective thought, where *objective thought* is thought directed at things being thus and so regardless of our taking them to be thus and so.[21] Thought that is subject to a "contrast of objectivity" between taking something to be true and it actually being the case, is all it takes for thought to be objective.[22] What the thought is about, its object(s), is always part of a context within which we can make sense of the object in contradistinction to some other object(s) in the same field. Objects do not present them-

18

SENSE

selves to us as absolutes, as isolated from all other objects, as this would, among other things, make it impossible for us to relate to them. Both the objects and the fields within which they appear (their fos) are real.

Objective thought is thought about objects that need not provide an account of itself. Successfully thinking that the moon is currently at such and such a distance from the earth does not essentially involve thought thinking itself, but successful thinking about objective thought surely does. Drawing a distinction between objective thought qua thought dealing with objects without dealing with itself on the one hand and thought thinking itself on the other presupposes a different kind of objectivity.[23] Its objectivity cannot be understood in terms of thought's directedness at mind-independent objects. Thinking about thought's engagement with reality therefore significantly affects our account of reality. On closer inspection, it obliges us to accept the full-blown reality of thought and to reject any worldview according to which mind-, thought- and language-independence are the mark of the real. We cannot even formulate the very idea of reality as mind-independent without thereby providing an account of our own relation to reality and, thus, of minds as part of what there is.

The idea that some fos are mind-dependent in the straightforward sense of essentially involving subjects (their minds, languages, consciousness, and social practices) is not designed to motivate any form of idealism. Being and thought are not one and the same, not even on the level of thought thinking itself, as I will argue in the pages dedicated to theories of subjectivity. We have no reason to believe that thought thinking itself is a paradigmatic example of an epistemic attitude that necessarily gets it right. The fact that there really are senses such that some of them are objective in a way yet to be explored ought not to mislead one into believing that reality as a whole is somehow encompassed by thought or "mysteriously trimmed"[24] to be graspable by thinkers like us.

If mind-independent objects qua target systems of first-order objective thought are real, then thought thinking itself is equally real at least in virtue of occupying the position of being its own target system. The status of being real is not conferred on objects in virtue of their mind-independence. Mind-independence (however one wields this ultimately problematic notion) is not the hallmark of reality. This is one of the starting points of contemporary renewals of realism under the banner of New Realism.[25]

SENSE, NONSENSE, AND SUBJECTIVITY

The chapter is divided into two parts. In the first part, I will bring my conception of realism about senses into conversation with similar approaches in contemporary Anglophone philosophy. It is not a coincidence that many of them draw either on Gottlob Frege's or on Edmund Husserl's conception of senses as real in the specific sense of non-psychological. However, both Frege and Husserl remain impressed by the existence of mind-independent objects and surprisingly grant them a privileged place in explaining the subjective sphere. In both Frege and Husserl, the existence of objects poses a challenge to their concept of senses—for Frege, because he does not want to think of senses (concepts) as objects; for Husserl, because he thinks of objects as potentially occluded by our access to them in such a way that the access conditions have to be clarified in order to achieve a transparent view of objects from a subject's overall ("transcendental") point of view. In my engagement with proponents of views adjacent to realism about senses, I will argue that they are still too mired in a problematic conception of reality as paradigmatically populated by mind-independent objects after all, thus still opposing the themes of mind and world, as if the mind were not always already part of reality.

I will work out how we ought to think of senses as extended in a way similar to the much-discussed extension of the mind into an organism's environment. What is extended, though, are not mental, subjective states, but rather the realm of senses of which subjects are a part. Apparently "subjective" mental states and processes, such as thinking and consciousness, take place "out there" just as much as the kinds of objects we easily recognize as being real. Thus, the issue of how the mind can be part of nature (i.e., the "placement problem"[26]) is replaced by an approach according to which senses exist in an unsurprising manner, such that we can place nature in the realm of senses rather than having to squeeze the dimensions of sense out of senseless material.

Realism about senses requires a reversal of a flawed metaphysical mereology: the senseless parts of reality are part of the realm of sense that encompasses them without thereby turning into mindless matter or purely physical information. Again, realism about sense ought not to be conflated with some fancy idealism, as it claims neither that there would not have been any senses had there been no subjects, nor that reality as a whole (the world) is constitutively open to human thought and inquisitiveness, as if it had been waiting for our discoveries.

20

SENSE

Realism about sense as spelled out in the first part of this chapter leads me to take a fresh look at both the motivations of FOS and the claim that fos do not form a totality.[27] Realism about sense is one of two basic tenets of my contribution to New Realism. The other is the "no-world-view," as I have been calling it, which maintains that there is no all-encompassing fos such that all objects (and fos) appear within it. The no-world-view is effectively a no-totality-view according to which there is no single absolute totality of all there is. Depending on one's metaphysics, one might think of all there is in terms of a totality of objects, of facts / states of affairs, or domains. The no-world-view rejects any such metaphysical conception of a whole of entities that assumes that there is a whole of which absolutely everything (maybe even including the whole itself) is a part. In FOS, realism about sense is thereby combined with *ontological pluralism* about fos. The real is intrinsically manifold in such a way that it cannot be reduced to a single fos. We are not tiny parts of a gigantic whole—be it a physical, mental, divine, or any other absolute whole (such as a unified realm of sense).[28] Hence, there is no longer any need to belittle thought, subjectivity, or the mind by thinking of it as a tiny episode in a grand scheme of the unfolding of spatiotemporal (or any other) reality.[29]

In the second part of the chapter, I present the no-world-view as a way of restricting sense. This allows me to clarify my version of radical ontological pluralism with a focus on sense. The realm of sense is restricted in that it cannot encompass absolutely everything. As I will argue, there is no fos of all fos. On this basis, we are led to recognize the possibility of nonsense, not as meaninglessness in the form of a violation of rules of sense-making, but rather as an independent dimension of reality that is not exhausted by objects appearing in fos.

In both parts of this chapter, I discuss and reject the widespread idea that senses are constitutively linguistic and, thus, somehow less real than they would be if they were parts of pure, non-linguistic thought. In this context, I discard the gist of the linguistic turn. Thought as such is not tied to linguistic expression or expressibility in any constitutive sense. The fact that we are capable of expressing and grasping thoughts that would be unavailable without specific linguistic capacities remains a source for much insight, particularly in the humanities. However, it should not be confused with the contentious and arguably false idea that thinking

21

as such is an exercise of linguistic capacities. To turn one of Heidegger's famous phrases on its head, being is the house of language, not the other way around.[30]

PART ONE: EXTENDING SENSE

Overcoming Dualist Metaphysics

The orthodoxy of contemporary philosophy is associated with a certain worldview. According to this worldview, senses—if they exist at all—are tied to conscious and non-conscious modes of representing reality. Reality itself is senseless; it merely is. Typically, this status of mere, senseless being is then identified with an overall metaphysical property of being a physical object, a part of the universe. This straightforwardly leads into a dualist metaphysics whose epistemological problems are generated by isolating mental representations from reality. If reality is primarily a realm of senseless beings (such as purely physical objects and processes) that come to be represented at later stages in its unfolding (by animals endowed with minds and, thus, with access to a realm of senses of their own making), how is it possible that the senses latch onto a reality that is categorially alien to the nature of thought and representation?

How could this be dualism, you might wonder? The answer is straightforward. If reality is identified with the senseless universe, how can senses be part of it? The basic tenet of dualism is that reality and the realm of sense turn out to be metaphysically distinct. It can take many different shapes, such as the dualism of mind and world, or a more sophisticated "linguistic" shape according to which reference and meaning are nothing but so many attempts at getting hold of elements and events in a purely senseless universe without themselves being part of it.

The ontological starting point of dualist metaphysics assumes that reality has two parts: a level of senseless objects, on the one hand, and somehow less real (or even unreal) subjects and their constructs who are in the business of tracking objects in their environment, on the other hand.

That this is flawed can be seen if one considers that the thought directed at the relationship between the objective (senseless) and the subjective parts of reality had better be assessable in terms of some theoretical criteria of success or other. Here, the very idea of a correspondence theory of mind and reality (truth and fact, language and reality, etc.) kicks in. But, if truth is essentially correspondence between the objective and the subjective, how can a relationship to the relationship between the objective and the subjective count as true in anything like the same sense in which truth is characterized within the same a dualistic metaphysics of intentionality? If dualist metaphysics were true, how could we access that truth without thereby thinking of our target-system (reality) as already involving both the subjective and the objective and, thus, as not identical with only one of these poles?

In order to circumvent construals that lead to dualistic metaphysics, it has recently become fashionable to strengthen the factivity link between knowledge and fact, or rather thinking and being.[31] In the wake of John McDowell's seminal contributions to epistemology and philosophy of mind, it has become common to think that the good case of our epistemic standing with respect to reality (or "the world," as they put it), ought to count as the paradigm of our self-understanding as thinkers. Qua rational animals, we are primarily knowers whose failures should be explained against the background of a massive wealth of actual knowledge. In the good case, our thought "does not stop short of the fact."[32] If someone knows that p, then p. Thus, the facts cannot lie on the other side of an unbridgeable epistemic gap (a "completely separating border,"[33] as Hegel famously and ironically put it).

But McDowell himself has never spelled out any ontology or metaphysics of senses or facts. He limits himself to a form of quietism designed to dissolve metaphysical questions rather than to address them head-on. I, like many others, am not convinced that we ought to take a therapeutic attitude toward philosophical problems. If McDowell really wants to make claims about mind and world at all, there better be some theory or other about their relationship that means that the factivity link has to be an indicator of a fact about the way in which thought and being actually hang together.

If we want to overcome dualist metaphysics and, thus, the opposition of mind and world altogether, we should revise both our ontology and our epistemology. In this regard, it is tempting to understand the structure of the good case of successful knowledge claims (i.e., knowledge) in terms of what I would like to call a *fusion of thinking and being*.[34] According to the corresponding fusion theory, the subjectivity of the owner of the thought involved in the good case disappears and the thinker turns into a purely syncategorematic effect in service of the fact that manifests itself, as Irad Kimhi has argued in his *Thinking and Being*.[35] Thus, one might think that in the good case, thinking and being are unified in a *fusion,* in the bad case a *fission* takes place that is at best explainable in terms of subjective sources of error.[36]

At this point of intersection between contemporary epistemology, philosophy of mind, and ontology, Mark Johnston has propounded an ingenious account of how things look if we fully commit to a fusion theory. In a way similar to FOS, Johnston draws on the ontology of the realm of senses to think of reality as essentially manifest. According to his proposal, the associated objectivity of our minds resides in the fact that something like the mind is itself an objective component of reality.[37] Here, what counts as sufficiently similar to the "mind" in order for it to be a legitimate denizen of reality is precisely a way for things to be presented, a sense.

Johnston rightly maintains that the fact that things are as we perceive and know them to be tells us something about the things themselves and not just about our epistemically successful standing with respect to them. Otherwise put, intelligibility is a full feature of reality and not just a construction or production of consciousness, the mind, the subject, language, thought, or whatever one identifies as the paradigmatic locus of manifestation of reality to a thinker.

He puts this idea by drawing a distinction between two self-conceptions: one where we identify ourselves as "Producers of Presence" and the other where we come to see ourselves as "Samplers of Presence."[38]

> On this hypothesis [that we are samplers of presence], Being is by its nature present; Being's fundamental activity is self-disclosure. All the modes of presentation of each existing thing, be they intellectual or sensory modes, all the possible *ways* of thinking and sensing each such thing, come into being with the things themselves, whether or not there are any indi-

SENSE

vidual minds to sample these modes of presentation, that is, to access them in individual mental acts.[39]

Johnston in this passage effectively offers a version of realism about sense. In general, *realism about sense* is the idea that modes of presentation (i.e., what Frege has labeled "senses" [*Sinne*]) are accessed, grasped, discovered, or found by beings capable of entertaining mental states with objective purport. Thus, sense is not made or produced, as a certain orthodoxy of our time presupposes.[40] We do not make sense of otherwise senseless things and facts, but rather figure out how things are by way of accessing the modes of presentation they offer us. Reality, according to realism about sense, is in principle disclosed to thinkers such that there are forms of disclosure we pick up in virtue of being part of what there is.

However, Johnston too quickly dismisses the subject in his admirable attempt to direct us to reality's sense-like manifestation. Thinkers of thoughts constituted by senses directed at objects, we are ourselves parts of the realm of sense such that subjective thought ought to be seen as one of the species of sense. And this is exactly where a decisive problem lies with the fusion theory. For what exactly is the relationship between the stock of objective senses and the fact that we access them "in individual mental acts," as Johnston puts it?

Johnston is wise to steer clear of a repetition of the opening move of the kind of dualistic metaphysic he rightly rejects. Thus, he cannot assume that reality consists of objects together with their mode of presentation such that beings who enter the stage at some point in the temporal unfolding of reality access an already existing, in itself complete sense structure from a merely subjective point of view. If such were his metaphysics, it would not fare better than the type of naturalism he rejects, i.e., the notion that brain tissue (or some other natural phenomenon) produces "natural representations," as if we were biological mirrors or *camerae obscurae*.[41]

If there is a dualism of objective senses and subjective access, we wind up in the same scenario as Frege who was not capable of understanding how we can actually grasp modes of representation from a subjective point of view.[42] In this way, we are still stuck in a form of dualist metaphysics, one that polarizes the realm of sense from within, as it were.

SENSE, NONSENSE, AND SUBJECTIVITY

As a next step, we need a theory of subjectivity that specifies the subject's position within the realm of sense. Subjects do not access the realm of sense from the outside, as it were, because this would require the establishment of a bridge from nonsensical subjectivity to the realm of senses. Making sense as such would thus always undermine its own success conditions in that a subject's grasp of senses distorts their objectivity. For this reason, the fusion theory has to understand subjects as tokens of individualized minds in terms of just more objective sense. Knowing how things are, i.e., fusing with reality, is an event that has to take place on the same playing field as the objective sense we harvest by way of being part of it.

This should lead Johnston to a flat ontology, according to which reality is a bunch of objective senses. The details of the content of given modes of presentation determine that something is a knower and some other thing a known. Similarly, the content of given modes of presentation is responsible for providing temporal structure. The process of writing this book differs from the atemporal fact that $7+5=12$ not by being part of becoming that is opposed to atemporal being. One of the differences between writing this book and the fact that $7+5=12$ is simply that writing this book has to be thought of in a tensed form, whereas it is not part of the senses combined in $7+5=12$ that this fact came into being.

Likewise, the difference between minds and their objective content boils down to a difference in content, which seems obvious once we realize that minds are, of course, part of the content we take into account when thinking about their relationship to non-mental reality. Hence, thus interpreted as a flat ontology, Johnston's version of the fusion theory has the clear advantage of solving the problem of how we can think of both minds and their non-mental environment without privileging non-mental reality as a paradigm case for objectivity. On a deeper level, then, Johnston's fusion theory can be seen as thinking of reality as a structure of senses S_1, $S_2, \ldots, S_n$ that, as far as their being senses is concerned, are on a par. Hence my characterization of this realism about sense as a flat ontology.[43]

But this raises some problems concerning the coherence of the metaphysical architecture of the realm of sense, which he does not address. What is worse, he even seems to fall back into an incoherent dualistic metaphysics when he claims that

26

> properly understood, there are no subjective phenomena. There is a host of events that fill our so-called subjective mental lives. These events are occurrent mental acts, which are objective psychological occurrences. . . . On this view our respective mental lives are just particular idiosyncratic histories of *accessing* modes of presentation. . . . The whole content of our minds is the contribution of the objects. When we speak of consciousness, we are systematically getting hold of the wrong end of the stick; the basic reality is not the fact of consciousness, understood as the inner achievement of a mind. It is the fact of the continuous and multifaceted disclosure of objects, which certain evolved animals are able to access.[44]

In this passage, he oscillates between a complete elimination of the subject from ontological consideration and the idea that we are evolved animals with idiosyncratic mental biographies. If we were mere loci of presence, it would be superfluous to add that there is anything idiosyncratic about this status. But if we are subjects after all (which involves the idea of idiosyncrasy, as I will argue in Chapter 3), we cannot be reduced to just being perfect windows onto the unfolding of reality's selfless manifestation. Johnston does not get the subject into view, as he faces a choice between purely objective senses and attempts to access them which by his lights are unreal and, thus, not really capable of being in touch with how things are.

The flaw lies in the very idea of *accessing* the realm of sense. How could we possibly access that realm from a subjective point of view, if that point of view were not itself already part of what there is? If Johnston accepts that we are already part of what there is, he ought to think of us as full parts of the disclosure of reality. But this undermines the idea that the "whole content of our minds is the contribution of the objects," because the minds themselves belong to the level of the objects insofar as they too are thinkables and knowables.

Let us call *refined fusion theory* the idea that minds cannot only fuse with non-mental objects through their objective senses, but that they can also fuse with themselves insofar as they are fully legitimate denizens of reality. Subjectivity disappears by fusing with itself so that we evade a pernicious notion of subjectivity that stands between us and how things are. This amounts to a full-fledged flat ontology combined with realism about sense.

This improved view faces an entirely different set of problems now associated with its inbuilt metaphysical impetus, i.e., with its drive toward a worldview according to which reality is a whole of objective senses. For we can now further develop the refined fusion theory on the assumption that it maintains a metaphysical worldview of roughly the following sort: Reality is a structure of self-disclosure where this means that what there is, is inherently tied to being intelligible in one of the manifold senses S_1, $S_2, \ldots, S_n$. These senses are in principle ready to be sampled by appropriately attuned subjects. But that raises specific logical questions concerning the coherence and consistency of the realm of senses. These specific logical questions follow from the idea that reality at this juncture turns into a *totality* of senses, a realm of senses that has to be credited with some overall structure or other. As we will see in due course, the realm of sense cannot be extended this far.

We cannot eliminate *subjective* senses from our account of reality by embracing the notion that there is an objective realm of sense. If senses are real in anything like the way envisaged by Johnston (who stands in the tradition of Frege), they cannot all be objective, since such a classification requires a response to the question of how we grasp the objective senses after all. Even if one thinks of grasping objective senses as just more objective sense (self-referential objective sense that gets a hold of itself), one has thereby committed to the existence of subjective sense that cannot be sampled. The language of production, construction, constitution, etc. that invites itself once we get to the point where we integrate ourselves into the realm of senses cannot be reduced to an explanation of the evolution of animals with idiosyncratic mental biographies, as Johnston suggests in the passage quoted above.

Reducing the subject to a mere event in the realm of objective sense (the evolution of mental idiosyncrasies), we lose track of our fallibility and, thereby, of the fact that we grasp objective sense. Understanding our grasp of objective sense requires a concept of fallibility according to which we can get it right or wrong. While objects radiate sense, this alone does not guarantee that we always get it right.

It is thus not enough to eliminate the subjective from within a fusion theory of thought and being, however attractive this might be as a model for the good case. Next, I want to argue that there is both objective and subjective sense and that we need a theory of how they hang together.

Objective and Subjective Sense

Many of our most cherished mental states turn on how they achieve their contact with reality. Here, contact is an interplay or interface between two kinds of senses, the one of the grasped, the other of the grasping. The grasping is never fully fused with the grasped, which is why we can even be wrong about being right and can become convinced that we do not know what we actually know.[45] That is why the concept of intentionality plays such a crucial role in the theory of what I call *subjective* sense, i.e., sense directed at how things are from a standpoint that contributes to the content processed.[46]

At this level of analysis, Hubert Dreyfus and Charles Taylor have recently followed up on the trend toward a New Realism by recovering the tradition of a *contact theory*.[47] The specific contrast at stake here is one between a *mediational* and a *contact picture* where a mediational picture "emerged in the idea that we grasp external reality through internal representations."[48] The idea of the mediational picture has it that we can explain knowledge (and cognate states) in terms of how we achieve access to reality through some inner state or other. Dreyfus and Taylor rightly insist that it does ultimately not matter if the mediational layer consists of mental images, brain states, or linguistic items such as sentences that are held to be true. The problem with all mediational theories is that they cannot make sense of how we can know that there is a mediational structure in the first place without assuming that we are in contact with the mediational structure in a way that categorically differs from the mediated nature of our knowledge of "external" reality. But that means that there is unmediated knowledge without which we could not be in a position to know that there is mediated knowledge. If this is the case, why postulate that knowledge as such is mediational? The postulate is clearly falsified by the theory conditions designed to make a case for the mediated nature of knowledge.

I have called this line of critique of mediational theories of our most cherished mental states "the argument from facticity."[49] In a nutshell, it argues that any theory according to which knowledge paradigmatically (or even exclusively) consists in a subject's attempt to achieve access to reality via media of objective purport, and that as such falls short of already being in touch with how things are, is incapable of making sense of itself. The grasp of the media that allegedly separate us from reality is already part of the reality in question, meaning the issue of how we can achieve access to reality at all is answered as soon as it is coherently raised.

Their critique of mediational theories leads Dreyfus and Taylor to endorse a specific contact picture that draws on the phenomenological (Husserlian and Heideggerian) tradition rather than on realism about (Fregean) senses:

> In what does the contact consist? In the fact that at the most basic, preconceptual level, the understanding I have of the world is not simply one constructed or determined by me. It is a "co-production" of me and the world. That's what it means to say that our grasp of the world at this level is not in us but in the interaction, the interspace of our dealings with things.[50]

In light of the idea of our dealings with things, Dreyfus and Taylor offer a *plural realism* according to which there are manifold different modes of contact. Yet, the plural realism offered by Dreyfus and Taylor presupposes the idea that there is such a thing as "the world as the all-englobing locus of my involvements."[51] Other than FOS, at this stage their pluralism is embedded in a monist metaphysics of the world. Their realism is supposed to be "an unproblematic realism with respect to the world."[52] In this regard, their plural realism is remarkably nonchalant about its ontological commitments. They hold that there is a multiplicity of modes of "interrogating reality"[53] without making explicit what exactly it means "that there are a plurality of revealing perspectives on the world (nature, cosmos, universe?)."[54] Their use of a variety of terms for the world (reality, nature, cosmos, universe) makes it clear that they are not speaking of the lifeworld of meaningful engagement here, but are thinking of the world as an object in the way rejected by FOS.

On the epistemological level, they "conclude that there are several ways of describing nature all of which may be true."[55] However, they do not let us know how the meanings of their terms "reality," "world," "nature," "cosmos," "universe" are connected and how the expressions designed to refer to the target domain that unifies different kinds of interrogation hang together with their phenomenological conception of the world qua locus of our involvements. In light of these shortcomings, it is unclear how exactly they want to combine realism and pluralism in their desired outcome of a realism retrieved.

At this point, it is useful to recall that realism, broadly construed, covers two overall ideas. According to its ontological and metaphysical dimension, realism is committed to reality's independence vis-à-vis our activity of grasping it by taking certain things to be true. In this respect, realism about a certain domain basically assumes that the facts about objects in the domain can come apart from what we take the facts to be. Call this the "contrast of objectivity."[56] Realism in that sense is rather modest or minimal, though it has regularly been contested on a local and a global level.[57]

As Crispin Wright points out at the outset of his seminal *Truth and Objectivity,* in a somewhat more demanding epistemological dimension, realism is a commitment to the "presumptuous thought . . . that, while such fit as there may be between our thought and the world is determined independently of human cognitive activity, we are nevertheless, in favourable circumstances, capable of conceiving the world aright, and often, of knowing the truth about it."[58] In light of the *ontological* thesis of realism, reality is introduced in order to make sense of the idea of an independence of the facts from our epistemic whims.[59] The *epistemological* thesis, by contrast, insists on reality's knowability. These two dimensions of the realism debate ought not to be separated: "realism" in its two overall senses is not fallaciously ambiguous, but rather concerns our twofold involvement with what there is. Qua knowers, we are part of every reality that we can meaningfully conceive of, such that we cannot really make sense of a part of reality that is in principle isolated from our effort to grasp it (including our capacity to cover parts of reality that are unknowable by way of *de dicto* thoughts about that reality as thus unknowable).[60]

One of the weaknesses of fusion and contact theories of the good epistemic case is that they fall short of providing an account of our fallibility, of

SENSE, NONSENSE, AND SUBJECTIVITY

fission and failed contact. It is not sufficient to spell out what it means for thought to latch onto reality if one misses the equally important fact that we often get things wrong. In this context, it is not enough to introduce the notion of objective (Fregean) senses or to integrate subjects into meaningful environments.

According to this concept, subjective experience of how things are from a given literal visual perspective is a manifestation of a reality that reveals its relational aspects. Reality is not hidden from view by the fact that we process it in terms of subjective glimpses. Rather, the very essence of reality is that it is processed thusly embodied thinkers. That our sense modalities can process a reality only by way of perspectival adumbrations is not a limitation but a manifestation of its essential sense-like structure. To the extent to which the sense modalities are part of a subject (an idea to be detailed in Chapter 3), the senses operative in our sense modalities can count as subjective.

Subjective senses are *subjective* to the extent to which they are part of illusions, where an illusion is a field potential for getting it wrong. Qua subjective they involve wrongness somewhere in the subject's mental life. When I speak of "subjective" and "subjectivity" I minimally intend to refer to the idea that our mental states typically represent things as being a certain way from our position. Our actual mental lives are always complex modes of overlapping mental realities. This is the case not only on the level of conscious perception but also for high-level exercises of our conceptual capacities, such as being engaged in mathematical thought. To the extent to which we think of our thoughts as subjective, we think of them as deviating in some way or another from the pure, objective facts. At the same time, they have to be in touch with the right objective facts (and, thus, objective senses) in order to deviate from them and to count as failures, mistakes, or in short modes of being wrong. This deviation is the origin of the varieties of being wrong, from the distortions of conscious perception to the constitutive failures and mistakes at the frontiers of our knowledge. At least, this is how I use the term "subjectivity," thereby opposing any of the traditions that think of the subject as an epistemologically privileged form of self-consciousness or self-knowledge.

To be sure, qua perceiving, knowing, and successfully acting subjects, we grasp *objective senses* as unclouded ways for things to be. The fact that $7 + 5 = 12$ and the related fact that $13 - 1 = 12$ reveal mathematical facts without invoking the makeup of a thinker. The senses by which $7 + 5$ differs from $13 - 1$ (having to do with elementary operations, algebraic number fields, etc.) are not perspectival or subjective. Rather, they are suitable for our analytic and synthetic capacities to identify elements in logical compounds. But our mathematical capacities are not reflected in our relation to the objects, at least not in the same way as in the exercises of our sensory capacities as ordinarily understood. Regardless of the details of the role of senses in mathematical thought (which was Frege's starting point), we can pinpoint the idea of objective senses by thinking of them as the kinds of senses that we grasp by successfully abstracting from our grasp.[61] Yet insistence on our capacity to grasp objective senses should not mislead us into rejecting the existence of subjective senses. Otherwise, we run the risk of a second-order revenge of psychologism.

Frege famously contributed to a pathbreaking generalization of the notion of a sense as a mode of presentation beyond the familiar case of perception. Simultaneously, and for similar reasons having to do with the foundations of mathematics, Husserl too provided a general theory of senses as modes of presentation of objects. While it remains unclear in which way we are allowed to map Frege's logical theory of sense onto the perceptual situation of embodied subjects, it is unclear how Husserl's theory of sense accounts for the specific objectivity of mathematical and logical thought. For this reason, both have been charged with (and to some extent suspected each other of) some form of psychologism.[62]

Here, *psychologism* is a name for the allegation that the objectivity of a given domain of thought is undermined by thinking of a thinker's relationship to that domain as subjective. In this context, "subjective" means that the relevant attitude the thinker maintains when in touch with an object cannot be shared by any other thinker (or not even by the same thinker at different times). In that vein, Kimhi has recently pointed out that Frege's rejection of what he calls "psycho-logicism" led him to "Psycho / logical dualism."[63]

> In contemporary philosophy the term *psychologism* denotes those programs which try to describe and explain human activity as a part of the order described and explained by the empirical sciences. (It is also used as a slur against ostensibly nonpsychologistic programs.) It is possible to be

"psychologistic" with respect to some parts of the mind but not others. For example, Frege is psychologistic with respect to phenomenal episodes including sensations and images, but not with respect to thinking. But this division of the mind into logical and subjective parts is itself characteristic of psycho-logical dualism.[64]

In order to circumvent this dualism that repeats the problems of psychologism on the level where the issue of the relationship between our phenomenal episodes and thinking arises, Kimhi argues that we ought to endorse a form of monism. According to "psycho / logical monism," "there is a sense of the 'I' in 'I think'" whereby "the 'I' is a logical word on a level with the logical connectives. For the monist, the unity expressed by the connective is the unity of self-consciousness."[65] What this means for the philosophy of logic is that we are supposed to think of logical compositions in terms of "acts of identifying our consciousness as agreeing or disagreeing with the combination (and their negations) displayed by the subordinate judgments."[66]

However, this conception of the nature of logical composition smacks of psychologism. In particular, it faces the following choice. The first option is that the "I" that is associated with consciousness and self-consciousness is such that we embody it as finite thinkers. In this case, how can we successfully abstract from the relevant details of our finite determinable nature as thinkers so as to arrive at a level of thought, where it does not matter who the particular thinker is? Who is this "I" if it is none of us? The second is that the logical "I" is not really the kind of thing we represent by way of thinking about ourselves as thinkers, but rather some other kind of thinker endowed with the prerequisites for performing the synthetic activity required for the unity of a series of thoughts. In that case, it is unclear why we characterize this other "I" as an I in the first place. Why not think of logical space as inherently structured by relations of compossibility that we articulate in terms of our symbolism? On what ground, if not in terms of a strategy designed to avoid the pitfalls of psychologism, do we postulate an "I" that we characterize in the (overtly psychological) vocabulary of consciousness and self-consciousness?[67] In any event, integrating an "I" into logical theory does not solve the issue of psychologism, but aggravates the situation by making it hard to see how the "hardness of the logical *must*"[68] does not involve too much of a projection of contingent circumstances of our practices of judging onto the structure of content as such.

To be sure, there is a sense in which our epistemically relevant embodied states are essentially not shareable and in that (Fregean) sense subjective. Clearly, the actual phenomenological and neurophysiological details of the state that I am in when perceiving are minimally different from the state that any other perceiver is in. They might be of the same type, such as seeing a banana. Yet, the actual mode of presentation of a given banana at a given moment will be fine-grained by parameters that are probably unique events in the universe. On this basis, one might think that the mode of presentation of a given banana at a given moment is subjective, utterly unrepeatable so that its classification as a mental episode of seeing a banana might be regarded as a model of an in itself highly singular token structure of physical events.

There might be a pattern such that your token of a banana perception and my token are sufficiently similar so as to make communication about the subjective states we are in possible. But they are never quite the same. Yet, when *I* think that there is a banana when confronted with said banana and *you* think that there is a banana, *we* are thinking about the same banana. The differences in our states that put us perceptually in touch with the banana are, as it were, filtered out in our thought directed at the banana. Thus, we achieve objectivity on the basis of subjectivity.

But if my perceptual relationship to the banana is subjective (just like yours), there might be a problem of how we achieve the level of objectivity required for thinking the same thought, for neither the perceptual state (which is subjective) nor the banana itself can guarantee that our thought directed at it is objective, communicable, shareable, and strictly repeatable.

This problem seems to disappear when we move to the realm of pure, logico-mathematical thought. If this is correct, Frege's concept of sense has the advantage of operating on a level of analysis where any potentially problematic impact of the subjective has been ruled out. Pure logico-mathematical thought is not subjective, which might be one of the main reasons why we can devise non-human computing systems that outperform us in calculative power.

However, this view of senses as exclusively objective has the disadvantage of creating a gap between the actual thinker and her logico-mathematical thoughts. For how can we grasp a Fregean thought with its internal sensemaking (or rather sense-grasping) structure without thereby bringing our subjectivity to bear on the situation? How can we bridge the ontological, categorical gap between an embodied thinker and her pure thoughts?

Another path, therefore, seems to recommend itself, namely to think of our actual lives as embodied modes of presentation. The literal visual perspective on a mountain or the juicy taste of an apple are not merely subjective. By way of exhibiting a pattern, an *eidos,* we can come to identify them as tokens of a type. Pure logico-mathematical thought could then be seen as a codification of eidetic patterns.

In this context, FOS offers a bridge between the idea of sense as a mode of presentation from a perspective or point of view and sense as a logical structure that characterizes content as such (and, therefore, regardless of its specific incorporation and manifestation in our lifeform). In FOS, "sense" is used univocally in the logical and the psychological case, but it picks out different domains or, as I put it, fields.

In the material, objective mode, a sense functions as a mode of individuation of a field. In virtue of a sense, a bunch of objects are related to each other in a given situation. A fos is a composition of objects that stand in relationships to each other such that these relationships are characterized as being of a certain kind. The characterization is the sense of the field in question, i.e., the way in which the objects are presented. The sense thus delivers a furnishing function for a field that accounts for the field's individuation in the context of other fields.[69] Just as in the case of mathematics, a field is a domain of objects (a "space") such that all points in that domain (the objects) share certain structural features, which accounts for the fact that they hang together in that field (rather than in some other). Yet, the idea of fields encompasses more than mathematical entities and their physical cousins. Reality is field-like beyond the reach of physics.[70]

In addition to the ontological layer of sense—without which there would not be any objects and hence nothing at all—there is a *psychological* dimension of sense that is, of course, in turn part of what there is. This psychological dimension consists in the fact that senses are objective features of objects that figure in thought as modes of presentation of thinkables.[71]

SENSE

The act of grasping a thought, i.e., of being in touch with content, is a psychological sense modality in at least the following two ways.[72] On the one hand, grasping a thought is an act that takes place in reality. Thus, there is a fos where thinking takes place. Thinking does not take place elsewhere, as it were. It is not a transcendent matter of peeping into reality through some kind of keyhole. The subject is not isolated from reality, let alone from her thoughts. On the other hand, thinking can get it right or be wrong in virtue of being directed at a reality not necessarily of its own making that is the fundamental concept of a sense modality. What one needs to add in order to make sense of the notion of thinking as a sense modality here is the notion that thinking's sensibilia are its thoughts, i.e., propositional contents whose structure is, of course, no less differentiated and fine-grained (in its own register) than that of the paradigmatically discussed sense modalities.

Yet, this does not mean that we ought to "naturalize" thinking. On the contrary, the idea of thinking as a process individuated by a sense, such that it takes place within reality, is an element in an argument against the misguided identification of thinking with processes that necessarily accompany it in animals (such as the dynamic wiring and rewiring of neural circuits).[73]

Thinking is itself a sense modality and, therefore, at least in part amenable to causal analyses.[74] Grasping a thought is both something that occurs on reality's level of sense and an activity that takes place at a literal interface that connects a subject with her non-subjective environment.

Notice that other subjects together with the whole array of fos "out there" belong to a subject's non-subjective environment. In this way, we avoid "psycho / logical dualism" by giving up on the idea that reality is fundamentally what it is in virtue of being "objective," i.e., "non-subjective." The reality of sense is rather both: objective and subjective.

Mind as an Interface

There is no good reason to believe that senses as such would not have existed had no thinker evolved in order to relate to an objective reality with their aid. On the contrary, the idea that we are not "producers" but "samplers of presence," as Johnston has aptly put it, has substantial explanatory advantages at the interface of ontology and epistemology.[75]

A prominent term for a realization of this interface is "mind." The idea of the mind is introduced at the interface between what there is and our higher-level epistemic attitudes that ought to be grounded in a basic contact with reality. The concept of a mind answers to the theoretical need to identify an interface at which subjective (distorting, deviating, wrong, illusory, etc.) and objective sense meet.

This connection between mind and the interface of objective and subjective sense is somewhat buried in the depth of the concept of a "belief" or a "propositional attitude" that should, after all, be understood as an actual mental state and not merely as an explanatory tool for getting a grip on the epistemically unmanageable complexity of each other's actual physical states. "The mind" is not shorthand for an immense calculation using physical concepts and elementary measurements; the mind is real and not a second-rate concept.[76]

In contemporary philosophy and neighboring mind sciences, there is a widespread tendency to either see consciousness as the mark of the mental or at least to admit that it poses some kind of deep difficulty. Part of this difficulty is that the concept of consciousness is treated as a purely psychological concept that tends to obscure its underlying epistemological and ontological structure of sense as the interface between an objective reality and its representation in an animal.

To be precise, it is unclear if consciousness is a psychological concept in the narrow sense of a concept that essentially belongs to psychology as a proper methodologically controlled discipline. There are legitimate worries that there might not be a single, unified natural phenomenon we call "consciousness" such that we can study it by way of the methods available to psychological science (see the discussion of the Lord Chandos problem in Chapter 3).

To be sure, this does not entail that consciousness does not exist. It might simply not be amenable to the kind of investigation that draws on the prior identification of natural / psychological kinds in order to study a given phenomenon in a controlled manner. Consciousness, in a word, might not be a natural kind at all, which does not mean that it does not exist.[77]

The problem with the psychological notion of consciousness at this stage of our dialectics is that it is a representation of the function of sense in improperly objectivist terms. Here is what I mean by this. From the standpoint of an actually existing full-fledged theorist—in our case, a human being—we are part of every possible situation in which we characterize circumstances that do not constitutively involve us. Roughly put, our mental map of mind-independent reality is itself mind-dependent. We cannot think of a reality without thereby playing a role in the activity of drawing a distinction between the conceptual and the causal aspect of things, as it were.

But that does not per se support the (ultimately unconvincing) case for the subjective idealists "master-argument" according to which we are incapable of conceiving of facts that are unconceived by us.[78] To put it in terms of Robert B. Brandom's helpful distinction between "sense-" and "reference-dependence,"[79] while the very idea of objectivity as tied to mind-independence is sense-dependent on the concept of a mind, the idea of an object involves the reference-independence of some objects with respect to the existence of subjects of any kind. It is simply not the case that the existence of minds somehow produces the conditions of existence of objects in general.

For similar reasons, it is equally misguided to detach objectivity from subjectivity and identify objectivity with access to an utterly mind-independent and therefore strange realm of potentially unknowable things in themselves.[80] We need not transcend the human standpoint in order to know how things really are: they are not screened off from us. Trivially, our best reasons to make knowledge claims must be sufficient to establish knowledge. If the concept of knowledge were the concept of an unattainable state of affairs (such as a view from nowhere or a view from everywhere), it would be an entirely useless fiction. Given that the concept of knowledge is devised so as to make the outlines of a distinguished set of (factive) mental states explicit in the context of epistemology, we are entitled to think of reality as essentially knowable without turning this epistemological insight into a metaphysical notion according to which "the world" is somehow embedded within a conceptual sphere tied to human concept articulation.

This does not entail that everything that is real is also knowable. Being and being knowable (let alone being known) do not coincide. This is one important way of stating a realist thesis. The realist in general accepts that it makes sense for there to be a contrast of objectivity between someone's taking something to be true and it actually being the case—but that does precisely not mean that we can draw a clear-cut line between what we know and what there is to know in principle.[81] In addition to known unknowns, whose overall structure can be figured out by identifying current limits of knowledge, there is an indefinite range of unknown unknowns. While this fact is itself knowable, it does not entail that we thereby already know too much about the unknown unknowns in order for them to be exactly what they are: unknowns.

Some objective sense is sense that would have been there had no one emerged in order to detect it. In contrast to this important part of the tapestry of sense, there is subjective sense qua sense that exists in virtue of our distorting presence in reality. For this reason, it is perfectly intelligible to say that the moon (up to a certain point in its astrophysical career) is what it is regardless of what we take it to be, whereas our so taking it to be on the basis of perception and scientific knowledge acquisition is not what it is regardless of our taking it to be so. A knowledge claim thereby differs ontologically from stardust, which evidently does not entail that knowers are detachable from their bodies.[82]

The problem of the identification of the mental with consciousness from the standpoint occupied here can be seen as an erroneous mode of thinking about the interface between objective and subjective sense. Replacing "consciousness" by a lower-level, non-conscious *mental* function or registration ultimately does not fare any better. What we need is the concept of mind as an interface that does not distort reality in such a way that we come to regard it as generally mind-dependent. This enables us to bridge both levels of sense.

Even though it has been an important step in recent philosophy of mind (notably taken by Tyler Burge) to insist that objectivity is a feature of mental states quite below the consciousness-level, this shifts the problem from one part of the psychological realm to another (albeit somewhat more tractable) level of sub-personal objective mental states. Whatever impressive feat an organism or some of its subsystems performs in its tracking correlations with its environment, we would not function at all if objective and subjective sense were not connected on the level of sense itself. If reality utterly lacked all the structure an organism produces due to its internal wiring, the organism could not even survive, because it would exist in two entirely separate realms:

SENSE

The illusory level of its surface experience of what there is, and the "true" reality of unfathomable processes that by their very nature cannot and must not make sense. If reality were metaphysically sense-less, entirely devoid of the modes of presentation without which nothing would be manifest to anyone, we could never be in a position to observe this stunning "fact."

A basic rule of epistemology in this context can be stated thus: never construct a theory of knowledge that makes it seem impossible to know how things actually are! This basic rule is a guide to ontology in that it postulates some connection or other between our subjective (factual and factive) mental states (paradigmatically: knowledge) and any kind of environment that is suitable for epistemic investigations.[83]

Prominent strands of the discussions surrounding "mind as consciousness" have created an air of mystery that can be dispelled if we can identify the reason why consciousness matters to core areas of theoretical philosophy. The main reason, I suppose, is that our modes of experiencing reality, on the one hand, put us in touch with how things are and, on the other hand, inform us about our distorting standing with regard to how things are. Consciousness, therefore, is both objective (part of what there is insofar as it is capable of revealing what there is to someone) and subjective (related to a subject). Recent attempts to dissociate consciousness from the subject can be seen as so many attempts to grasp the pure realm of objective sense from a self-effacing subjective perspective—which in my view is an unnecessary flight from subjectivity.

These claims can be made more intelligible by exploring the interface idea with recourse to the widespread notion that animal conscious perception is a narrow-minded look into complex physical systems. It is certainly true that conscious perception is tied to the organically realized capacities of a given organism. The colors, shapes, and smells I can consciously process reveal only a tiny fraction of physical reality to me. This fraction of reality that is revealed to me has been selected over long stretches of evolutionary adaptation of members of my species to their environment. In that specific respect, then, we can draw a distinction between the objective senses that can be made visible in terms of scientific models of reality that outstrip conscious perception and the subjective modes of presentation that enable us to know anything about said reality in the first place.

SENSE, NONSENSE, AND SUBJECTIVITY

What does not follow from this distinction yet, though, is the more contentious idea that the subjective modes of presentation insurmountably distort reality. On the contrary, the more we know about the relationship between objective senses and our subjective experience of how things are, the better we understand how subjective senses fit into the broader landscape of reality. Redshifts and other color phenomena have long served as proper pieces of scientific evidence because there is a correlation between objective and subjective senses. Similarly, objective mathematical structures are sufficiently tied to our capacity for producing algebraic formulations for our mathematical methods to be impressive devices for tracking objective structures that clearly outrun our individual and collective capacity for knowing how things are in the mathematical realm (if a single realm it be).

Grasping objective senses requires exercises of epistemic capacities. These exercises restrict the scope of our interest to a proper subset of in-principle available data. Thinking about this or that in terms of its being such and so necessarily relies on selection functions. These selection functions are realized in our minds in the form of consciously available glimpses of reality. Insofar as consciousness is essentially tied to subjectivity (a matter I will discuss in detail in Chapter 3) and, thus, to being wrong, discourse about consciousness can be reconstrued as a manner of speaking about *subjective* sense.

Subjective sense connects someone to objective sense. Subjective sense is objective sense processed by a specific, embodied thinker. We experience reality from somewhere in virtue of being amid the kinds of objects we are capable of grasping as being such and so. Among other things, this means that we cannot be metaphysically distinct from the structures we grasp when effectively dealing with how things are.

For this reason, it is insufficient to think of objective senses as belonging to a realm that is categorically distinct from the realm we occupy as embodied thinkers, i.e., as animals. Being a thinking animal cannot preclude access to how things really are. On the contrary, animals (not just human animals) are paradigmatic thinkers. They are in touch with how things are from their specific standpoint. To the extent to which this standpoint can be classified as "conscious," they process reality in a subjective, fallible mode. Unlike the subjective mode of information processing that accounts for our fallibility, objective senses are not the kinds of things that can be fallible. "2 + 2" as one of the senses of "4" or the literal visual perspective on Mount Vesuvius from a certain angle are not fallible. However, even the most skilled mathematician and the best painter are fallible with respect to senses of mathematical objects and literal visual perspectives.

What transforms an objective sense into a fallible, subjective one, therefore, need not be construed in general as an insurmountable distortion of content. Rather, fallibility resides in the relationship between a given content and its inferential environment. Animals relate to content as being of a certain kind, classifying content in terms of exercises of their conceptual capacities. These conceptual capacities transcend what is actually given to the animal by a long shot. Without this transcendence, *we* would not get reality in view that does not entail that we produce a second reality by which we (mis-)represent first-order reality.[84]

Concepts of the mind are concepts of how objective sense is accessible by way of subjective sense. They are concepts of the interface of objective and subjective sense, an interface which is itself part of the realm of sense. Our mentalistic vocabulary serves the function of specifying such an interface. From the theory position of New Realism discussions of the mind can be seen as a contribution to a better understanding of the architecture of sense rather than as psychological clarifications concerning those states in a given animal that are essentially non-shareable and mysteriously conscious. This is one theoretical advantage of extending the mind by extending sense rather than consciousness.

Objective Sense and (Linguistic) Meaning

In general, a sense is a mode of presentation of an object. There are different kinds of modes of presentation. These different kinds are instances of the overall concept of a sense. But they do not form a single architecture. Reality consists of a bunch of fos each of which is individuated in contradistinction to other fos by the senses that account for the fact that there are rules for including objects in their fields. For something to be an object, there has to be at least one fos in which it appears. Thus, there are not any objects without an associated relation of sense that maps them onto their domain.

SENSE, NONSENSE, AND SUBJECTIVITY

This conception of sense raises some important issues, in particular when it comes to the interface where the subjective and the objective meet. To account for the fact that we are capable of articulating how things are as seen from within subjectivity and our shared linguistic practices of communication, we introduce the concept of "meaning." In speaking about reality, we come to fuse intersubjective (linguistic) meaning with objects and facts without thereby having to assume that our linguistic meanings are mind-independent and in some such sense objective (naturalizable) entities.[85] To the extent to which linguistic meaning can be seen as unproblematically expressing thought grasping objective sense, it is indeed part of any full account of how subjective (here: linguistic) and objective sense are connected.

Accordingly, I now want to focus on the relationship between realism about sense and (linguistic) meaning. In this context, Jocelyn Benoist has recently pointed out that there is a problematic anti-realist inclination built into some of the semantic foundations of so-called analytic philosophy of language.

> This anti-realism was characteristic of its semantic phase, when, even as it purported to be realist, it essentially placed the world at a *distance from us,* something which we could access only by *referring* to it—as though there were always a referential distance between us and the world. In fact, AP [analytic philosophy] had its own struggle to recover the thought that things, even when we speak of them and even *in* speaking of them, are not mere objects of reference but things that possess *other ways of being* (than to be referred to) just as we have more ways of relating to them than merely referring to them.[86]

This problem is encapsulated in the idea that reality should be identified with the referents of some privileged class of terms (such as proper names) rather than with the senses or linguistic meanings that at most serve as modes of accessing language-independent reality. This assumption has produced strange effects, not the least of which is Frege's own idea that whole thoughts (well-formed propositions) designate one of two objects: the true or the false.[87] He explicitly endorses the idea that thoughts are proper names of truth values—an idea not really taken up in his wake.

In the semantic tradition drawing on Frege, linguistic meaning is usually construed in terms of a reference relation whose paradigm is the relationship between a sign and what it designates.[88]

It is commonly assumed that one can read Frege's sense-reference distinction as a contribution to semantics or the philosophy of language more generally construed. According to this understanding, senses systematically correlate with meanings of words embedded in sentences. Yet, at this point, one ought to be careful not to identify senses with meanings. If senses were identical with meanings, there would not be any senses in the absence of meanings, hence no objective senses at all.[89] Whatever the conditions of production of meanings in natural languages, they would at the same time be conditions of production of sense. Given that it is very plausible to assume that the use of language constitutes an important part of the meaning of words and sentences, the genealogy of a given use of language would provide us with conclusive insights into the realm of sense, which could not stretch any further than the meanings actually available to competent speakers.

If all senses were meanings, non-linguistic reality would not be structured according to the kinds of rules of field-constitution that are open to us in virtue of our competent use of language. There would be a categorical difference between meanings and the realm of non-linguistic structures that they relate to (paradigmatically by way of semantic aboutness).

The first problem with this view, which is associated with various versions of a linguistic turn beginning in the eighteenth century, is that it makes it hard to grasp how we can understand a reality that is in itself devoid of linguistic meaning.[90] Here, it is not sufficient to insist with Benoist that "reality *simpliciter* is just *what norms apply to*. As such, it is what it is, whether a norm is applied to it or not."[91] Replacing referential distance by *"logical distance"*[92] is still a version of the idea that reality essentially differs from our ways of articulating a relationship to it. Surprisingly, Benoist at some point even introduces the notion of "reality itself" that he distinguishes from "intentional reality,"[93] as if intentional reality were ultimately less real.

I surmise that this is an expression of a tension in Benoist's conception of realism. His acceptance of an Aristotelian conception of "the ontological grounding of truth" turns out to counteract his otherwise laudable insight that "the majority of the real things that play a part in our lives are not physical things—or at least not things that are *only* physical." Why, then, rule out that linguistic meaning qua sets of norms or rules exists in the full-blooded sense of the term, all the while accepting that "social reality possesses a terrible robustness of its own"?[94]

The rules that constitute mountains as a topic for conversations imply that mountains, for instance, differ from valleys in such a way that there is something that holds them together in a meaningful way. The fact that mountains and valleys are related to each other, however, is not itself a *linguistic* fact. This is even more evident in cases where we are dealing with natural kinds or the joints of nature, as the saying goes. Let us assume, not at all implausibly, that there are some elementary particles or other whose defining properties are adequately captured by existing physical theory. Then there is a complicated rulebook with which we make these properties explicit in terms of equations, referring terms, non-referential (inferential) items, operators, Dirac distributions, and so forth that constitute our physical vocabulary. This rulebook is supposed to provide us with explicit, understandable clues concerning the behavior of entities that we rightly treat as non-linguistic.

What we believe to discover with the help of experiments, measurements, theories, etc. are properties of the things themselves. If there were a categorical difference between the rules of the vocabulary that we deploy in order to make natural kinds available to understanding and explanation and the regularities we thereby attempt to codify, we would have to be in a position to assume that the non-linguistic items with which we are dealing substantially differ from the way in which they are presented to us. At least, they could not have the features we attribute to them on the level of meaning. However, we use predicates in order to express properties in such a way that the proper names for the objects and the predicates designed to individuate them correspond to a distinction in non-linguistic reality. The sense of "spin" might be complicated to grasp (it takes quite some mathematical training to understand what spin is). But once we grasp it, it appears to be the case that we understand something about reality for which it is not essential that we use linguistic code in order to articulate a structure of thought.

In the visual case, this is even more evident than in more sophisticated theoretical scenarios that put us in touch with so-called unobservables.

SENSE

If I see an object, such as the typical philosophers' table, my literal visual perspective on the table is not a linguistic item. While one might claim that our linguistic competence shapes our perceptual experience, this still much-discussed claim should not be stretched so far as to entail that no one has perceptual experience of objects without linguistic training, for receiving any kind of linguistic training presupposes perceptual awareness (in whatever sense modality is available to a given trainee) of the trainer, their overt actions, sounds, etc.[95] We could not ever become members of a speech community without already being equipped with sensory modalities that are operative in providing us with access to a realm of non-linguistic senses (such as literal visual perspectives). In short, objectivity and veridicality originate below the threshold of linguistically structured awareness.[96]

That there are objective senses does not rule out that linguistic meanings are produced by communities that use language and transmit uses via complicated and highly dynamic chains of tradition. Natural languages come into existence and evolve. In that sense, linguistic meanings are produced and reproduced, but the senses that are associated with meanings are not thereby produced and reproduced by the same "grammatical" principles.[97]

The idea of an objective realm of senses that stretches indefinitely beyond any given linguistic community and their expressive powers does not mean that all senses are real in virtue of being what they are regardless of our relationship to them. Some senses constitutively involve us. The literal visual perspective I have with respect to a table or the perspective I gain on a political speech act I abhor by classifying it as "propaganda," say, involve my subjectivity. As a subject I bring along a socially conditioned lens through which speech acts or other strings of socially symbolic code are identifiable as propaganda. Thinking of something as propaganda implies a value judgment that allows me to discern certain patterns of (linguistic) behavior as objectionable. The linguistic meaning of terms such as "propaganda" is tied to subjective sense. Without the historical, recorded experience of making sense of the practices of propaganda, we would not be able to understand what we are talking about when we talk about propaganda. However, subjectivity, like any other object that I can direct my thought at, is itself embedded in the realm of sense. The presence of subjects in the texture of fos contributes to the

47

extension of the realm of sense. We modify the realm of sense in virtue of being present in it.

This modification does not mean that we are never in a position to grasp non-linguistic reality without somehow distorting it due to subjective factors. The distorting factors (subjectivity) are not in turn distorted by our attempts to see through them. Rightly condemning something as propaganda is not necessarily involved in some kind of inevitably propagandistic speech act. The critique of ideology is not necessarily ideological; not everything is politicized. If we suspect language of distorting non-linguistic reality by producing a realm of sense that does not correspond to the way things really are, the suspicion itself has to be couched in terms that undermine its plausibility. We cannot suspect language to be misleading when it comes to how things are without thereby suspecting the linguistic texture of that thought as well.

To be sure, the adherent of the linguistic turn could reply that language itself qua object of linguistic analysis is exempt from the suspicion of distorting non-linguistic reality, because in dealing with itself it is precisely not dealing with non-linguistic reality. But how does one explain this surprising epistemological difference between the necessarily successful application of our linguistic capacities in the case of self-reference and their surprisingly systematic failure in the face of non-linguistic reality? Why is language speaking about itself more reliable than language speaking about objects and processes in our environment with which we believe ourselves to be in touch regardless of the details of our linguistic equipment?

Another important dimension of the still ongoing debate with respect to the scope of the linguistic turn concerns non-human animals, infants, and other candidates for the status of thinkers who relate to how things are without using language as the medium of making sense of how things seem to be. It is wildly implausible to assume that non-human animals, infants, and so on do not relate to reality in such a way that objects are presented to them in a certain way. If there were not any senses without linguistically structured awareness, thinkers would not relate to objects that are presented to them in a certain way, which is an incredibly implausible model of the pre-linguistic mind.[98]

Against reducing senses to (subjective) linguistic meaning, in a recent book, Harald Atmanspacher and Dean Rickles have proposed a "field theory of meaning" explicitly drawing on FOS. In particular, they argue that the concept of meaning connects "the mental and the physical" in that it derives "from a domain of reality transcending their separation."[99] In this context, they use "meaning" to cover both Fregean reference (which they call meaning's "surface structure") and Fregean sense (the "deep structure of meaning").[100] According to their account, sense is the glue that ties the object of a reference relation to a thinker. Sense is "experienced" "by understanding"[101] in such a way that the idea of thinking as a sense modality (see the section "Thinking Thinkers") is connected with a solution to the looming threat of rule-following regresses. In order for us to be in a position to refer to something in particular, we notoriously need to be able to individuate objects. We manifest concept possession by way of exercises of discriminatory capacities. But that famously requires that we transcend any given causal scenario where we could think of the reference relation as being in principle reducible to a causal flow between an embodied thinker's neural endowment and the object affecting her sensibility.[102]

This allows us to think of the reference relation as a paradigm case for the mind-body-problem, whose generality must not be confused with the hard problem concerning the nature of the relationship between neural tissue and consciousness. Thus, the solution space for the various regress problems and shortcomings of a "purely" causal theory of the reference relation provides a logical pattern for the solution space of the hard problem—a semantic fact that is already half of the solution (or dissolution) of the hard problem. If there is meaning at all, it covers both the object and the subject of the reference relation. Given that the reference relation cannot solve this alone, as its embodiment can indeed be characterized in "purely" causal, physiological terms, we require additional vocabulary to so much as successfully characterize sensory episodes underlying actually embodied instances of successful semantic contact with how particular objects are.

The additional vocabulary seamlessly flows from the recognition of the existence of sense. If there is sense, the subject and object of the reference relation hang together in that the object does not as such differ from its modes of presentation. Rather, its modes of presentation are among its properties. To be Mount Vesuvius is to be visible both from Naples and from Sorrento. If we approach it from different angles and literal perspectival scenarios, we experience its properties of looking like this from here and like that from there. The additional indexicality is a manifestation of the presence of the thinker but need not be seen as a distorting factor—a mistake that is at the heart of denying the existence of meaning.

Based on the solution space provided by a full recognition of realism about sense, Atmanspacher and Rickles rightly point out that the "Cartesian split" "of the mental from the physical is not part of the fundamental ontology."[103] What they call "meaning" and what I call "sense" here is more fundamental in both an epistemic and an ontological respect. Epistemically, our mode of processing objective sense (including mind-independent physical facts) requires acts of abstraction and understanding of patterns we can discern as independent from us. In part, reality is presented to us as thus independent. Stating the independence presupposes recognition of the reciprocal sense-dependence of subjectivity and objectivity, to use Brandom's insightful distinction again:[104] the concept of mind-independent reality depends on the concept of mindedness without it being the case that mind-independent reality thereby surreptitiously turns into something mental. The Cartesian split is real, but the split is mind-dependent in at least the trivial way that it is supposed to cover a distinction between the physical and the mental. What we experience as understanding, moreover, is a manifestation of our presence in fos, which cannot be reduced to physical contact between a bunch of bodies. Space is furnished by way of functions that constitute relations among objects in a given fos. These functions are objective senses, and their subjective repercussion has a hermeneutic component which can be gleaned from the *reductio ad absurdum* of meaning denialism: in the absence of meaning facts, we have to think of human linguistic communities as chance behavioral sequences rather than as social formations of communicators.

To be sure, this presupposes that the "meaning facts" of whose existence the Kripensteinian skeptic despairs "[transcend] the public-private distinction,"[105] which does not make them less real, because reality must not be confused with mind-independence. Meanings really "just ain't in the head,"[106] which is not to say that they are "outside of our head" and, thus, are somehow reducible to a combination of social and causal factors, as Hilary Putnam's originally semantic externalism maintained.

Atmanspacher has rightly pointed out to me that the concept of sense in FOS cannot, therefore, be identical to Fregean sense, for Fregean sense

SENSE

is indeed entirely on the objective side. His "third realm" excludes thinkers whose self-investigation is relegated to the leftover, imaginary position of "psychology."[107] This is a consequence of his two-tiered ontology of meaning which leads him to the idiosyncratic use of "reference" (*Bedeutung*) according to which reference is not quite a relation, but rather one relatum, namely the senseless object.

This invites the worry of the unity of the proposition that was hotly debated in Frege's time: If propositions are sense structures (as Frege thought) that are correlated with various "references" depending on the level of analysis (the decomposition) of the full proposition into parts, then how do the parts so much as hang together in the proposition?[108] Frege's best answer is the notion of the sense of a whole proposition that correlates with a truth value as an object (the true and the false). While this kind of semantic holism has some welcome features, it does not solve the problem of the reference of individual terms identifiable via one of the many decompositions of a proposition.

Let's take the proposition *that Mont Blanc is a mountain*. The sense of the proposition correlates it with the object called "the true" (let's bracket the thorny issue of how we can name that logical object). Now, we can decompose the proposition into various structures such as *that . . . is a mountain* and *that Mont Blanc is a. . . .* These decompositions force us to recognize a sense of proper names and of concepts if we do not want to think of the reference relation as entirely causal on that level, which aggravates the unity of the proposition problem (as Fregeans rightly argue against the Russellian / Wittgensteinian "chemical" notion that facts are dissolvable into bunches of objects). But how do the manifold senses we discover by reflecting on the meaning of given truth-evaluable utterances hang together in one single proposition?

Atmanspacher and Rickles argue that we need a third term which transcends the semantic version of the Fregean split. They use "meaning," for which they provide a field theory which is closely allied with FOS. This made me aware of the fact that what I call a "sense" on this level certainly diverges from Fregean orthodoxy, because it allows me to think of the unity of the proposition to be a constellation of fos. The whole proposition is embedded in larger scenarios that form wholes of which the various decompositions are parts. What Frege lacks is the concept of a field and, thus, the concept of a field theory of meaning (or sense).[109] His notion of a sense is tainted by his attempt to imbue it with some relevant features of the reference relation, which is manifest in his famous allegory of the telescope.

> The referent of a proper name is the object itself which we designate by its means; the conception, which we thereby have, is wholly subjective; in between lies the sense, which is indeed no longer subjective like the conception, but is yet not the object itself. The following analogy will perhaps clarify these relationships. Somebody observes the moon through a telescope. I compare the moon itself to the referent; it is the object of the observation, mediated by the real image projected by the object glass in the interior of the telescope, and by the retinal image of the observer. The former I compare to the sense, the latter to the conception or experience. The optical image in the telescope is indeed one-sided and dependent upon the standpoint of observation; but it is still objective, inasmuch as it can be used by several observers. At any rate it could be arranged for several to use it simultaneously. But each one would have his own retinal image.[110]

Surprisingly, in Frege's stage-setting the connection between sense and the referent (the reference relation) is represented as a feature of the telescope itself whose orientation produces a "real image" (an interface, after all!) in its interior. Thus, there has to be some causal story of how the sense is produced, which is surprising given the official "location" of Fregean propositions in a third realm, which does not seem to be part of the causal order (as ordinarily construed).

Frege should never have detached the subject from the object in such a way that he can only link them indirectly by way of introducing a third term (the reference relation) that hovers in between the object and the subject. Rather, he should have thought of sense as the real sense of a situation we actually find ourselves in when we begin to analyze our thought episodes into structures, some of which rightly count as propositional, i.e., as truth-evaluable and therefore conducive to logical investigation in the now usual sense of the term. But that would have required the notion of a subjective sense and of the activity of thinking (grasping objective sense) as both real and irreducible to the psychologistic notion of Fregean "representation" (*Vorstellung*).

We can circumvent the traditional conundrums of how Fregean sense, reference, and linguistic meaning are related (which have shaped many a development of analytic philosophy of language for a century), by leaving behind the idea that meaning is a subjective phenomenon socially produced in order to put us in touch with how things are. Here, I endorse Benoist's diagnosing much of analytic philosophy of language as being ensnared in the idea of a logical distance from reality. According to that picture, thought and language as such stop "short of the fact,"[111] as McDowell has famously put it. Once the mind is excluded from the world, we cannot reintegrate it in terms of our capacity to designate objects "out there." Language—understood as a socially produced toolbox for the construction of reference relationships—won't heal the ontological wound of modernity.

Sense and Consciousness

Time to return from language to being. Realism about sense is an ontological doctrine in that it maintains that for all intents and purposes there really are senses. I have now argued that we do not have to reduce them to a linguistic (or any other) level for them to exist. Senses are modes of presentations of objects. Insofar as they are objective, they constitute fields within which objects have their properties in relation to other objects. Objects are thereby organized in light of overarching structures that cannot be reduced to their brute individual arrangement. Rather, objects are bound to each other in virtue of sharing properties in their respective fields of sense, and insofar as they are individualized they at the same time repel each other. Insofar as senses are subjective, they exhibit a distorting feature which indicates the presence of a fallible thinker, a subject capable of getting it right or wrong.

New Realism sets out by repudiating the notion that the objectivity of thought is grounded in an objective reality, such that the hallmark of said reality is to be mind-, thought-, language-, and theory-independent.[112] Given that minds, thoughts, languages, and theories exist, reality as such cannot be mind-, thought-, language-, and theory-independent.

To be sure, this does not entail that reality is mind-, thought-, language-, and theory-dependent. Given that both the kinds of things one is inclined to classify as mind-independent and those usually deemed to be mind-dependent are real, the issue of mind-dependence / mind-independence turns out to be a red herring in the context of ontological realism. In this chapter, I have been articulating this point in terms of realism about sense.

In order to spell out the idea of realism about sense more thoroughly, it is crucial to overcome an obstacle built into the amphibious concept of consciousness. The term "consciousness" is amphibious in that it sometimes characterizes mere phenomenal episodes and sometimes refers to the kind of intentional aboutness definitive of some mental states and articulated in linguistics.

"Consciousness" is a paradigmatic title for the ultimate representational layer of our minds. The ultimate representational device is the one without which we could not be in a position to specify enhancements of our finite, parochial perspective. The paradigm of such enhancements are technical artifacts such as macroscopes and microscopes. Theories, models, propositions, utterances, pictures, artworks, in a word, the whole gamut of representational devices extends our consciousness by specifying contents that would not have been available otherwise. Astronomy and microphysics are enhancements of our consciousness concerning objects at different scales of the universe. They would not mean anything to us if we were not conscious in the first place.

Consciousness thus plays the role of an ultimate layer of our mental life without which we could not be in a position to transcend our parochial perspectives and extend our minds. However, given that this extension of consciousness is at the same time a modification of the bedrock of our subjectivity, it is tempting to conceive of consciousness as a surface whose contact with structures of ontological depth seems to be questionable—a problem I will explore further in Chapter 3.[113]

From the perspective of FOS adopted here, the problems of consciousness derive their force from an often-unarticulated ontology of sense. Consciousness is a subjective placeholder for the deeper problem of the interface of objective and subjective sense. The concept of amphibious consciousness—a phenomenal layer of our mind which at the same time somehow stretches beyond itself and presents our non-subjective environment in a qualitative, distorted medium—is a misplaced concretization of the analogous logical dimension of sense.

To appreciate the force of this claim, let us take another fresh look at the problem of sense and reference. It originates in a setting where the identity of an object under different modes of its presentation is at stake. In the *visual case,* there is an object of perception which can be seen from different literal perspectives; in the *logico-mathematical case,* there is some object or structure undergirding expressions of identity without which there would be no equations; in the *linguistic case,* we can refer to the same object with the aid of different descriptions. What these three paradigmatic cases have in common is a setup where a given object can be identified in different ways without thereby endowing a subject engaged in an activity of identifying with a necessary grasp of the identity relation that holds across a number of different modes of presentation. Someone might be surprised to find out that $e^{-3\ln(5)} = 0.008$, not to mention all the much more powerful equations that express spatiotemporal structures of the observable universe. Some other person might competently think about her friend Jim (say) without knowing that he is Banksy (I, for my part, do not know Banksy's real identity).

An illustrative example of the confusion of sense and consciousness is Donald Hoffman's claim that consciousness as such obscures reality, an idea which he spells out as a "case against reality." This serves as an illustration of the dangerous conceptual features of the idea of consciousness as a mental interface.

Hoffman sets out to defend the idea that perception "is not a window on objective reality. It is an interface that hides objective reality behind a veil of helpful icons."[114] He goes on to say that "if our senses hide reality behind an interface, then what is that reality? I don't know."[115] Paradoxically, this combination of claims (which are defended in the book on the basis of a metaphysical interpretation of a theorem in evolutionary neurobiology) leads Hoffman to speculate that "perhaps the universe itself is a massive social network of conscious agents that experience, decide, and act. If so, consciousness does not arise from matter.... Instead, matter and spacetime arise from consciousness—as a perceptual interface."[116] Hoffman goes to great lengths to defend the idea that reality does not consist of spatiotemporal objects that we manage to perceive. For him, this layer of our experience is an illusion which comes into existence as a side

SENSE, NONSENSE, AND SUBJECTIVITY

effect of evolution. However, he does not question the experience under-lying the illusion. On the contrary, the layer of subjective sense, which he rightly thinks of as a perceptual interface, is for him the fundamental layer. This amounts to his *"conscious realism,"* according to which "the world consists entirely of conscious agents."[117]

The combination of a denial of realism in the epistemological sense and a robust realism about subjective sense (called "consciousness" by Hoffman) amounts to a blatant contradiction. While Hoffman argues that we cannot know how things really are because, for him, consciousness is an interface that hides reality, he surprisingly comes to the opposite con-clusion as soon as he gives up on the notion that objective reality has to be spatiotemporal.

> The interface theory of perception contends that there is a screen—an interface—between us and objective reality. Can we hope to pierce that screen and see objective reality? Conscious realism says yes: we have met reality and it is like us. We are conscious agents, and so is objective reality. Beyond the inter-face lurks no Kantian noumenon, forever alien and imper-vious to our inquiry. Instead, we find agents like us: conscious agents.[118]

Hoffman believes to have resolved the contradiction by calling it "a new ontology."[119] But why deny the existence of an objective reality on the ground that we need an interface (of subjective sense) to be in touch with it in the first place? And why deny it at all if the conclusion is that we can grasp it as it is in itself?

According to the level of ontological analysis adopted here, Hoff-man's mistake is to eliminate objective senses and replace them with subjective ones. If reality consisted of senseless and meaningless items, so-called objects or spatiotemporal objects, we could indeed not know any-thing about them by way of our perceptual interface. I agree with Hoffman on that point. Our perceptual interface, which provides us with subjective sense, cannot be in touch with a layer of senseless objects; such is the cru-cial insight behind Frege's and Husserl's shared concerns behind their in-troduction of the concept of sense as mode of presentation. What we think about consciously is given to us under specific conditions. Yet, these specific conditions need not and ought not to be understood in terms of a construction or production of their objects. This is only attractive to the extent to which one postulates a notion of "objective reality" according to which objective reality is objective because it contains senseless objects.

Hoffman's book demonstrates that there is a profound insight in John Campbell's and Quassim Cassam's claim "that physics seems to push sensory experience into the head."[120] As soon as we think of sensory experience as taking place at a distance from a three- (or four-) dimensional physical universe, which by its very nature does not contain consciousness, we are screened off from reality. The best we can do at this stage is to inflate the subjective layer into an ontology, which is reminiscent of earlier forms of subjective idealism.[121]

In Chapter 2, I will argue that this is a nonsensical position. In the context at hand, what matters is the idea that consciousness as a purely qualitative layer through which we perceive non-conscious objective reality (whether it exists or not) is a manifestation of an unbalanced account of sense. It results from a thorough exclusion of sense from the objective realm, so that we are first pushed into our heads and then turned into pure surfaces of qualitative experience which simply do not manage to refer to non-conscious objects and processes in their environment. In particular, it misconstrues the thinker by identifying it with the conscious subject.

If we resolutely want to avoid a dualist metaphysics of mind and world, it is not sufficient to extend mind as consciousness (as Hoffman's new ontology of conscious realism does), for this leaves us with the unresolved issue of non-mental objects that should not be reduced to consciousness or panpsychist proto-consciousness. Not all that there is, is conscious. Rather, we should extend sense so that it covers both objective sense and our modes of registering it, the senses.

Thinking Thinkers

An important dimension of our thinking is in propositional shape and, thus, differs from the type of content presented to us in terms of lower-level forms of consciousness. In this context, the notion of a graspable thought, a thinkable, is introduced in order to account for the fact that two subjects can think the same, such as that $7+5=12$. This is one of the grounds of a distinction between the subjective and the objective: Whereas the objective is straightforwardly shareable, the subjective amounts to an individualistic standpoint that no one can ever fully share from the outside or from sideways-on. What it takes for me at any given point in my mental biography to think that $7+5=12$ differs from what it takes for any other individual subject to think that $7+5=12$. But if thinking is subjective in that fairly undemanding sense, how is it capable of grasping something that is objective? How can the subjective and the objective merge in one overall mental state, that of successfully thinking that p where the content of p neither directly contains nor indirectly implies or presupposes references to the subjective?

Associated with this problem, which Frege famously underestimated, is the fact that thoughts can be composed in different ways. These different compositions manifest the work of a thinker who analyzes their synthetic thought into analytic units, as Kant famously put it with his distinction between an analytic and a synthetic unity of consciousness.[122] While the paradigms of objective thoughts should not be misconstrued as containing subjective microelements, we should also not throw the baby out with the bathwater by ignoring the fact that subjects actually grasp thoughts. Our grasping of thoughts manifests itself in our capacity to decompose them without losing sight of their unity. Kant thought that we therefore had to put the thoughts together before we could grasp them, which rightly triggers the antipsychologistic response that this threatens to undermine the objectivity of thought and thinking alike. The unity of the thought differs from our synthetic and analytic capacities. Yet, that does not make those capacities subjective in the sense of a layer of mental reality that in principle separates the subjective from the objective. Given that mental life is part of reality and, thus, already part and parcel of the articulation of the realm of sense, the subjective must not be reduced to the mess of an utterly unstructured first-person confusion.

The orthodox Fregean conception of sense sets out from the observation that propositions or thoughts, for that matter, can be decomposed in multiple ways.[123] In this context, the idea emerges that the decomposition of a thought specifies an object on the one hand and a concept on the other hand such that for a given decomposition, the concept cannot play the object-role. The thought that Oscar is a racehorse can be decomposed along the lines of a subject-predicate form so that *Oscar* is the grammatical subject and *— is a racehorse* the predicate. *Oscar*'s role in that decomposition is to replace the — so as to yield a whole thought which can then be evaluated as true or false respectively.[124] Frege certainly is right in insisting that incomplete thoughts are not assessable in terms of a propositional truth value. Hence, it seems inevitable to think of *— is a racehorse* as incomplete and, thus, as not quite true or false respectively. So much for the broad strokes of orthodoxy.

Whatever one's preferred take on this line of thought, which is famously susceptible to paradox (as we seem to turn a concept into an object whenever we refer to it, thereby making it impossible to get it into view as such, i.e., as concept), we ought to distinguish our response to the difference between an object and concept in a decomposition of a thought from the notion that senses do not (at least not always) function as objects.[125]

And this is where thinking enters the picture. Thinking qua grasping or having of thoughts is sense that in its function as sense cannot be objectified. Once we objectify it, we do not grasp it as sense but as object. This is not a mistake but a change in category that allows us to integrate the thinker as subject into the expression of a thought recognizing, for instance, that I think that *p*.

The issue of the multiple decomposability of thoughts is a road to thinking as a sense modality. The principles of a given decomposition of a thought articulate the senses that jointly constitute the whole thought, as it occurs in someone's mental life. Thinking of Oscar's contribution to a truth about him in terms of Oscar's objecthood allows us to specify the sense of the properties we are in a position to ascribe to him. That does not make "Oscar," let alone Oscar senseless: In order for Oscar to contribute anything to a thought directed at him, he cannot be conceived as a pure referent (a "reference magnet,"[126] as the saying goes) that we are attempting to get a hold of by way of conceptual vehicles of apprehension. Thinking of an object cannot be a blind flight. Senses are not subjective means of shooting at an otherwise unknown target (the object) in the dark.

The activity of decomposing a successfully entertained thought into elements which exhibit logical regularities presupposes that we are already in touch with the right object. This is important for the all-too-underdeveloped theory of false thought. If *S* falsely thinks that

SENSE, NONSENSE, AND SUBJECTIVITY

Oscar is a racehorse, there is something about the target, namely Oscar, that S must get right in order to be so much as wrong about Oscar. For instance, Oscar might really be a donkey and the mistake is explainable in terms of S's ignorance concerning the relevant bits of zoology. False thought about an object requires a good enough grip on the object and, therefore, only takes place against an indefinitely large background of true thought concerning the object at hand. The more true thoughts we collect in the form of humanity's knowledge store, the more false thought thereby comes into existence as unintended collateral damage of knowledge acquisition. By necessity, there is unintended epistemic collateral damage wherever a subject makes a knowledge claim, because the knowledge claim is embedded in the subject's overall mental life (the epistemic and non-epistemic biography of their mind). In that context, no belief that is formed by exercising one's epistemic capacities is ever fully isolated from the subject's overall belief systems. And it is impossible for there to be an actual such subjective belief system that does not contain false thought at some point or other in its unfolding. If there were a thinker who does not at some point or other in their engagement with reality get it wrong, the thinker at the very least would not be a subject of knowledge claims.[127]

When we understand a given decomposition of a linguistically coded thought-expression or a mathematical expression such as $e^{i\pi} + 1 = 0$, we grasp the senses that allow us to identify the structure of the thought. Precisely because the senses articulated in a given decomposition by way of symbols defined in the context of a code (such as $i = \sqrt{-1}$) can be as complex as it gets, our understanding of an expression can be limited despite the fact that we grasp its sense. Just as much as I can be wrong about the backside of an object that presents itself as a blue cube (its backside might be red or any other color), I can be wrong in different ways about the solution space of equations involving complex numbers. Grasping a sense and, thereby, being in touch with the objects that appear within its scope does not grant anyone absolute epistemic authority concerning the object.

For this reason, the widespread tendency to reject the very idea of *understanding* as grasping senses on account of the suspicion of questionable claims to infallibility in the vicinity is unfounded. Senses as vehicles of acquaintance are not instruments of infallibility. On the contrary, they

SENSE

account for our fallibility to the extent to which the paradigm of senses in perceptual experience can be generalized.

In the case of perceptual experience, senses are perspectival modes of presentation of the objects of perception. Thus, content in perceptual experience is tailored to the literal perspectives available to a thinker from her point of view. Perceptual intentionality (beyond the much-discussed case of vision) is imbued with content that indicates the position of the subject. The content presents its object without ever disclosing the entire object—an old chestnut from the heyday of first-wave phenomenology. Content, i.e., sense in perceptual experience, discloses its object in such a way that it thereby conceals parts of the object that could not have been selected for processing due to the limiting factors of the organism involved in selecting parts of objective reality for subjective representation.[128]

Mutatis mutandis the same applies to the mathematical case and, thus, to pure thinking, where the sense of a symbolic expression does not immediately disclose all its logical relations to neighboring mathematical structures. The sense of a function such as *arccos(x)* evidently yields results for the definition range of the function, which is tied to other mathematical, in this case, geometrical structures that are not automatically disclosed to a competent human user of the trigonometric functions. Mathematical objects are like perceptual objects in that both are given to thinkers via a sense which allows them to be in touch with the objects. However, successful contact with the object never exhausts all the objects' properties, as any object is embedded in indefinitely many relations to other objects in the same fos or to other fos within which the object exists.[129]

Senses both relate us to objects and can in turn be objects within FOS. In modified Fregean terms: senses operate on the level of sense as well as on that of reference (at least insofar as they make their appearance within the scope of metaontological investigations such as the one at hand). Insofar as they shape the relationship between a thinker and the objects she is thinking about, they belong to her thoughts.

This leads us back to the set of problems associated with psychologism. We had better avoid any account according to which senses belong exclusively to thoughts that we grasp as objects. According to this orthodox Fregean picture, we run into the problem that the thinker's subjectivity tinkers with the objectivity of the thoughts-qua-objects she grasps.

One way to resolutely avoid psychologism is to postulate that the grasp of the thoughts-qua-objects has objective sense. However, if the grasp of the thoughts-qua-objects has objective sense, what is the relationship between the sense of the thoughts grasped and the sense of the grasp? That there is a problem here—which motivates my introduction of the concept of subjective senses—comes out more clearly if we translate the metaphor of a grasp into the (dead) metaphor of a concept (etymologically derived from the Latin word "*con-cipere*," meaning to grasp together). The senses of thoughts can be interpreted as concepts that structure thoughts. If we needed a concept of those concepts in order to think a thought, the concepts inherent in a thought would be mediated by a further set of concepts whose function it would be to put a thinker in contact with her thoughts. Maybe the kind of concept that can perform such a function belongs to the category of concepts of thinking, such as __ *is thought by S*. Then, the concept which puts a thinker in touch with her thoughts might simply be such that the thought falls under a concept of thinking. On the one hand we would have the thoughts, $\{p, q, r, \ldots\}$, on the other hand, the categories of thinking, {is thought by S, is believed by S, is rejected by S, ...}. The fact that one thinks that p indeed requires that the activity of thinking take place on the same level as its thoughts-qua-objects. An actual thought has the form that S *thinks that p* or S *thinks p*, for short. That S thinks that p is itself a thought with nested senses.

Yet, the problem this analytic strategy now faces is that the concept of thinking still has to be implemented in the embodied reality of the thinker, S. If S's reality as a thinker was categorically distinct from S's reality as an embodied subject, we could not understand how S's causal integration into any reality that can be sensorily registered contributes to the contents of their thought. Notoriously, this has led many to postulate that there is some difference between a pure (transcendental) and an empirical subject, an idea I wholeheartedly reject.

And that means that S's thinking that p cannot merely be a concept. It must be an embodied activity—unless it is possible to think of the embodied activity of thinking as conceptual in a sense not commonly in view in contemporary debates concerning the relationship of an embodied thinker to her thoughts. That is exactly what the idea of thinking as a sense modality allows us to do. We ought to think of thinking as an embodied reality without either reducing it to the brute materiality of the objectively available aspect of thinking (such as neural patterns) or to the subjective in the philosophical sense of some private first-person arena. The activity of thinking connects subjective and objective sense in the complex reality of a subject's mental life.

Frege did not consider the option that a thinker's actual thinking might be a movement in the realm of sense. This sets him clearly apart from full-blown Platonists who, since the heyday of the Platonic academy, have regarded the realm of sense as no less than as a form of life.[130] By contrast, Frege locates the thinker's mental (subjective) state in the realm of representations (*Vorstellungen*) that are at most the objects of psychological or other empirical investigations into the workings of an individual mind and its biography. Thus, Frege lacks the concept of subjective senses, as he restricts sense to a semantic dimension of objective propositional structure. Mental biography on this Fregean construal does not consist in a series of events in the realm of sense, which is non-temporal and non-dynamic. Rather, it is seen as belonging to a different realm that categorically differs from the realm of senses.

Once we integrate the thinker into the factual realm of sense, it is straightforward to reconstruct the good case of thinking as one where a subject thinks a true thought in the right way. The good case can in turn take many forms, which epistemology ranks in light of their proximity to the optimal success notion of knowledge. A thinker who thinks a true thought is considered a knower if she meets some further conditions which have as yet not been unified into a single theory. Yet, most epistemologists agree that the right way of knowing is a question of the form of justification at stake in a claim that things are thus and so.[131] Claiming that things are thus and so and being in a position to justify the claim when challenged in an appropriate manner are essential for the practice of defending a knowledge claim—a capacity in turn tied to knowledge.

For this reason, knowing differs from accidentally getting things right. True belief is not sufficient for knowledge, as Plato famously pointed out. Knowledge is more demanding in that it requires a specific relationship, a λόγος, that binds a thinker, her thought, and how things are together.[132] And this is what I have been calling an "interface."

In the good case, then, a thinker is straightforwardly embedded in the realm of sense qua part of a concept of concepts. The "concept of a

SENSE, NONSENSE, AND SUBJECTIVITY

concept" here refers to the idea that thinking a thought amounts to conceiving of a thought which can be analyzed into its conceptual components some of which are subjective senses, senses tied to subjects and, thus, to thinkers who in one way or another get something wrong so that the good case is never good all the way down. The good case would be good all the way down if the subject not only knew that p but at the same time also knew that all conditions for her successful knowledge claims were met. This would require knowledge of too many conditions (ultimately concerning the entire causal infrastructure of the knowledge claim, from the quantum level of the universe to the neuronal circumstances that correlate with the execution of the knowledge claim and beyond) and cannot be a plausible requirement for actual knowledge.

The concept of thinking requires a thinker: S. Qua concept, S can only be instantiated if actual thinkers are in good enough ontological shape to replace a variable. Given that nothing can replace a variable in a concept without having some sense or other, any given subject of an act of thinking has to be embedded in a fos to which it belongs in virtue of the sense of subjectivity operative on the level of thinking. Hence, there clearly is no such thing as a logical space that is hard or even impossible to access for finite, embodied thinkers. We cannot differ categorically from the thoughts we are thinking. Rather, we are part of any situation that is thinkable for us.

Yet, this does not mean that the set of thinkables is coextensive with the set of thinkables-by-us. The realm of sense outstretches our actual capacities to conceptualize it in detail. We cannot embrace all of logical space simply in virtue of conceiving of the concept of logical space as encompassing all concepts and, therefore, all thoughts that are in principle thinkable. Trivially, we cannot know enough about what we do not know in order to draw an all-encompassing landscape for logical space.

This is evident from the practice of mathematics, as we know it. Mathematics has not come to an end, and there are very good mathematical reasons to believe that mathematical research will never be able to solve all mathematical problems that could be raised in principle. There are just excessively many mathematical structures, a fact about mathematical objects that clearly came into view in the last centuries' various incompleteness and independence theorems.

SENSE

Similar things can be said about *logics* qua discipline dealing with logical structures. As we now know, just as there are different, equally respectable formal systems of set theory, mereology, and so forth, there are equally respectable formal systems in logic that differ from each other in virtue of the axiom sets that govern their fundamental parameters.[133] We currently do not know if it even makes sense to identify a common ground of the plurality of logical systems that would allow us to specify the intrinsic structure of a privileged logical space in terms of axioms, rules of inference, modes of composition, and so forth. In any event, the issue is wide open.[134]

The issue of logical pluralism is relevant to any ontological theory that makes claims about reality. Ontological claims about reality are couched in terms of structures that at least stand in a relation of analogy to a logical case. Whatever the outcome of ontological research concerning the architecture of reality (if any), assumptions about the expressive structure of the ontological theory ought in turn to be made explicit. Ontology qua discipline investigating the essence of existence (if any) and related concepts is practiced from a theorist's point of view. Any theorist will implicitly or explicitly commit to a bunch of rules that allow her to rank alternative theories within a space of options limited by formal and informal criteria of rational plausibility. If we knew that there was a single "background" logic governing all theory-rankings as such (regardless of the specification of a given topic) and if we knew which kinds of rules ought to be expressed in the context of making the singular "background" logic explicit, we could certainly rule out many options by showing that their prima facie conceivability was illusory.[135]

Thinking, even pure thinking (in logics and mathematics), is embedded in fos inhabited by subjects that are suitably attuned to the senses that structure their field of attention. Due to the answerability and, therefore, fallibility of thinking directed at objects in specific fos whose structure potentially outruns any given intellectual evidence a thinker might have, we become aware of the contrast of objectivity, i.e., the potential divergence between taking something to be true about the domain and its actually being true. In this fundamental respect, then, thinking is sufficiently like any other sense modality for us to overcome the dichotomy of perception and cognition and realize that we can grasp

65

concepts in the context of the activity of thinking—an activity which is in no relevant way sealed off from reality.

PART TWO:
RESTRICTING SENSE

So far, I have introduced a form of realism about sense. In light of New Realism's basic tenet according to which being real is not reducible to being mind-independent, I then argued that it is possible to draw a distinction between objective and subjective sense which allows us to integrate the (embodied, fallible) subjects of knowledge claims (and lower-level exercises of epistemic capacities) into the realm of sense.

While in the first part of this chapter I articulated the theoretical virtues of extending sense into the ontological realm, I will now turn to sense's inherent limitations, its bounds, thereby restricting sense. This will lay the foundation for the concept of ontological nonsense discussed in Chapter 2.

In what follows, I will elaborate on the idea that there is an in-principle upper limit to how much sense we can make of how things are. The upper limit is defined by the notion that there cannot be an all-encompassing fos. An all-encompassing fos (the world as an absolute whole) would be such that all objects either directly appear in it or in one of the manifold fos that appear within it as objects encompassing further objects and/or fos. The arguments designed to show that there cannot be a totality of fos and, thus, that the world as a whole does not exist, hinge on the idea that we cannot make sense of any position from which anyone could grasp such a whole. Thus, the notion of sense is central in the articulation of its own upper limit. The no-totality- or no-world-arguments then move from a diagnosis of epistemological limitation to a recognition of an ontological incompleteness: Reality cannot be exhausted from any point of view, as it is intrinsically and radically manifold. Such is the thesis of *radical ontological pluralism,* as I conceive of it.[136] Here, the radicality manifests itself in giving up on the idea that the manifold of fos is grounded in a singular overarching conception according to which absolutely everything ultimately hangs together. The realm of sense cannot extend beyond itself, as it were, so as to encompass absolutely everything. Yet, the reason for this limitation is not that there is a realm of pure referential materiality, a causal realm of nature "out there" that at best impinges on us, inhabitants of the realm of sense. Rather, the limitation is constitutive of the realm of sense whose upper bound is the no-world-view, which I will unfold in this second part of the chapter as an account of the bounds of the extension of sense.

Fundamental Concepts of FOS

Before introducing some novel ideas, it will be useful for readers not familiar with FOS to rehearse some of the opening moves of FOS with respect to the topic of sense. FOS defines "existence" as *appearing in a fos*. One of the reasons for this choice is that objects which we identify as existing are parts of contexts. They stand out from a context in which their similarity to other objects as well as relations of identity, difference, inclusion, exclusion, and so forth are provided to us. A fos is an arrangement of objects in a given field that is subject to certain rules. If we abstract from the rules, the objects lose their membership in their context and dissolve into sense- and meaningless items. They turn into what I would like to call "mere metaphysical atoms." The rules of inclusion and exclusion that allow us to reconstruct the furnishing functions of a fos are the field's senses. For instance, it can be constitutive of a field to be a scalar and for another field to be a vector field. In the first case, a number, and in the second case, a vector is assigned to each point in its domain. The actual numbers or vectors that make their appearance within the field are objects, whereas the fact that the space is populated by scalars or vectors, for that matter, is its sense. *Mutatis mutandis* for fos of an entirely different character, such as the fos of contemporary US-American politics, which contains two major parties, a congress, political scandals, tax regulations, and many other objects that are subject to a range of senses that can be articulated in political, legal, social, and economic terms. Those terms have their own senses that span theory spaces (in political science, the law, sociology, economics, media studies, etc.) within which specific objects (such as Joe Biden, the White House, the GOP, and state tax rates) make their appearance.

SENSE, NONSENSE, AND SUBJECTIVITY

Sense is an ontological concept. It has its home in the theory of existence. It plays a foundational role in ontology in that it contributes to the solution space of certain riddles concerning basic concepts such as existence itself, concept, identity, difference, structure, whole, and many others. The basic idea of FOS has it that to exist is to appear in a fos where an appearance is a mode for given objects to be arranged in, in potentially informative and intelligible ways—regardless of the actual presence of thinkers. Senses individuate their respective fields by particularizing their objects. They characterize the relations that obtain between objects within a field, but they can also cut across many fields. As I have argued in the first part of the chapter, some senses are objective, others are subjective (in virtue of constitutively involving a subject).

An *object* is something which is embedded in a fact. A *fact* is something that is true of an object. In the paradigmatic (though not fundamental) atomic case, we can think of a singular object we might pick out linguistically by a *proper name* that instantiates a property, which we articulate linguistically as a *predicate*.[137] In the case of reference to non-linguistic facts, the object is, of course, not identical to the proper name, and the property is not identical to the predicate. It is misleading to think of the relationship between a proper name and its objects, a predicate and its property, and an atomic sentence and its fact in terms of isomorphism, let alone mirroring. Though Wittgenstein, among many others, in the *Tractatus* rightly pointed out that a proper name, a predicate, and a sentence are in turn objects that hang together in a particular way, this by itself should not convince us that in the fundamental case the objects of linguistics are as such in the business of representing non-linguistic objects. There is no fundamental case in the first place. The paradigmatic atomic case structure is not itself a candidate for a mirror of reality or a privileged mode of representation of reality. The fact that there are some facts whose structure we articulate in terms of a single, one-place predicate which applies to a given object, is not evidence that reality is a complicated whole composed of building blocks that resemble categorical judgments of an elementary type. The elementary position of simple categorical judgments of the "S is P" type in our thinking is just a side effect of textbook presentations of logics since its earliest beginnings in the Platonic academy. To be sure, we can think of some logical structures such as $p \wedge q$ as a compound of p and q so that p and q seem to be more ele-

SENSE

mentary than the compound. But this at most mirrors our elementary practice of calculating the truth value of the compound by producing truth-tables rather than a composition structure in non-linguistic reality.

This is particularly pertinent when it comes to negation. $\sim p$ is not a composition of an elementary proposition p that holds in reality together with an absence designated by $\sim$ that somehow creeps into p's vicinity in order to turn it into a falsehood. Moreover, p, q, and so forth do not wear it on their sleeves that one might be inclined to think of them as having the paradigmatic form Fa or S is P (whatever one's preferences for articulating the age-old Platonic ὄνομα-ῥῆμα-schema). The variables p, q, and so forth are propositional variables that can be as intricately structured as the entire *Principia Mathematica (PM)*.[138]

Objects do not differ from the facts in which they are embedded. An object is identical through all its facts in virtue of being the glue that holds them together. Objects would differ from the facts in which they are embedded if they could be embedded in facts that undermine their being embedded in the facts we happen to find them involved in. Let us say that o is F, G, and H. In light of a paradigmatic (but not fundamental) way of counting the facts, o would be embedded in the following three facts:

(f) *Fo.*
(g) *Go.*
(h) *Ho.*

We can articulate (f), (g), and (h) in indefinitely many ways depending on a choice of language (including all the natural languages capable of expressing facts (f)–(h)). Let o be Angela Merkel. Then we could think of (f)–(h) as, for example,

(f) Angela Merkel is married on August 19, 2021.
(g) Angela Merkel is a head of state in 2021.
(h) Angela Merkel is a human being.

Angela Merkel is identical through (f)–(h). The predicates F, G, H are tied to her, as tradition rightly has it.[139] Any proposition (f#) which undermines (f) is thus ruled out by the facts. It could not be true about Angela Merkel that she got a divorce on August 19, 2021. None of the objects which is such

69

that it got a divorce on August 19, 2021, is Angela Merkel. *Mutatis mutandis* for all the facts in which Angela Merkel, or o for short, is actually embedded.

What holds factual structures such as (f)–(h) together, is the object itself. The object itself cannot escape the facts, as it were. If it were detached from any of its facts, it would be a different object, since the facts about an object deliver its identity.

A fact is governed by senses. The sense of being a head of state differs from the state of being human in various ways. To be sure, those facts hang together in that currently only human beings are capable of being heads of states (if "head of state" picks out certain roles defined by legal procedures rather than some broader notion of a hierarchy that might very well be instantiated elsewhere in the animal kingdom). A fact presents its objects in a particular way.

Now, if objects cannot differ from their facts, which are ways in which objects are presented (in virtue of the sense of a fact), it is reasonable to ask if they are identical to their facts. To be sure, someone at this stage might be puzzled by many things, such as how I can claim that objects are presented by their facts even in the complete absence of thinkers from the scene we are envisaging. But there is a shortcut to relieving this worry, which I take to hold across many levels of reflection at which a worry of this form can take hold. Let us call this the *transcendental worry:* how can we claim that objects are presented in various particular ways if no one is around to be conscious of said presentation? Otherwise put: how do objects look if no one actually perceives them? The form of the answer to these questions is that objects are the way they are presented to us when we actually grasp them as they are. The transcendental worry only arises at the level of false presentations that seem to put the object at an epistemic distance from a subject who wrongly takes it to be embedded in a fact ($f^{\#}$) where it really is involved in (f) such that (f) and ($f^{\#}$) are incompatible.

In false thought, the object and the mode of presentation partly come apart. A subjective sense is involved. Again, in the paradigmatic (non-fundamental) case, one can think of o that it is $F^{\#}$ while it is F. This is a paradigmatic form of a mistake in that one will have mistaken o for some other object which is $F^{\#}$. This paradigmatic mistake is not a building block in an architecture of more complicated, compound forms of mistake.

SENSE

Just like categorical judgments of the Aristotelian "*S* is *P*"–form are not building blocks of the logical universe, paradigmatic mistakes are not building blocks of a realm of illusion that is ontologically isolated from reality.

Let us assume that it makes sense, then, to ask if objects are identical to the whole of the facts in which they appear. Given that they cannot be embedded in other facts, this certainly seems plausible. I actually take it to be the case that objects are essentially involved in the facts we find them to be embedded in, which is one motivating line of thought behind the *bundle theory of objects*.[140] According to that theory, objects are bundles of facts. Otherwise put, an object is identical to everything that is true about it. If anything in the bundle were different, the object would be different.

In order to sidestep the atomistic mistake of building a universe of entities by confusing a paradigmatic case for a fundamental one, I hasten to add that facts are typically richer than an object instantiating a property. A fact such as the one expressed by the time-dependent Schrödinger equation is complex (pun intended) on many levels. It cannot be broken down into elementary facts, which consist in an object being a certain way. The objects involved in the target-systems which triggered the formulation of the equation in an appropriate mathematical code certainly are embedded in facts one might think of as paradigmatic such as "This electron is a fermion." But this paradigmatic form by itself does not reveal the complexity of the fact-structure without which the electron could not be a fermion. Some relevant complexity is encoded in the sense-structure of the terms of any proposition that we can express in our paradigmatic form. Nothing is so simple that it really just is F. There is no o such that it is F and nothing else. Hence, the idea of a fundamental, elementary fact structure from which we could somehow build an entire universe of meaning is illusory and does precisely not correspond to the facts. While full reality can be decomposed into local matters of fact, this should not mislead us into thinking that reality is made of elementary building blocks that enter into more or less contingent, more or less constitutive relations.

This is straightforwardly entailed by the basic concept of ontology, as I understand it, that of existence. If there were a singular object characterized by instantiating just one property, the object and its property, i.e., the fact, would constitute a fos. In order for that fos to exist, it in

SENSE, NONSENSE, AND SUBJECTIVITY

turn has to appear in a fos. This even holds in the following extreme case, which I do not have to rule out at this stage of the thought.

As Graham Priest has correctly brought out in an ongoing conversation about fundamental ontological issues concerning objects and existence, I accept that a fos can appear within itself.[141] Therefore, there are some loops in the realm of sense: it is (at least in part) non-well-founded. This opens up the possibility that there might be singular fos, where a *singular fos* would contain one object which is one way: *Fo.* That object would be identical with the singular fact in which it is embedded. If the singular fos is non-well-founded, it appears within itself. We can call a singular, non-well-founded fos a *monad.*[142]

Now, even monads are embedded in some fos* which differ from their self-contained fos. For the self-contained fos of a monad differs from the kind of fos* which are not thus self-contained, such that there is some fos** in which monads differ from non-monads which we can call the *polyads.*

To be sure, one might be inclined to go all out and present a full-blown monadology according to which there really only are monads which do not compose anything. Then, objects would be identical with a singularizing property that, together with the object, form a fact that appears within itself without excluding or including anything that would take place outside of this extremely dense point-like structure. As soon as one admits that there are many monads, there is too much they have in common in order for them to be sufficiently isolated so as to be thoroughly self-contained.

FOS, then, is a form of fact ontology grounded in realism about sense. Some of the facts recognized by FOS are subjective in virtue of involving subjective sense tied to exercises of the epistemic capacities of fallible subjects. The realm of sense and its fact structures do not form a world to which the mind needs to find some kind of access or other, as the mind is always already part of what there is. This excludes the possibility that minds might be brains in vats, activities that are essentially isolated from their environments and incapable of so much as referring to something external to their mental episodes, as such a view of us does simply not correspond to the facts. An important part of the facts is that we are subjects of knowledge claims which are answerable to reality by virtue of being part of it.

SENSE

Sense and the No-World-View

We cannot combine (fuse) all objects into a single fos.[143] Any position which gets objects into view remains insuperably incomplete, because there is no sense attached to the idea of getting all objects together with one's view on them into view. Given that this premise carries substantial weight in the architecture of the main argument for the no-world-view, allow me to rehearse the main argument in light of the concept of sense here.[144] Within FOS, the argument serves as a conclusion of negative ontology which sets up the conditions for the positive view of FOS.[145]

If to exist is to appear in a fos and, thus, to be an object, for the world to exist it has to appear in some fos or other. If it appears in a fos that is not itself the world, then there is a whole that encompasses the world such that it too has to be encompassed by the world that appears within it. However, that new whole would precisely have to be the world, as it would be the maximal whole of all fos. Hence, the world, if it exists, appears within itself. It has to be a self-including totality of all fos. That presupposes that there is a set of senses that constitute the world in such a way that we can think of absolutely everything as subject to a set of senses that cannot exclude anything. We need to help ourselves to a position from which it would be possible, in principle, to get everything into view. Yet, we have no conclusive evidence that any worldview gets the world as whole as an object that appears within itself into view. At most, we are able to devise formal ontological structures (such as non-well-founded mereologies) that allow us to delineate the structure the world would have to satisfy in order to exist as a fos of all fos. However, this does not suffice to show that we are in any of those logically possible scenarios. At most, then, metaphysics as the theory of absolutely everything—of the world as a whole—amounts to a description of a formal, logically possible scenario without us ever being in a position to actually determine if our reality is part of such a metaphysical scenario.[146]

It should not come as a surprise that sense plays a crucial role in the argument. An important part of FOS is the idea of *ontological descriptivism* according to which are no objects outside of the purview of some sense or other.[147] An *object as such* would be an object that is not individuated in virtue of being such and so. Such an object would be senseless. To the extent to which being such and so is a function of having properties,

73

SENSE, NONSENSE, AND SUBJECTIVITY

ontological descriptivism can be read as an endorsement of the widespread idea that objects necessarily have properties.[148] Objects are what they are in virtue of standing in relations of determining exclusion to some other objects, relations that are structured by senses that constitute fields.

Notice that this does not rule out being an object as a non-determining property. Being an object, being self-identical, being different from some other object, being self-similar, being similar to other objects, and so forth might very well be non-determining properties. They hold for all objects, which, of course, does not entail that there is a special case of objects whose being is exhausted by their non-determining properties. Given that the idea of non-determining properties in Plato led to the formulation of the first category theory in Aristotle, we can call the non-determining properties *ontological categories*.[149] To the extent to which they are objects of factual propositional thought directed at them, the ontological categories are ontological objects.

But ontological objects are not objects as such. For one thing, they differ from each other in virtue of being one of the properties that differ from other categories. Identity differs from difference and so forth. Being self-identical does not distinguish an object in a given fos from any other object. Yet self-identity differs from difference such that the object we call "identity" thereby exists under the description constitutive of identity.[150]

None of this should lead to metaphysical ontology, as I call it. *Metaphysical ontology* thinks of existence (or being, for that matter) as the highest genus. All other things are located on a lower level of a tree whose crown is existence. The level of reality right below existence consists of the ontological categories that are the highest species of existence. Moreover, such a picture is metaphysical insofar as it thinks of the tree of existence as encompassing absolutely everything, including non-existence and the objects that it characterizes. In such a scenario, there is a single, all-encompassing reality whose architecture corresponds to a maximal *arbor porphyriana*.[151]

From the standpoint of FOS we are adopting here, the problem with the traditional view of a chain of existence arises when we ask the question concerning its own sense. How can we make sense of the idea of a tree-like, all-encompassing reality while at the same time being aware of our position within it? This worry is not an optional epistemological afterthought about a stable metaphysical situation. Under which conditions can we actually know that we are on some branch or other of a maximal *arbor porphyriana* (however rhizomatic in detail it might turn out to be)? Given that there is a myriad of alternative views of reality (a plurality of metaphysics is prima facie possible), it is evidently not satisfying to insist that we have weak prima facie intuitions of the form that we are part of a whole that has to have some structure or other.

And this holds in general: The fact that there are many competing (formal and substantial) worldviews, some of which satisfy the formal criterion of being consistent and non-well-founded, while others think of the world as involved in dialetheism (i.e., as involved in true contradictions), requires that we describe the position from which we make sense of the world as an object of inquiry. And that, the no-world-view argues, is impossible.

We can thus generalize from an inherent epistemic limitation to the non-existence of the world as a whole. One of the reasons why arguments of this form go through within New Realism is precisely the integration of the subject into its concept of reality. We must not misconstrue reality as a world "out there" ready to be grasped (or misrepresented) by subjects whose ontological standing as minds, consciousness, or what have you is somehow ontologically suspicious. Once we recognize that any conception of reality has to include us as subjective thinkers, the fact that no position is available from which to actually make sense of the world in such a way that we can substantiate metaphysical claims beyond the cognitively empty gesture of a formal ontology is itself relevant ontological evidence. Radical ontological pluralism (according to which there is no category structure of reality grounded in an overarching fos or general concept of existence) is thereby combined with realism about sense. Extending sense so as to include subjects in reality generates an upper limit. At this stage of the dialectics, the right way of extending sense is thus effectively restricted. This allows us to postulate a new category of ontological non-sense as a constitutive complement to the realm of sense.

Reality: Why It Is (Roughly) What It Seems

At this juncture, one might wonder how such a no-world-view is compatible with realism? Might the no-world-view be an anti-realist intruder, as it were, a remnant of the major anti-realist, nay, postmodern theme of "the world well lost," to quote a famous paper by Richard Rorty?[152] How can we be realists without assuming that there is a somewhat unified reality with an inherent architecture?

In contemporary philosophy (both analytic and continental), the concept of reality has received considerable attention. Philosophers as different as Kit Fine and Jocelyn Benoist maintain that reality is the hallmark of realism.[153] To be a realist is to make room for reality. In this context, the term "reality" is designed to pick out an ontological thickness that Benoist interestingly characterizes as noise (*bruit*), a notion to which I will return.[154]

Benoist worries that the kind of realism about sense which I have been advocating does not do justice to reality.[155] As a matter of fact, what he calls reality (*réalité*) is indeed largely absent from FOS, apart from the role it plays in its notion of an epistemic account of objectivity. Here, I use the notion of reality (*Wirklichkeit*) in order to identify the possibility of getting it right or wrong within the sphere of thought and judgment. Reality corresponds to the very idea of an independent domain such that our judgments ought to be measured in light of it. On the basis of this consideration, reality is not opposed to normativity, let alone to sense, as Benoist thinks. On the contrary, reality is precisely conceived of in terms of its contribution to thinking without thereby being reduced to it.

Here, allow me to call "naïve realism" the view according to which reality is just there, a brute in-itself that we either register or don't. According to such a "conception," the fact that we relate to reality (from within itself) plays no role at all for its concept—and this is where I begin to disagree with Benoist and Maurizio Ferraris, two of my fellow New Realists. Both Benoist and Ferraris believe that they can detach reality to a certain extent from our attitudes and practices, which generates the worry that it becomes unclear how our normative attitudes can be in line or out of touch with reality in the first place.[156]

The concept of reality is constrained by epistemological considerations, which is not to say that reality would not have been what we find it to be in specific cases, had we not directed our thought and action at it. Epistemology does not stand in ontology's way. Rather, overhastily detaching epistemology from ontology either leads to a resuscitation of skepticism or to ignorance with respect to the role that knowledge acquisition plays in the shape of reality.

SENSE

Skepticism returns if we think of reality as the metaphysical other of knowledge. If reality simply is what it is—entirely independently from the way in which we take it to be—it becomes unclear how we could ever hope to know enough about it to straightforwardly rule out the very possibility of skeptical scenarios.[157] Reality, therefore, must be credited with some form of intelligibility or other. The fact that it is knowable (at least in part and, therefore, in principle) does not only tell us something about our access to it, as our access to reality is itself part of it. We access reality from within and cannot approach it from a "cosmic exile."[158]

If we downplay the epistemological requirements on an intelligible notion of "reality" by emphasizing the easiness by which we apply norms to reality, there is hardly any room for a full recognition of the existence of our minds as parts of the causal order. The mind boils down to practical normativity that leads to a dualist metaphysics based on what I have called "the deontological difference."[159]

Thus, we need to make room for some form of *transcendental ontology* or other. Subjectivity and human mindedness are parts of reality, such that reality comes to know itself in part through some of its parts.[160] While this should not mislead us into metaphysical conceptions of reality (worldviews) according to which it is some maximal whole or other after all, it should also not be ignored on pain of a relapse into naïve realism according to which the status of reality consists in there being "obstacles to free passage,"[161] as Charles Travis wittily put it.

According to FOS, reality is an epistemic category which plays an indispensable role in our self-conception of knowers. Reality, after all, is a concept, albeit one deployed in order to make sense of a distinction between our ways of taking things to be a certain way and the way things are. Thus, reality in that sense involves "mind-independence" without excluding the mind. The concept of reality is the self-concept of ourselves as answerable to something in such a way that we can get it right or wrong.

Here, *answerability* refers to the idea of an objective constraint which manifests itself in the potential divergence between how things are and how we take them to be, including ourselves and our mental states. This does not mean that minds are not minds. Minds are trivially mind-dependent in virtue of being identical to themselves, but they are not thereby mind-dependent in some more demanding sense of the term often associated with the idea of the self-referential incorrigibility and transparency of some cogito or other.

Reality does not in general or in principle differ from how it appears to us. This follows from the fact that it is not ultimately unified into a world. Instead of using any notion of reality as a block, FOS allows us to be more precise and think of it as the unfolding of the multiplicity of fos such that their individuating senses are only in exceptional cogito-cases (if any) identical with their being grasped as being such and so by a thinker.

This means that a popular contemporary route to metaphysics is unavailable. Let us call this standard route *meta-physics*. According to meta-physics, reality is not what it seems (to us) which is celebrated as a scientific discovery.[162] Throughout the course of modern physics, we have learned to identify patterns and regularities that seem to contradict common sense. The immensely and no doubt impressively successful mathematical tools of modern physics reveal connections and structures in physical reality which oblige us to revise many of the beliefs concerning reality we would hold if we did not take physics into account. While entirely true on one level, this culturally dominant narrative supposed to justify the transition to a naturalistic metaphysic fails in a crucial respect, which nicely comes out in a famous story told by Elizabeth Anscombe. In her *Introduction to Wittgenstein's Tractatus,* she remembers the following conversation:

> I can illustrate the method from Wittgenstein's later way of discussing problems. He once greeted me with the question: "Why do people say that it was natural to think that the sun went round the earth rather than that the earth turned around its axis?" I replied: "I suppose, because it looked as if the sun went round the earth." "Well," he asked, "what would it have looked like if it had *looked* as if the earth turned on its axis?"[163]

In my reading of this passage, the point of Wittgenstein's observation is that reality does not look to naïve observers as if it did not exhibit the kinds of patterns encapsulated in the mathematical equations of modern-day physics. Rather, the equations and overall theories of modern-day physics at best provide us with a deeper understanding of how reality appears to us, as many quantum theorists since the early heyday of philosophical speculation about quantum mechanics have pointed out.[164] Reality looks exactly the way it is in that its looks are part of it. Still, we can be wrong about reality and mistake it for something it is not.

Physics does not disprove "common sense," which actually does not even exist. It is simply not the case that reality strikes uninstructed observers as geocentric, Aristotelian, or Newtonian for that matter.[165] Geocentrism, Aristotle's physics, or classical mechanics are full-scale theories of physical reality and not articulations of an alleged common sense that is constitutively led astray by the appearances, in dire need of modern correction.

Moreover, the appearances cannot lead us astray in principle.[166] Otherwise, we could never overcome the limitation of our access to what there is in order to observe the alleged metaphysical discrepancy between common sense and a physical worldview which reveals a hidden nature full of funky processes.

On the epistemological level of observation, senses are vehicles of acquaintance. They put a thinker in touch with how things are. For this reason, they should not be represented as modes of access to a mind-independent reality, as this potentially undermines their epistemic function of manifesting reality in the first place. In order to know anything whatsoever, a thinker has to be in a position to select content for her relevant epistemic attitudes. The selection of the content is not generally itself part of the content, as this would lead to a vicious regress. A thinker need not represent her mode of representation in order for her to represent how things are from her point of view.

In this regard, we can endorse a modified version of one of Kimhi's main ideas, according to which the logical I is a syncategorematic expression.[167] As vehicles of acquaintance, senses present reality in a certain way to a thinker. Typically, they are not thereby represented among the objects they present. Yet this should not mislead us into thinking that senses substantially differ from objects in that they cannot be represented on the level of the objects—a line of thought constitutive of the orthodox Fregean conception of the realm of senses.[168]

Reality is thus in part manifest. It is neither as such a form of manifestation and thereby metaphysically tied to the existence of minds, nor does it love to hide itself. It is precisely neutral with respect to the fact that we sometimes get it right and sometimes get it wrong, which is why we invoke it as an epistemological category in order to account for our fallibility and our answerability alike. Detaching reality from its epistemological home leads to unwarranted metaphysical musings which can and ought to be avoided.

Thinking of a unified reality is still a leftover from the attempt to create a worldview. As a metaphysical concept, reality seems to be a unified block which the mind tries to grasp by way of producing concepts and maintaining social practices of knowledge-production. This leftover disappears once we replace the vague notion of "reality" by insight into the ultimately irreducible plurality of fos without giving up on objective and subjective sense. Objectivity need not and should not be hypostatized into a reality, an external world, with which we poor finite, fallible conceptual creatures must grapple.

Facts without Objects: The Road to Nonsense

In this concluding section of this chapter, I address the worry that the strategy of extending sense might lead to an extreme form of the primacy of the proposition according to which reality's fact- and sense-like structure is propositional through and through. This worry is related to the language of a realm of sense insofar as it draws on the Fregean tradition. Frege's starting point was the case of logical and mathematical thought and its analysis into what he called "thoughts," i.e., into structures that are in propositional shape.

Evidently, the senses involved in thinking about formal structures that are suitable for mathematical, symbolic modeling are as clear-cut as it gets. They are definite. But is their logical nature really a guide to ontological truth concerning objects that lack the conceptual granularity constitutive of maximally rigorous thought and discourse?

At this point, Gregory Moss has recently addressed the interesting question to FOS of whether there could be facts without objects. According to FOS, an *object* is something about which something is true. A *fact* is something which is true of an object. But what about truth itself? Could it be the case that something is true without being true of an

SENSE

object? Could there be a different kind of truth (such as metatruths about truth that do not involve an object about which anything would be true)?

I am sympathetic to a version of the distinction between *propositional* and *revelatory truth* which corresponds to Hegel's and Heidegger's notorious distinctions between correctness (*Richtigkeit*) and truth (*Wahrheit*).[169] Along one conceptual axis, the explanatory function of the distinction consists in the difference between a non-epistemic and an epistemic aspect of truth. Whereas we can express propositions about objects without knowing their actual correctness value, truth is the position we are in when relating to objects within a given field that is disclosed to us. The disclosure of each field is itself to some extent indeterminate in that we do not relate to neighboring fields in such a way that we always deal with closed fields. Famously, the visual field is not delineated in such a way that it has sharp boundaries that distinguish it from neighboring fields. Vision is constitutively blurry. Disclosure is, thus, not fully disclosed, functioning only in virtue of obscuring some aspects of a scene within which facts obtain.

This motivates the phenomenological vocabulary of unconcealedness and adumbrations, which is designed to articulate the circumstance that our position within reality is dynamic, open, and fluid despite the fact that we are able to identify objects within fos so as to express propositional truths about them that happen to be correct.

If this line of thought captures a relevant distinction within a genre of truth in general (that is divided into correctness and disclosure), could we not begin to think of metaphysics as a discipline which reveals reality as a whole to non-propositional thought? Non-propositional thought could then be regarded as a human prerequisite for accessing the realm of propositional senses.[170]

In Chapters 2 and 3, I will explore this option further in the context of my accounts of nonsense and subjectivity. Here, it opens up the possibility of *ontological blurriness,* which differs from *semantic vagueness.* Usually, vagueness is discussed in the context of intrinsic limitations of propositional thought, i.e., thought directed at objects embedded in facts.[171] However, it is hard to see how the objects involved in the semantic phenomenon of vagueness could themselves count as vague. Be that as it may, semantic vagueness is a red herring in this context anyhow, since thought directed at seemingly vague objects is normally construed as straightforwardly propositional.

In light of this basic consideration, ontological blurriness, if anything, is a form of indeterminacy rather than of semantic vagueness.[172] The indeterminacy at play could be classified as a background phenomenon in a phenomenological sense: In order for us to get specific objects in view, we have to focus on them. A given focus on an object such that we can think of it as suitably embedded in a fact can be expressed in propositional form. However, the act of focusing on an object or constellation of objects presupposes a prior selection which is not yet subject to propositional articulation.

On the level of consciousness, we experience a moving and blurry background from which specific objects emerge so as to become targets of propositional articulation. Phenomenology notoriously bases its theory construction on the dynamic, temporally unfolding, open-ended flux of mental life. From this perspective, it is natural to think of objects as correlates of consciousness. Objects are targets of a subclass of mental states that is characterized by a focus. Phenomenology correctly warns the thinker not to overgeneralize on the basis of a world in focus. The world, from the standpoint of the phenomenologist, certainly is not some stable structure of objects. If anything, it is a lifeworld, something we experience as a temporal flux without clear-cut borders. The propositional or "apophantic logos," as the Heideggerian saying goes, does not represent reality as such or as a whole (be it of objects or of facts). At most, it establishes correctness conditions for utterances that can be reconstructed as targeting facts and thereby objects as their fundamental constituents which account for their aboutness.

A classically minded phenomenologist in the wake of Husserl and Heidegger could argue that statements concerning the world (such as that it exists or does not exist) are not about any object at all.[173] They are neither correct nor incorrect, but rather belong to a different kind of non-propositional expression. What they express are the outlines of non-propositional truth. Saying that there is a world as a whole, in this context, could be regarded as a way of expressing the thought that correctness only gets a hold of objects if there is a blurry context from which objects qua intentional correlates of a subset of mental episodes emerge.

However, this phenomenological line of thought does not support the case for the existence of the world. At most, it ascribes a meaning to the phrase "the world exists" that does precisely not stipulate the correctness of a proposition about the world as object. A phenomenological interpretation of utterances containing "the world" in fact avoids ontological commitments on the level of objects in virtue of its idea of not treating the world as an object.

Moss's recourse to the correctness/truth distinction does not, therefore, put FOS on the road which leads to what he calls absolute dialetheism.[174] Dialetheism in general is the view that there are true (correct!) contradictions. That the world exists and that the world does not exist, is not one of those. If the first conjunct is motivated through the use of the correctness/truth distinction just outlined, it is not a proposition about an object at all. And according to the second conjunct, the world is not an object either (about which more later). Hence, Moss cannot draw on a combination of phenomenological and FOS considerations in order to produce a dialetheic proposition.

But what about sense itself? An influential line of thought in the phenomenological tradition treats sense as thoroughly non-objective. According to that construal, sense is something that is essentially tied to consciousness and consciousness cannot ever become a proper object. Consciousness is instead a dynamic field from which objects emerge.[175] As Alison Gopnik sums it up in a different context: "Consciousness isn't a transparent and lucid Cartesian stream. Instead, it's a turbulent, muddy mess."[176]

The phenomenological idea that there are truths without object, such that the world might be located in a realm different from that of propositional sense, is a paradigm of a commitment to ontological nonsense, as I will argue in Chapter 2. Ontological nonsense is neither linguistic meaninglessness nor some form of mistake, but a way of manifesting an important feature of reality, namely the fact that reality is not reducible to a network of propositions. However, this truth should not mislead us into thinking that we are thinking about the world after all—albeit indirectly, poetically. As we will now see in Chapter 2, ontological nonsense does not reveal how things are.

2

NONSENSE

SINCE THE HEYDAYS of the Vienna Circle, it has become standard to think of nonsense in terms of meaninglessness. According to that overall approach, an utterance, proposition, thought, thought expression, or sentence is nonsensical if it falls short of some relevant standard of meaning constitution. Theories of nonsense-as-meaninglessness cover issues of the violation of basic syntax, category mistakes, overgeneralized metaphysical concepts, unverifiable speculation, and the resolute nonsense of mere gibberish.

The original goal of this type of nonsense research—paradigmatically represented by early Carnap and early Wittgenstein—was to demonstrate the meaninglessness of metaphysics. Ideally, only *logics* as investigations into the very forms of meaningful discourse and *science* as methodologically controlled empirical inquiry into (physical) reality were supposed to be entirely free from nonsense. All other manners of speaking and thinking (in ethics, aesthetics, the humanities, the arts, etc.) were supposed to be infected by nonsense.

On closer inspection, the theoretical underpinning of the specific articulations of nonsense-as-meaninglessness offered from Carnap and Wittgenstein to Gilbert Ryle, with his account of category mistakes, turned out to be largely flawed or limited in scope.[1] They were based on highly questionable distinctions (such as that between the analytic and the synthetic, logical form and empirical content, propositional thought and mere expression of feeling in terms of propositional semblance, etc.) and turned out to be metaphysical and, thus, meaningless by their own lights (an infamous theme in the *Tractatus* and the literature it generated).

A century later, it is fair to say that the standard view in philosophy with respect to the nonsense-as-meaninglessness approach deems it a failure. For this and other reasons, metaphysics has made a comeback within self-described analytic philosophy. While the extent to which the return to (analytic) metaphysics can claim fully respectable epistemic and semantic standing remains contested, the relevant worries are no longer formulated by drawing on the conceptual toolbox of the early days of analytic antimetaphysics.[2]

As laid out in Chapter 1, FOS's framework is antimetaphysical for different, that is to say, for *ontological* reasons. The no-world- or no-totality-view argues that metaphysics, in its ambition to deliver a formal or substantial theory of absolutely everything, a theory of "how things in the broadest possible sense of the term hang together in the broadest possible sense of the term,"[3] is a form of failure. In this context, I have already alluded to the idea that metaphysics is involved in nonsense. As will become clear, by "nonsense" I do not intend to refer to forms of linguistic meaninglessness that can be categorized in such a way that we could in principle envisage a language reform or ideal language within which metaphysics cannot even be expressed.

In this chapter, I will argue that ontological nonsense is an important source of errors that constitute subjectivity. Here, "nonsense" will turn out to be a type of *confusion* that does not exclusively describe the mental states of a subject that precede and condition false thought or judgment. Rather, the idea of ontological nonsense emerges out of objectively existing forms of confusion that characterize our mode of being as subjects.

Reality in itself—at the very least insofar as it encompasses subjects—is in part confused, which manifests itself, among other things, in the good old paradoxes of change, vagueness, and temporality that the Greeks rightly associated with the topic of being wrong.[4] This chapter in part considers how these paradoxes are tied to our experience of reality, which in contemporary terms is associated with consciousness.

SENSE, NONSENSE, AND SUBJECTIVITY

One way, then, of avoiding these paradoxes is to sidestep the issue of subjectivity resolutely by adopting an eternalist point of view, by practicing metaphysics as if the world were primarily or even exclusively a stable stock of entities, facts, or pure physical events. Any such conception of reality as an eternally stable block universe encompassing all entities ignores *ontological nonsense,* as I will conceive of it in this chapter. At most, it reduces nonsense to a "subjective" phenomenon, thereby ignoring the objective existence of subjectivity, i.e., subjective sense, which is part and parcel of the unfolding of reality as we know it.[5]

This chapter develops the concept of ontological nonsense in three steps. First, it introduces the overall notion of *field confusion* in order to argue that metaphysics as a theory of absolutely everything (the world) leads to global forms of nonsense. Second, it demonstrates that diagnosing and eliminating *global* nonsense does not automatically solve more *local* versions of nonsense-as-confusion, such as the very idea of reducing consciousness to its neuronal correlates or the notion that knowledge as a factive mental state is a fusion of thought and being. Third, it culminates in the idea of ineradicable, yet meaningfully expressible ontological nonsense, which leads me to the final topic of the book: subjectivity.

First-Order Metaphysics as Field Confusion

Where sense is invoked, the possibility of nonsense is to be expected. Nonsense is a form of error that paradigmatically involves subjects and their practices of dealing with sense. For this reason, nonsense is revealing and not mere gibberish. It makes traces of subjectivity and, thus, a constitutive part of our lives as specifically minded animals intelligible. In light of this idea, I will now look at the phenomenon of field confusion.

The account offered here contributes to a clarification of the issue of category mistakes. The idea is to show that category mistakes (not to be confused with syntactic failures à la Carnap, which is but one theory of category mistakes) are possible because reality itself is structured in a meaningful way. To confuse categories is to be wrong about reality itself.[6] This does not lead back to a dualism of subject and object according to which the object (reality) is free from confusion, while the subject can get it right or wrong from a perspective that does not fit into its conception of

NONSENSE

reality. Given that subjects are real, ontological nonsense is also part of the totality of reality about which subjects can *be* confused.

But how can we conceive of nonsense in an ontology of fields of *sense?* Realism about sense, as developed in Chapter 1, presents us with a variegated landscape of sense ready (though not literally waiting) to be discovered by subjects, which seems to leave no room for nonsense. In the context of realism about sense, subjectivity and, therefore, the evolution of human thinking in terms of socially orchestrated trial-and-error processes might seem to disappear in favor of an ontologically grounded infallibilism about getting it right.[7] Against that picture of realism about sense, I will argue that ontological nonsense can be accommodated by FOS and actually lead to a theory of subjectivity.

One particularly prominent form of worldview I will discuss here is metaphysical naturalism, which captures the idea that all of reality, including the mind, could be turned into an object of natural-scientific investigation. Its more specific version, meta-physicalism, posits that the material-energetic universe is a big physical object of which absolutely everything is a part. Given its picturesque mode of representing the whole of reality as a big spatiotemporal system that evolves at any point in time according to merciless deterministic (or not so deterministic, quantum) laws of nature, it serves as an illustration of the structure of global nonsense and the associated subjectivity that attempts to dissolve itself in anonymous processes of nature—a paradigm case of confusing our "oceanic feeling"[8] of belonging to a gigantic whole with a given overall architecture of reality as such.

On a less existentialist note, one can illustrate the gist of my argument in epistemological terms. The family of worldviews associated with metaphysical naturalism confuses the specific field of sense of idealized, futuristic physics with the overall field of human knowledge acquisition.[9] Meta-physicalism in particular results from an epistemological field confusion. As a doctrine, it rests on reducing all methods of coming to know about what there is to just one single type of knowledge acquisition, namely physics as it is portrayed by the meta-physicalist. Many things we know clearly cannot be found among the kinds of things under investigation by physics. If I know, say, that Anna Karenina is a famous literary character, my knowledge does not deal with facts that can be meaningfully studied by a physical research project. Thus, to assume that absolutely everything is somehow within the purview of (futuristic) physics is a global confusion of different fields of sense. Physicalism as the doctrine that futuristic physics will provide us with a theory of everything that reduces all natural sciences to (more or less simple) physical equations, might be a meaningful and, thus, possibly correct view of nature's intelligibility, but as soon as it turns into a metaphysical view (integrating subjectivity into the meshwork of fields of physical forces under investigation by quantum theory, say), it becomes global nonsense by fusing everything there is into one all-encompassing fos of all fos. Such is the nature of global nonsense.

I call the underlying phenomenon, which has both a global manifestation and more local manifestations, "field confusion."[10] *Field confusion* combines mutually incompatible forms of sense by collapsing separate fields into a single field, which leads to various, never-ending forms of incoherence. Nonsense, then, is an important source of being wrong, rather than something that undermines an attempt to get things right *or* wrong, a distinction that should make it clear how FOS's approach to ontological nonsense differs from prominent contemporary Wittgensteinian treatments of nonsense that think of it as outside of the realm of truth-aptness altogether.[11] One corollary of the theses about nonsense developed here is that nonsense cannot be fully eliminated: we cannot "see the world aright."[12]

Nonsense raises a particular set of worries in the context of realism about sense according to which reality as such does not impose limits on knowability and intelligibility. To a certain extent, being is intelligible, which does not mean that "the totality of facts is conveniently (but mysteriously) trimmed to ensure that there is nothing that outreaches human inquisitiveness."[13] Reality does not impose limits on its own intelligibility and knowability, but this should not mislead us into thinking that it could be a subject's goal to fully transcend its own subjectivity by replacing all false beliefs with true ones in the epistemological realm or becoming a moral saint in the practical realm.[14]

This is one of the respects in which I have labeled my approach "*realism* about sense": The landscapes of fos are made up of facts about which we can be wrong. At the same time, this is no reason to think that reality is an object that we might get entirely wrong, that we might be detached from what there is by virtue of our very epistemic and practical capacities. For this reason, New Realism has no truck with skepticism.[15]

Contrary to an influential line of thought in modern and contemporary philosophy, though, I do not believe that the intelligibility of reality means that subjectivity and objectivity can ever fully merge on the level of a metaphysical thought directed at reality as a whole in its most general (categorial) outline.[16] Nevertheless, I do not reject ambitious metaphysics by questioning the objective intelligibility of reality. On the contrary, New Realism endorses an epistemological thesis typically associated with realism, namely the idea that reality is open to our thought, not somehow separated from our best ways of either making sense of it or limning the architecture of sense already within it.

Rejecting the epistemic accessibility of reality, i.e., skepticism, is itself a prominent form of global nonsense that manifests itself in various guises in the theory of subjectivity. Typically, it begins by stating some fallibilist thesis or other and attempts to generalize this to a metaphysical picture according to which we might be screened off from reality itself. Doubts that are actually intelligible given the sense constitutive of a given field (such as doubts based on insights into perceptual illusions) are spread over all fields we might come across such that, for instance, consciousness is seen as just so many ways of distorting reality, which might mislead one into thinking that there is absolutely no knowledge based on perception.

Ontology, the theory of existence, provides us with the right kind of methodology for diagnosing a central source of nonsense. My starting point is an earlier claim that "the world is a source of nonsense" (*Unsinnsquelle*), as I put it in *Fields of Sense*.[17] What I had in mind there is the idea that first-order metaphysics—the theory of absolutely everything there is—does not and cannot have an object, because the world as an all-encompassing whole simply does not exist. Thus, any attempt to state alleged facts concerning such a whole are doomed to fail. Their failure is an expression of nonsense and precisely not a mistake about reality as an object, as there is no such object, full stop.

The idea that first-order metaphysics is global nonsense produced by the world (or rather by a worldview) as a source of nonsense, is not an attempt to exorcise nonsense from logic. We do not have to engage in that activity, as logics indeed "takes care of itself."[18] Logics cannot be unclear—and it cannot be clear either. It just is what it is and thereby contributes its norms to the regimentation of our mental lives.

SENSE, NONSENSE, AND SUBJECTIVITY

I would now like to explore the idea further that first-order metaphysics leads to field confusions, such as the identification of the world as a whole with the most-encompassing possible object of natural science, the universe as a material-energetic system.[19] Contrary to some of the currently influential literature on Wittgensteinian nonsense, I believe that we can begin to taxonomize forms of robustly existing global (metaphysical) and local nonsense and show that they are grounded in different sources of illusion, delusion, and perceptual mistakes. Otherwise put, nonsense is the target system of a legitimate form of ontological and epistemological theorizing. I agree with the Wittgensteinians that metaphysics is a paradigm case of nonsense, but I differ from them by arguing that the reasons for rejecting object-level, first-order metaphysics are ontological. To be sure, there cannot be a formula of nonsense, a single source, or an all-encompassing category. Rather, we face an open-ended proliferation of various kinds of field confusion. And this means that nonsense is not something we can hope to leave behind by either overcoming philosophy altogether or at least certain modes of philosophical discourse located at lower rungs of the ladder. We need philosophy not just to be on our guard against the real and sometimes even dangerous forms of nonsense that *inevitably* pervade our discourse but also to be able to explain *why* they do.

As has been discussed for centuries, "metaphysics" has many meanings. I mostly use the term in three ways:

(1) *Meta-physics* is the discipline that deals with objects and facts that cannot be located in the universe, where "the universe" refers to the maximal whole under investigation by physics. If mathematical objects (or at least some mathematical objects) are not part of the universe, the part of mathematics investigating them by definition belongs to metaphysics, as do philology (for instance, insofar as it studies fictional objects) and political science (insofar as elections, geopolitical strategies and political institutions do not fall within the field of sense of physics, i.e., the universe). FOS is part of meta-physics too.

(2) *Meta-Physics* is the part of philosophy of science that is in the business of uncovering the meta-physical aspects of physical theory. Physical theory at some point or other makes assumptions without which it cannot ontologically commit to there being certain entities within the reach of its vocabulary. Meta-Physics is a part of meta-physics.

Meta-Physics is a highly developed subdiscipline of the contemporary philosophical landscape, which historically unfolded in accordance with the shifting background ontologies articulated within physical theory. Meta-Physics studies, among other things, the nature of space, time, and space-time; the interpretations of quantum mechanics; the methodology of physics; and the applicability of ontological concepts (identity, essence, substance, process, object, fact, modality, etc.) within physics.

(3) *Metaphysics,* finally, in the objectionable sense is the theory of absolutely everything, a theory that (a) ranges over physical and non-physical objects alike and (b) assumes that they all belong to a singular, all-encompassing field: the world, being, nature, the universe, reality as a whole, the cosmos, etc. I will continue calling the all-encompassing field (however construed in detail) "the world."

A *metaphysic* in my sense is a worldview. There is a plurality of meta-physics. Some metaphysicians straightforwardly make claims about the world as an object, such as David Lewis, who famously opens his *On the Plurality of Worlds* with the claim that the world is "a big physical object."[20] In the wake of Post-Kantian idealism, metaphysics of this sort used to be called "dogmatic" and Spinoza was usually regarded as the paradigmatic representative of dogmatic metaphysics.[21] In this vein, I call *first-order metaphysics* the discipline that thinks of the world (or rather "the world") as an object of direct investigation. Typically, first-order metaphysics depends on the availability of conceptual methods that allow us to achieve synthetic (genuinely informative) insight a priori into the fabric of the world.[22] Wittgenstein's *Tractatus* (as I read its non-destructive parts), Aristotle's *Metaphysics,* Spinoza's *Ethics,* or most of the work in contemporary analytic metaphysics are first-order meta-physics in the intended sense.

In contradistinction to dogmatic, i.e., first-order metaphysics, there is *higher-order or critical metaphysics,* whose defining feature is that it thinks of the world as embedded in thought as embedded in the world. Higher-order metaphysics respects the methodological demand of "transcendental ontology," i.e., the idea that any successful account of the world must integrate the thinker into the world-picture whose blueprint she draws.[23]

SENSE, NONSENSE, AND SUBJECTIVITY

The ontological ascent from first-order to second-order metaphysics has been a form of progress in that it identifies metaphysics' overall Achilles' heel (its dogmatic ontological commitment to a worldly totality graciously given to thought and theory) and tries to shield itself from the associated objection that even if such an all-encompassing world existed we could not come to know it.

It is possible to generate the meta-physical ascent from first-order to higher-order metaphysics from within a given metaphysic. For any specific metaphysic that is not capable of providing an account of the subject supposed to know that it is a part of a maximal whole makes its incompleteness felt to the theorist. If subjectivity is nowhere to be found in the worldview, the (imagined) world begins to feel like a lonely, meaningless place. If this existential hole is filled by some kind of speculation about the universe's marvels, the subject reenters the scene and asks for an account of its existential position within the meaningless vastness of its worldview. This typically leads to the notion that subjectivity is consciousness, a form of local representation of what there is that disturbs the meaningless reality of what there is.

For any honest metaphysician who tries to base their thought on known physical facts, it is obvious that there are objects that are not within the scope of physical investigation. For, trivially, the impressive success of modern physics is encapsulated in its conceptual recipe to construct mathematical coordinates that represent objects and forces within mathematical parameters that allow the most precise predictions of the behavior of physical systems possible. Contrary to what popular folklore about the uncertainty principle and the objective indeterminacy of the quantum world would have us believe, quantum theory is no exception to that rule, as it results from extending mathematical ingenuity into regions previously inaccessible to theory and measurement. Mathematical physics has no room for a kind of indeterminacy that does not have a mathematically precise location within the theory. Stochasticity in quantum mechanics, concepts of objective chance and randomness, the measurement problem, and their ilk are far from undercutting physics' mathematical architecture. Thus, if there weren't any mathematical objects, how could we even begin to explain physics' tremendous success in thinking about the universe in terms of mathematical structures at all?[24]

NONSENSE

In this context, it is possible to defend an extended physicalism that thinks of mathematical objects as parts of physical reality, where "physical reality" is not reduced to the material-energetic layer accessible to our causally intervening measurement systems.[25] Extended physicalism sets out to deny that there are objects that are not within the scope of physical investigation by bringing numbers into the physicalist world-picture. Such a view would not be meta-physical in that it reconstructs the apparently non-physical parts of the universe in physical terms (for instance, by treating the mathematical structure of reality in terms of measurable information).[26]

At this stage, it is important to remember that objects are elements that appear within fos. Fos, insofar as they appear in other fos, can also function as objects in that fos. Some fos overlap, some are disjoint. Fos can also be embedded in other fos, either as fos or as objects. Insofar as we can think of a fos as an object, it is a candidate for the position of the Fregean referent (*Bedeutung*). To be an object is to serve the function of ending a field-regress. The concept of an object isolates structures (that might have an intrinsic multiplicity) from other structures like a node's logical core from its position in a network.

We can now begin to unearth the deeper ontological structure of field confusion. Two fos are confused if it is unclear whether they are disjoint or share some of their objects. An illustrative example of confusion arises from the fiction / reality distinction. On the one hand, we imagine some fictional objects to be real items (for instance, by identifying Paris as Paris while reading Proust's *Recherche*). On the other hand, we know full well that Paris in the *Recherche* has properties that the actual Paris does not have so that it can at most be a modal counterpart to Paris (i.e., something similar to it): it is populated by many people whom we easily recognize as fictional in the sense both that they are imagined to populate Paris and are not populating the actual Paris. Here, a confusion arises when we think that Proust's *Recherche* presents us with Paris, for we accept both that fiction and reality are disjoint and that some objects presented by an artwork differ from other objects presented by the same artwork (and in the same way) by being real.

Field confusion occurs at the intersection of fos; it is a phenomenon of the in-between. It can take both an epistemic and an ontic shape.

Epistemic field confusion results from the lack of an overview. It is easy to confuse two (or more) fos if we are not in possession of sufficiently clear concepts and information to delineate the senses that individuate each fos. *Ontic* field confusion is the ground of epistemic confusion: error participates in the objective confusion of fos and does not merely consist in misrepresenting how things are with a "mind-independent" reality. For some fos are dynamic, temporal, and historical in such a way that their borders dissolve. Their senses are objectively unclear: there is nothing we can do to fix that. Sometimes, fos morph into other fos. This happens in conscious experience all the time. Conscious mental states fuse into each other, and they are not clearly delineated. Our epistemic shortcoming in individuating conscious mental states is a feature of consciousness itself. That we cannot freeze conscious mental states and represent them as atemporal snapshots of reality is itself a fact of consciousness and, thus, does not merely lie in the eye of the psychological or neuroscientific beholder.

First-order metaphysics are paradigmatic cases of global, maximal-scale field confusion: All fos fuse into one. This, among other things, is what makes metaphysics interesting for philosophy, because they are mistakes at the heart of philosophy itself—though they are constantly committed outside of the barriers of professional philosophy too. However, that does not make them less philosophical, as philosophy should not be confused with the reigning conceptual trends and technical exercises characteristic of its academic practice. The fact that many scientists (physicists, neuroscientists, biologists, etc.) both in their popular writings and, sometimes, within their academic research are subject to metaphysical field confusion must be taken into account in order to fend off the naïve positivist assumption that we can cleanse human thought of category mistakes by replacing philosophy with a mode of scientific or logical expression sufficiently incapacitated so as not to be able to express metaphysical propositions.

Metaphysics in the objectionable sense at some point or other reduces all fos to one fos, the world. This either works by way of ontological elimination or by embedding all fos into a singular, most fundamental fos. Ontological elimination maintains that in reality there is just one fos encompassing all the objects. All objects, then, are such and so, for instance, physical. Ontological reductionism claims that all fos are in one way or another grounded in a fundamental fos such that we can in principle develop a theory (or a whole tree of theories) that account for the emergence of less fundamental levels or layers of reality that, combined, constitute the world.

As an exemplar of this operation, metaphysical physicalism (that I called meta-physicalism above) is the position that all objects are physical and, thereby, subject to a single explanatory pattern (the scientific method). One way of making a case in favor of metaphysical physicalism is by hinting at a reductio of the opposite view (i.e., anti-physicalism). Physics' modern success lies in the human mind's ability to produce or grasp mathematical structures that allow us to build coordinate systems. These coordinate systems are such that we can map elements from one set onto the set structured by the rules of our coordinate system. Now, mathematics potentially has infinitely many conceptual or structural resources to set up coordinate systems and define operations that allow us to dissolve anything that has a geometrical structure at all into figures in coordinate systems. Arguing that there is a limit to that activity of translating the structure of elements in a given set (such as events we witness) to a mathematically regimented coordinate system (that is part of a physical theory) easily becomes an uphill battle, as all conceptual structure as such is amenable to logical reconstruction and, therefore, to mathematical modeling. If there are ontological limits to physics, they must consist in nonconceptual, non-structural features of reality while supporting real phenomena. It is not enough to insist that qualitative experience cannot easily be measured so as to associate vectors with conscious forces and construct a rigorous theory. Rather, we need a positive argument to the effect that non-physical objects can do some heavy explanatory lifting while not being amenable to the type of mathematical modeling definitive of physics.

And here is where FOS comes to anti-physicalism's rescue. For it argues that there cannot be a theory of mathematical functions such that all senses are reduced to one kind of sense (that of mathematical functions), which would allow us to map any set of given objects onto a mathematical space in the narrow sense of the term. Something or other must escape our mathematical grasp due to the impossibility of reducing all senses to one kind of sense. If there were just one kind of sense, all objects would be mapped onto a single fos. Yet, this is ruled out by the arguments for the

SENSE, NONSENSE, AND SUBJECTIVITY

no-world-view. Hence, meta-physicalism (like any other first-order meta-physic) fails due to a formal ontological difficulty that cannot be overcome by further research. In this context, its failure can be further specified by identifying the particular types of global confusion that give rise to different shapes of meta-physicalism.

Mutatis mutandis, non-physicalist first-order metaphysics fail too. For instance, subjective idealism is the metaphysical view according to which all objects are either mental contents (intentional objects) or minds. Subjective idealism, in that respect like physicalism, maintains that there really is just one kind of sense: *esse est percipi vel percipi posse.*[27] But, again, this cannot be true as it requires the kind of maximal closure that is ruled out by FOS's no-world-view. Similarly critical comments apply to any other form of monism, however strict. The idea of fusing all of reality with the One or Being with a single non-physical object with which we as subjects somehow fuse is just the more abstract version of subjective idealism. It arises once we fuse all mental content into the mind's self-consciousness, which is a consequence of denying that a material-energetic (or some other non-mental "external" world) contributes to the unfolding of the mind.

Traditionally, what seemed to speak in favor of subjective idealism was how it allowed a subject to reflect on itself as ground of reality, in a way that made the subject a promising candidate for the entity that performs the "strange loop" of non-well-foundedness.[28] If reality is mental content and if mental content is tied to a subject who can conceive of itself both as one of its contents and as the ground of all content, we can create a circular structure that encompasses absolutely everything—as long as we do not bring in the notion of content that transcends the subject's grasp.

The problem with subjective idealism arises (at the latest) when it tries to account for the fact that it does not initially seem to be true. To "natural consciousness," as the saying goes, reality seems as if it presents us with objects that are not merely intentional. Many objects appear to be mind-independent in the sense that they have features not revealed in conscious experience. Plus, there are many objects whose features are not revealed in conscious experience at all, so that we can easily grasp the concept of a mind-independent object. In their attempt to demonstrate that we are in the logically possible scenario of subjective idealism, subjective idealists have to construe this as a form of illusion. Idealists, therefore, have a hard time vindicating their position. Such vindication depends largely on demonstrating that their opponent gets a large-scale a priori truth wrong by placing their faith in empirical phenomena that, on closer inspection, are supposed to be unreal.[29]

In extreme cases, this leads to a flat denial of the very existence of sensory, perceptual, a posteriori knowledge. Knowledge, then, if anything, would have to be absolute knowledge, knowledge entirely detached from the alleged grounding of our internal information processing of an external reality. Such is the price for closing the circle around the subject to deliver a thoroughly non-physicalist first-order metaphysic. This makes subjective idealism prima facie *logically possible,* but *empirically impossible.* If subjective idealism were true, there would not be any actual sensory or perceptual experience: there would only seem to be. However, the seeming would require the conceivability of a posteriori content, something the subjective idealists needs to deny, as they are in the firm grip of a form of global nonsense.

Each of these extreme, opposite ways of carrying first-order metaphysics to its logical conclusion—meta-physicalism on the one end and subjective idealism on the other end of the spectrum—thus leads to nonsensical expressions. The idea that reality is just the unfolding of mathematical, point-based structures that are transformed into new shapes according to laws articulated in the form of equations leads to nonsense, as it winds up denying the existence of the level of abstraction at which its alleged truth manifests itself to the mind trying to embrace meta-physicalism. Similarly, subjective idealism becomes nonsensical once it faces up to its own theoretical expressibility. Claiming that absolutely everything is either mental content or a mind undermines one of the concepts needed in order to state the view one is trying to deny, namely that there are some mind-independent objects that reveal their features in sensory or perceptual experience.

First-order metaphysics do not have an object. Surprisingly, metaphysics lacks a world. Each metaphysical worldview compensates for this lack at the moment of its closure, by postulating something or other (a divine mind, futuristic physics, or some other demon) that finishes the job the metaphysician cannot actually bring to an end and, thus, adds insult to injury.

Local Confusion: Consciousness and Nonsense

First-order metaphysical confusion is global: It fuses *all* fos into one (be it one fos merely containing objects or a manifold of fos all contained in an all-encompassing fos). Showing that first-order metaphysics is nonsense flowing from the world as a source, however, does not suffice to tackle local field confusions.

In this section, I want to look at issues surrounding consciousness that generate a local form of nonsense. In this context, it is possible to specify one source of first-order metaphysics already identified by Kant's transcendental dialectics in the *Critique of Pure Reason*. First-order metaphysics can be seen as arising from consciousness thus: It identifies the mental operation of synthesizing one's conscious mental states over time with the idea that reality is somehow synthesized on its own, simply by being the world. Here, we can follow the Kantian line of reasoning that sees in the world a mirror onto which consciousness projects itself, thereby missing its nature as essentially non-objective.[30]

But how can consciousness be essentially non-objective? Scrutinizing this prominent line of questioning provides us with access to the phenomenon of local field confusion. Following a famous proposal by Tononi and Edelman, neuroscientist Anil Seth argues in his book *Being You* that the content of consciousness is maximally informative, where "information" is "reduction of uncertainty."[31] "Every conscious experience ... delivers a massive reduction of uncertainty, since *this* experience is being had, and not *that* experience, or *that* experience, and so on."[32] He goes on to infer from this concept of highly (or even maximal) informative content that a certain form of extreme phenomenological holism is correct, which he characterizes thus:

> On this view, the "what-it-is-like-ness" of any specific conscious experience is defined not so much by what it *is,* but by all the unrealised but possible things that it is *not.* An experience of pure redness is the way that it is, not because of any intrinsic property of "redness," but because red is not blue, green, or any other colour, or any smell, or a thought or a feeling of regret or indeed any other form of mental content whatsoever. Redness is redness because of all the

things it isn't, and the same goes for all other conscious experiences.[33]

The problem with this extreme form of holism comes out when we look at the shortcoming of what Brandom has labeled *"strong individuational holism"*:[34] If something is only what it is in contradistinction to everything that it is not, there is no positive content at any of the nodes in the network. If node $N=_{\text{def.}}$ not-N^* and not-N^{**}, ..., not N^{*x} and *mutatis mutandis* for N^* ..., N^{*x}, then nothing is anything. Strong individuational holism is incapable of stating what N is such that *it* is different from everything *it* is not. In short, the nodes must have intrinsic content (such as *that* redness) to fulfill their function of repelling other nodes from consciousness. That is the very idea of qualia that Seth claims for himself.[35] It thereby comes into view in the context of metaphysical theorizing.

The case of qualitative, phenomenological consciousness is instructive, as it already led Leibniz, Baumgarten, Kant, and others to postulate intensive quantities. Here an "intensive quantity" is a quality that can come in degrees with which we are immediately acquainted in virtue of being in the relevant state represented by the concept of a quale.[36]

And this is where a general concept of confusion emerges. Ramon Llull influentially discusses the notion of "intensitas" as something that indicates itself (*"ens, se ipsum indicans"*[37]). This corresponds to the idea that phenomenological content is informative. It can still rightly count as the paradigm of evidence or of what Kant calls "Anschauung (intuition)," i.e., the immediate representation of an object.[38] The immediacy of evidence in that sense is not compromised by the fact that phenomenal content is mind-dependent (in the way described by Seth's "controlled hallucination" reading).[39] But what if, as Llull, Leibniz, Baumgarten, Kant—just like their predecessors and successors—did, we take *time* into account as the transition from one slice of consciousness to the next, from one conscious state to the other? Bergson, Husserl, and all those who insisted that, if anything, consciousness is not a series of atemporal snapshots of reality but a temporal unfolding (appearing) of objects and processes, put their finger on precisely that point.

And this is where Llull interestingly brings in the concept of *confusion:* "Confusion is the principle, in which the movement of coming into being and of destruction originate" (*Confusio est principium, in quo motus generationis et corruptionis inceptus est.*).[40] Different qualitative contents differ by being neither isolated objects nor reducible to the node-like position within a network of purely negative codetermination. Yet, it is also not sufficient to insist that qualitative content carries intrinsic information such that our acquaintance with the part of reality that appears to us in such and such a way guarantees an intrinsic determination that stops the looming regress. Given that consciousness unfolds temporally, it produces a confusion. Any given, allegedly maximally determinate phenomenal content (which is what is in contradistinction to all other actual and possible content) immediately fuses with other content such that actual, always temporal consciousness confuses one apparently fully determinate node in a network with some other node and, thus, turns phenomenal points, as it were, into a temporal line.

For this reason, we need a concept that serves the function of a temporal bridge. This concept cannot be derived by adding more of the same. If the transition from one conscious state to the next requires a mediating state of the same type, we have not achieved anything but only multiplied our problem ad infinitum. This is where the concept of confusion enters the picture. Conscious temporality is essentially blurry. Despite their intrinsic content, conscious states are not isolated. They are also not part of an all-encompassing, totally informative conscious state (unless, of course, we accept a full-blown metaphysical version of Brahma as a cosmic consciousness of which all conscious states are illusory parts).[41]

In this way, the topic of consciousness and its place in a broadly nonconscious, meaningless universe brings in confusion, which raises the problem of how the local confusion of consciousness (the experience of time as tensed) fits into the broader metaphysical worldview which at last stumbles over its own subjectivity.

Once sense has been extended into an ontology of fos, we can see the world as a confusion of all fos into a single referent of thought and action, a big mind-independent object to whose parts we are attempting to refer by designating them, by putting word-labels on the items that make up the proverbial "furniture of reality."[42] But this confusion takes place in consciousness, which readily gives itself over to the oceanic feeling of merging with reality.

As I maintained in Chapter 1, thinking about consciousness is a practice space for thinking about sense. While sense extends beyond consciousness, we are easily acquainted with its reality in virtue of being conscious. Consciousness reveals the structure of reality in virtue of being a self-conscious case of being that, of course, should not mislead us into thinking that everything actually or potentially is conscious. What is special about the topic of consciousness is that it leads to a sense directed at itself as real. This special self-referential status of consciousness—which is the ground of the perennial attraction of the cogito and its manifold variations—lies in the fact that, in consciousness, appearing is being.

Having said that, self-consciousness cannot be a revelation of clearcut sense, because on closer inspection, consciousness is a paradigm case of a confusion. From consciousness we can learn that confusions arise between fields; they are transitory. We experience reality as confusing insofar as we are part of its temporal unfolding in the form of our conscious mental processing.

In that respect, mental contents differ from objects, let alone from individuals who are defined as defined, i.e., as *entia omnimode determinata*.[43] Objects are the kinds of things that can be self-identical, i.e., they can replace the variable x in "$x = x$." In contrast to objects, subjective senses fulfill the function of furnishing a given field with objects. For this reason, the essential mathematical concept of a function rightly served as the breeding ground of Frege's realism of sense.

In FOS, senses are furnishing functions that position a thinker to give an account of why certain objects appear in a given field. Senses prepare the ground for the existence of objects. Now, consciousness is neither merely one of its objects nor is it a furnishing function of a given field, as it constitutes different fields while it continually recreates itself. Consciousness is essentially blurry and indiscrete. Otherwise, its temporality would be frozen. If there is a unity of consciousness across different contents at all, it cannot consist in being one of its manifold contents. That is the truth in higher-order theories of consciousness: to be a conscious state is to be a phase in a transitory process of a manifold of conscious states unified by something that does not appear on the level of its objects, namely subjective consciousness. It is not an accident, therefore, that subjects are in the position of confusing fields, as consciousness—one of their supposed hallmarks—is by its very nature in the business of field confusion. The term "consciousness" on this level captures an important aspect of our pre-ontological experience of reality as blurry, indeterminate, confusing.

One prominent way of trying to fix this, of turning the experience of being someone into an object, gives rise to my paradigm case of local field confusion, namely the identification of mind and brain (or consciousness and its minimal neural correlate). This case is local in that it need not be motivated by an independent acceptance of a metaphysical, materialist worldview according to which in reality (in the world) there really are only physical objects. Such a global materialist outlook creates problems for the local idea that the mind is the brain, as the brain's very existence is threatened by the kind of microphysicalism that usually accompanies contemporary materialist (or physicalist) metaphysics. Local nonsense need not rest on global nonsense.

Notice that the account of nonsense as field confusion does not treat nonsense as mere gibberish or linguistic meaninglessness. Not all nonsense fuses into one unintelligible block either. Nonsense is always in part intelligible and even motivated by considerations that lie outside of the narrow realm of propositional thinking. Thus, we can diagnose and articulate the conceptual infrastructure of local nonsense without committing the mistake of using a language that is meaningless. Our ladder is stable, and we do not have to throw it away after using it to climb to a higher position of self-critical philosophical thinking.

Propositional thinking in all its forms (including the sensing and perceiving of objects in sense modalities other than the grasping of thoughts) takes place in the context of (human) lives.[44] The context of (human) lives is such that sense and nonsense as field confusion intersect: We constantly move from one fos to the next and experience the unfolding of fos in terms of the fluctuation of conscious mental content (or the stream of consciousness, if you will). Similarly, the contours of our actual thinking have been drawn and redrawn by the manifold empirical modern discoveries in psychology (including evolutionary psychology), behavioral economics, cognitive science, etc., which time and again have shown that thinking is quite far from our distinguished activity of drawing inferences and avoiding fallacies. Clear, logically disciplined, propositional thinking is only a miniscule portion of our actual mental lives—a statistical, empirical fact that does nothing to demonstrate that we are somehow ultimately "irrational" or "much less rational" than we thought, as Steven

Pinker has recently pointed out in his attempt to correct some of the in-coherent overgeneralizations of the famous findings on the role of biases and other flaws in human judgment.[45]

Nonsense emerges at the intersection of fos. Confusion is a real process, not limited to our minds. Just as sense is as real as it gets, we need to integrate nonsense as confusion into what there is. Otherwise put, first-order metaphysics is a real temptation insofar as reality unfolds in such a way that a given plurality of fos always collapses into one insofar as fos, in order to exist, have to be objects in other fos. Yet, being an object and functioning as sense are mutually exclusive (which is what I call the the-orem of the functional ontological difference).[46] Reality itself is confusing.

Nonsense creates friction between fos, which leads to a crossing of boundaries. It emerges when fos intersect and overlap in such a way that their delineation turns out to be blurry, leading to the gradual disintegra-tion of our epistemic sense of clarity. Here, we must not forget that sense in FOS is real, where sense's reality is not merely logical, semantic, or lin-guistic, let alone "subjective." One of the reasons why mathematics' effec-tiveness in physical science is not "unreasonable," as Eugen Wigner put it in a famous article, is that the universe (qua fos of physics) is in itself structured by senses. However, the senses constitutive of mathematical theorizing (articulated as definitions, concepts, functions, categories, operations, etc.) are not identical to the senses operative in nature to the extent that there are some senses in nature that have no equivalent in our models. By the very nature of physics as an epistemic enterprise, we cannot know how far nature (the target system of physics) deviates from the sense we have made of it in terms of mathematical modeling. The difference between the (known and knowable) universe and nature's un-known (and unknowable) fos is incommensurable, i.e., not meaningfully measurable by the theories subject to its effects.[47]

Our actual mental lives are necessarily confused, as they consist in our ways of dealing with the unfolding, the manifestation of reality. That unfolding itself is confused, mixing propositional episodes with nonsense as field confusion. *Global* confusion is the impression that the world as a whole has revealed itself to a thinker. *Local* confusion works similarly to its global cousin in that it confuses the thinker and a part of her environ-ment so that the distinction between her subjective fos and the objective senses she is dealing with collapses.

SENSE, NONSENSE, AND SUBJECTIVITY

There are two paradigm cases of local confusion that succumb to a similar pressure from nonsense: *neurocentrism* and *infallibilism*. Neurocentrism is the idea that our candidate subjective mental states (combined into the ultimately confused category of "consciousness") are at bottom identical with their minimal neural correlate of consciousness (MNCC). I say "at bottom identical" because hardly anyone today actually goes all-in with a full-blown identity theory. Prominent contenders for identifying a consciousness meter on the basis of a sophisticated account of the MNCC all stop short of an identity theory. For instance, integrated information theory (IIT) presents us with a candidate for the substrate of consciousness and otherwise remains in the realm of tight correlation (without assuming identity), whereas global workspace theory is closely allied with illusionism in its desire to eliminate consciousness from genuine reality.[48]

Neurocentrism contains at least two local confusions. The first confusion is the fusion of all conscious mental states into one type of state or process: consciousness. The second confusion is the at-bottom identification of consciousness with its (hitherto largely unknown) minimal neural correlate. Let us take a closer look at both of them.

The mental states we tag as "conscious" ex hypothesi are wildly different. They therefore contain information, i.e., they have fine- and coarse-grained content. There is nothing that two conscious mental states actually have in common on the level of their fine-grained phenomenal content. For this reason, consciousness, if anything, has to be a feature of all conscious mental states that precisely does not occur on the level of its fine-grained content. For, if consciousness thus appeared among its fine-grained contents, it could not be the same across two or more different conscious mental states, which is self-undermining. If anything, consciousness must be a fos in which the unfolding of conscious mental states takes place. For this reason, neuroscientists eager to identify the MNCC tend to be fascinated by the concept of *pure* consciousness and its association with the minimal condition of intelligibility, i.e., otherwise contentless pure space.[49] But if consciousness were otherwise contentless, pure space within which specific or, rather, individual mental content appears, such that it counts as conscious in virtue of appearing in this way, then how could consciousness acquire its specific content? Answering that question would require a solution to the binding

104

problem, which would explain how a plurality of different brain regions are integrated into the consciousness field. We would need an empirical equivalent of Kant's synthetic unity of consciousness that would go beyond the identification of the MNCC with the help of a first-person meditation on the nature of pure consciousness.

This gives rise to another series of problems. If consciousness as such were identical with pure consciousness, we would need an account of how pure consciousness acquires content. But that account would have to postulate a different MNCC for each conscious mental state other than pure consciousness (assuming that it makes sense to think of the MNCC of pure consciousness as one single type or set of tokens of an arrangement of neural tissue). For each content, there would either have to be some neural supplement to the MNCC for pure consciousness or some entirely different MNCC for each conscious state. At the end, we wind up with a spatiotemporal map of parts of the brain whose resolution exceeds everything that is currently feasible with recourse to existing imaging techniques. As we approach an ever better understanding of the details of the synchronized and causally coordinated behavior of the neural system of systems under investigation, it will indubitably turn out that the actual circuitry across the population of certainly conscious subjects differs to such an extent that the various MNCCs of different states (from pure consciousness to the conscious state of interpreting a Jackson Pollock painting) turn out to be different to such an extent that the very idea of a singular phenomenon of "consciousness" disintegrates. The neural tokens might form certain patterns whose details are bound to vary across individuals. This includes the MNCC (if such there be) of pure consciousness. This entails that consciousness either is not ever quite the same in two individuals (or one individual over time) or that the identity conditions for consciousness differ from those of its MNCC, which would amount to a commitment to a form of dualism (or pluralism) according to which consciousness is sometimes somehow correlated with neural states—which is the minimal view no one doubts.

Here, we encounter the problem that we do not quite know what "consciousness" means, so it is unclear what we are looking for when we search for its MNCC. This triggers the confusion at hand: Given that different speakers call different things "conscious," we distribute various meanings of "consciousness" over the brain by partitioning it into local conscious states somehow connected by being integrated into an overall

SENSE, NONSENSE, AND SUBJECTIVITY

consciousness. In this way, we achieve access to the behavior of subsystems of the neural systems in terms of their correlation with states independently classified as "conscious," understood according to several different meanings of the term.

This is a case of what I have called "the hardest problem of consciousness":[50] Given that the meaning of "consciousness" varies historically (within one language and across languages), how can we distinguish between meanings for which it makes sense to try to find a neural correlate at all and those for which this is nonsensical? For instance, if my current perception of my computer screen is a conscious mental state of which my computer screen (and not just a mental representation of it) is a part, it would simply be nonsensical to search for a MNCC of that very state. If a neuroscientist or neurophilosopher at this point just pushes perception into the head by going all-in and claiming that there aren't any conscious representations of objects such that the objects themselves are part of the representation, then this response exhibits a pattern of confusion. For it confuses the fos of mind-independent objects with the fos of their representation in a way that severs representation from its content. In any event, no such conceptual maneuver could be justified by more closely inspecting the empirical results of the spatiotemporal unfolding of neural circuitry presumably correlated with whatever meaning of "consciousness" is at stake.

In light of these considerations, neuroconstructivism can be given a place in a logical architecture of local confusion about consciousness as such. Here, "neuroconstructivism" refers to the family of views that think of consciousness as some form of "controlled hallucination"[51] where neural circuitry is in the business of constructing an internal world that at best serves as a kind of map an organism draws on in its adaptive behavior. Yet, this view is famously incoherent, as we see upon applying even the most lenient test of self-application to its motivation. A key part of the motivation of neuroconstructivism is that it purports to have discovered some feedback loop structure in brain regions associated with our consciousness of an external reality. One way of stating this is the "predictive coding" account according to which the brain is busy predicting certain patterns in its environment such that our mental contents are internal simulations run to predict the mesoscopic, human-scale behavior of potentially dangerous objects and processes. Thus, no one ever sees a lion, but always only a lion-hallucination which might or, rather, might not resemble an actual lion "out there." Yet, this paradoxical (and untenable) result can only be arrived at via empirical research into patterns of neural circuitry. If we can never see a lion but can only infer that there is some danger or other out there on the basis of a controlled hallucination, then this applies to neural circuitry, fMRI technology, and computers too. Neuroscience itself would be a series of controlled hallucinations on the basis of which we somehow try to pierce through to reality itself.

Facing this problem, some neuroconstructivists courageously bite a bullet already recognized by Nietzsche in his response to fashionable forms of neuroconstructivism in the wake of Schopenhauer, Helmholtz, and others.[52] Here is Donald Hoffman on an exchange about this very problem between himself and no lesser a figure than Francis Crick:

> But then I set up my paradox. If we construct everything we see, and if we see neurons, then we construct neurons. But what we construct doesn't exist until we construct it (too bad; it would be much cheaper to move into my dream mansion before constructing it). So neurons don't exist until we construct them.[53]

To which Crick supposedly replied as follows:

> It is a reasonable hypothesis that a real world exists of which we only have limited knowledge and that neurons existed prior to anyone observing them *as neurons*.[54]

Evidently, Hoffman and Crick here enter shaky epistemological terrain, as is betrayed by the fact that Hoffman goes on to invoke the old chestnut of Kant's distinction between things in themselves and appearances, which—through Schopenhauer's influence—happens to be one of the origins of local neurophilosophical nonsense.[55] If a neuroscientist winds up with the claim that the existence of neurons prior to their observation is merely "a reasonable hypothesis," many other things must have gone awry. For neurons are a particular type of cell that evidently existed before anyone observed them. The existence of neurons (and we might add of neurons *as neurons*) prior to their observation is as obvious as the existence of lions, trees, and dinosaurs

SENSE, NONSENSE, AND SUBJECTIVITY

prior to their observation, which is why Hoffman has to question the existence of basically anything prior to its observation in order to come to terms with the paradox he has generated out of his local confusion of the fields of pure consciousness with its contents.

That neurocentrism (the idea that at bottom consciousness is just a part of the brain) is typically associated with neuroconstructivism (which can range from more modest claims about the difficulty of grasping reality through our neural, constructed representations to outright denials of the existence of an external reality) is not a coincidence. Rather, it is the consequence of having to push too many states into the head in order to create the heuristic framework for unhampered research into the MNCC of all sorts of conscious states. Neurocentrism is primarily a heuristic and, thus, methodological failure. Pushing consciousness into our heads presupposes an entirely nonscientific (at least non-natural-scientific) decision concerning the selection of relevant target meanings of "consciousness." Therefore, the paradigm within which neurocentrism operates generates local confusion that can never be overcome by just further extending the limits of technoscientific resolution of brain functions.

The standard version of *the hard problem*—from Leibniz's mill to Chalmers's zombies—is thus only one manifestation of local nonsense flowing from *the hardest problem*. For the hard problem only arises when we look at neural circuitry from the third-person, scientific standpoint and compare it with its alleged correlate in the form of first-person experience. What it is like to be in a certain conscious state and how the neural circuitry looks in a brain scanner's model (such as on a computer screen) are indeed two separate fos that cannot really be converted into each other, let alone just straightforwardly identified. But that does not entail that there is an actual hard problem for neuroscience, but only that a certain ultimately confused research project cannot ever achieve the impossible goal of dissolving consciousness into neural tissue.

Reality begins to look like a hallucination only if we accept a given, profoundly confused meaning of "consciousness" into our vernacular in order to then identify its correlates in neuroscientific terms. But that decision is not grounded in neuroscientific insight or empirical findings. Instead, it conditions them by constructing a questionable and ultimately confused research paradigm.

It is tempting to wonder, as Hoffman does, "how neural activity causes conscious experiences, such as my experience of red?"[56] But that very question generates the conundrum that we think of two correlated kinds of things (substances, processes, events, or whatever one's ontology needs to fill in for the generic "things" here) when we think of neural activity and conscious experience. If they were but one thing, it would not make sense at all to wonder how neural activity causes conscious experience, as this would amount to wondering how neural activity can cause itself (or, for that matter, how conscious experience can cause itself). At most, it seems to make sense to wonder how some part of neural circuitry influences (causes) some other part of neural circuitry, a spatiotemporal organization that could in principle be a candidate for an overall cause of consciousness. On the supposition that neural activity and consciousness are one thing, it makes no sense to ask how one can be the cause of the other, but it does make sense to specify causal links between different bits of the circuitry. However, this entails that it is nonsense to see the overall organization of these intra-circuitry causes as a cause of consciousness.[57]

In that scenario, we must think of the discovery of a MNCC as the discovery of an identity and, thus, of a necessity. Now, famously, the fact that we can all too easily think of conscious experience without thereby transparently thinking about its MNCC makes it hard to figure out in what sense we can establish an identity theory whose claim to necessity can be cashed in despite appearances.[58] How can two things that certainly look and feel different (neural circuitry on the one hand and conscious experience on the other hand) be the same?

To be sure, there is no shortage of answers in principle, many of them based on versions of the Fregean sense-reference distinction: we can think of the identity of the MNCC and consciousness in terms of a reference-identity that is split into a sense-difference. Consciousness would then be the kind of thing that looks different when experienced as opposed to how it looks when studied neuroscientifically. But what is the nature of the object in the target-system that provides the reference for the identity statement?

Identity theories are usually attractive in the context under discussion, because they are associated with eliminativism or, at least, with illusionism about consciousness.[59] They seem to make the problem go away. In that case, though, the identity statement merely claims that some

SENSE, NONSENSE, AND SUBJECTIVITY

neural circuitry is what it is, which is why the notion that consciousness is an illusion in the sense of a mistaken ontological commitment is simply misbegotten: there just is no such thing as consciousness, though it might not "seem" that way. For this reason, subtler identity theories recognize that you need a third, neutral term such that neural tissue and consciousness are both modes of presentation of that third term, the psychophysically neutral.[60]

The conclusion of this whole line of thought is that neurocentrism confuses the subjective and objective, such that we wind up with muddled thought. The unclarity and aporetic nature of the position of neurocentrism (the largely unquestioned metaphysical dogma of mainstream philosophy of mind) is a manifestation of nonsense.

Enter *infallibilism*. Infallibilism too confuses the subjective and the objective by thinking of the epistemological good case (paradigmatically knowledge) as a fusion of the thinker and her objective thought. In the good case, the thinker knows that p (where p is true and her propositional attitude is sufficiently justified to somehow guarantee the truth of p). In the good case, what the thinker thinks cannot be about herself in such a way that no other thinker is in the same position to grasp it. In the good case, the knowing subject fuses with reality.

In light of these elementary considerations, infallibilism about knowledge insists that the good case cannot be one where a thinker S is still fallible. S has made up her mind, acknowledged the truth of p by judging that p and has the kind of reasons for so doing so that warrant our describing her factive mental state as knowledge. S who thus knows cannot get it wrong. So far, so good, as one must indeed not deny that this description corresponds to a conceptual layer of the good case.

Yet, even in the good case, there has to be a kind of claim (be it in the form of perceptual registration, of tacit judgment, or an overt speech act of claiming knowledge that p). While in the good case the claim by definition succeeds, it can only count as a claim if at least a third person can (wrongly) think of the claim as a failure. Thus, what is logically infallible (in virtue of being an example of the good case) can be rightly seen by a second-order (or third-person) judge as potentially right and potentially wrong. The logical or epistemological point about the nature of the good case does not demonstrate that a given actual case of knowledge is such that the knower necessarily got it right. The conceptual nature of the good case as a series of instances of getting it right should not be confused with a logical, let alone metaphysical, insight into the intrinsic necessity of reality's revelation to the knowing subject.[61]

In general, the identity of a thought's content cannot be constituted by its actually having the truth value it does. For this reason, different people (or the same person on different levels of their commitments) can have divergent takes on their actual thoughts, claiming them to be true or false respectively without thereby misunderstanding their very content. Yet, this does not undermine the basic idea of the factivity of knowledge according to which the mental state of knowing is such that the knower counts as knowing, among other things, in virtue of the truth of their claim. That someone who actually gets it right might have gotten it wrong makes it possible for us to be wrong about our knowledge. Knowledge claims and knowledge do not fuse, they always potentially come apart, which is why knowledge is not iterative as such: knowing that p is not always knowing that one knows that p.

What makes the claim a successful one is, therefore, not detachable from the fact that S judged that p and has been successful. Hence, even in the good case, subject and object cannot fuse: there is still a logical distance between S, the judging I, and p, what S judges. Thinking and being never fully coincide, at least not on the level of knowledge.[62]

At this point, contemporary infallibilists rightly insist that self-knowledge (or self-consciousness, as they tend to say) is different. If S knows about himself that he knows that p, it seems to be the case that he cannot get that wrong, not even as portrayed from the outside. However, as long as p is a proposition about something other than S's self-knowledge, there is always the possibility of describing S's position as fallible. To isolate S from their fallibility, then, is to stipulate conditions such that the state that S is in has no content other than her knowledge of the state she is in. Yet, it is questionable whether there is such a state. What could a state in which the subjective and the objective coincide in the subjective look like, i.e., a state where the subject qua thinker is its own object?

Famously, discussions of self-consciousness in Kant's wake (that deal with this issue) amount to the idea that there is pre-reflective immediate consciousness of oneself, a "feeling of life," an idea recently revived by the neuroscientist Christof Koch.[63] Infallible self-consciousness thus has no content whatsoever by which the subject is in touch with an objective

SENSE, NONSENSE, AND SUBJECTIVITY

sense. But that means that subjective and objective melt down into a state that is highly subjective after all, as it just names the subject as such: Fichte's "I = I," to which the earliest rejoinder (by both Hölderlin and Schelling) already had it that it is entirely unclear in which sense we are dealing with a subject here at all rather than a pure, contentless state of "being."[64]

The problem with the fusion theory of infallibilism is that it cannot make sense of the objectivity of the good case, i.e., of the conditions under which it can be an achievement in contrast to a failure. A pure achievement, self-consciousness, cannot be a fusion of subjective and objective, as the objective just drops out of the equation. But if self-consciousness is pure subjectivity (without any further content), it cannot ever count as embodied. This avoids the neuroconstructivist's problems of correlation and identity on pain of stipulating a meaning of "subjective" that cannot refer to anyone in particular. Resorting to calling the anonymous thinker (who is no one) a "transcendental ego," at this point, boils down to explaining *obscurum per obscurius*.

Kant famously thought that the soul, the world, and God are on a par with one another as sources of nonsense. He classified the associated nonsense (the transcendental illusions) as paralogism, antinomy, and ideal respectively. I agree with him insofar as confusions about ourselves do not go away once we transcend metaphysics, i.e., once we give up on the existence of the world. Diffusing global nonsense alone does not suffice to avoid nonsense's local avatars. If we think of ourselves as a part in a whole of which absolutely everything (including the whole itself) is a part, global confusion involves a local state of affairs (namely our thoughts directed at the world-whole and our place in it). Yet, regardless of this metaphysical mode of being confused about ourselves, there is the local counterpart that cannot be derived from the global paradigm. In light of this, in this section I have chosen the basic infrastructure of philosophy of mind as a road to a broader notion of nonsense.

Ontological Nonsense

Realism about sense has been charged with an unhealthy proximity to idealism. In particular, Benoist worries that I follow in Hegel's footsteps, who famously stated the following:

> "Sense" is this wonderful word which is used in two opposite meanings. On the one hand it means the organ of immediate apprehension, but on the other hand we mean by it the sense, the significance, the thought, the universal underlying the thing. And so sense is connected on the one hand with the immediate external aspect of existence, and on the other hand with its inner essence.[65]

According sense a central ontological role threatens to spill linguistic meaning over an itself meaningless and senseless reality, as it were. We should indeed be wary of dissolving Fregean reference in the fluid of sense. Such a dissolution would be a form of nonsense, something to be diagnosed and ideally overcome with recourse to some form of linguistic analysis or other.

Fending off the charge, I now want to argue that this reproach draws on resources that make it liable to its own embodiment of nonsense. Then, more positively, I will address the issue of the role of reference in FOS. In this section, I will present the idea that the Fregean referent (*Bedeutung*) points to nonsense in a way that Frege could not conceive of, as he was indeed caught up in the problematic heritage of idealism.

At the dawn of modern analytic philosophy, the Kantian notion of critical philosophy as overcoming nonsense has been transformed into an account of category mistakes. The idea in Carnap, Wittgenstein, and Ryle was to show that pseudo-problems are generated if we confuse categories and, therefore, stop making sense.[66]

This tradition, then, construes nonsense as a semantic or broadly speaking psychological phenomenon. If we only managed to cleanse natural language of its inherited tendencies to create "inference traps" and to speak nonsense (as in poetry, novels, and other manners of speaking where propositional truth and sensemaking do not provide the ultimate norms of meaningfulness), we could finally "see the world aright."[67] Notoriously, all attempts at setting the record of sense straight once and for all by developing methods for identifying and eliminating nonsense altogether, failed by contributing nonsense in their attempt to get rid of it. In this regard, Wittgenstein is just the most outspoken of those who would like to create a language that is free from what they perceive to be its shortcoming, namely that language is neither exclusively nor primarily a

SENSE, NONSENSE, AND SUBJECTIVITY

stock of conceptual and propositional building blocks for construing a world-picture.

At this point, my argument significantly goes beyond the correct observation that our linguistic resources ought not to be limited to a narrow and ultimately incoherently constructed layer of pure propositional sense. What we do with words is indeed more than what the logical puritans wanted language to do. In contrast to that tradition, I will now continue my case for the acceptance of ontological nonsense: just as sense is an irreducible part of what there is, so too is nonsense. Nonsense is an ontological problem in that reality itself *is* confusing.

In order to flesh this thought out, remember that reality according to FOS is a hypercomplex proliferation of fos. The reason for this is that there cannot be an overall architecture of all fos; they just do not form a world. But that means that any model of reality that is not simply identical to it in some way or other misses out on this peculiar absence or incompleteness at its very core. The new step taken here in the development of FOS is the recognition of the existence of nonsense as real.

Nonsense's reality is, among other things, an objectively existing confusion of fos. We saw this in the case of consciousness. To think of oneself as conscious is to be confronted with a temporal unfolding of mental events that is by its very nature confused, as a manifold of fos fuse, intersect, melt, and reemerge in ways that are in principle inaccessible to any kind of theory that expects that there are overall patterns constituting the flow of consciousness as such.

If reality just made sense, we would never make mistakes. Mistakes literally happen when we think of one thing as in part something it is not, thereby believing ourselves to have something in view while we have some other thing in view. In short, there is being in being wrong. A simple example can be derived from the experience of mistaking someone for someone else. For instance, the day before I wrote this sentence, I intended to meet a certain person I had never met in real life but only online. I was slightly late for the meeting and looked for the person in a café on the Stanford University campus. In this context, I confused two people in a row who were present in the café with the person who I thought was expecting me. It turned out that my contact was late for reasons similar to mine, which then solved my problem, as he recognized me more easily in a crowd where no one looked quite like me, but at least two other people resembled

NONSENSE

him in some relevant respects. For these reasons, I mistook two people for a person I wanted to meet. In order to be thus confused and to make that particular mistake, the two people with whom I confused my contact had to at least look enough like him in order for me to be confused about the situation. Mistakes presuppose that reality is not entirely transparent and that we therefore have to process the sense that is manifest to us. Reality is, in part, obscure.[68]

Being mistaken is a paradigmatic form of being wrong. In order to account for a given mistake we need independent means of identifying the target system or the object that we mistook for something it turns out not to be. The independence of these means is twofold. On the one hand, the judgment of others is always capable of correcting ours. We cannot correct ourselves in the act of judgment, as that act is a wholesale commitment to things being the way we take them to be in that judgment. We can only ever be corrected by another thinker. On the other hand, reality can correct us by dragging another judgment out of us—a transaction which requires prior social training, i.e., prior internalized correction by others. Before reality can correct us, we must learn how to judge while being open, in principle, to correction. The reality principle is not a mere given of the mind (part of its innate conceptual infrastructure) but something learned by our engagement with others in the everyday situation of human triangulation (the birthplace of objectivity). In this way, we learn to think of the same object as something that can be seen differently. Different points of view can present us with the same object as if it were different.

This is where Frege's distinction between sense and reference (which arguably harks back at least as far as Spinoza[69]) unfolds its explanatory power. If the concept of identity is grounded in the concept of the presence of a single object potentially presented in different modes, the fact that we literally see things differently is part and parcel of the concept of reality. Reality is that which can be seen (be made intelligible) in manifold ways.

At this point, the worry is that realism about sense has no room for Fregean *Bedeutung*. This seems to follow from the principle of the functional ontological difference according to which objects are bundles of senses, such that to be an object is to be in the object position of a given fos while not being an object (but rather a fos) in some other fos.[70] Otherwise put, nothing is just an object, an ontological point in reality to which we can at most point. To be an object is for something to appear in a fos,

SENSE, NONSENSE, AND SUBJECTIVITY

and for something to be anything is for it to appear in a fos (which includes fos). Objects, therefore, are neither absolutes nor givens that we register in terms of fos. As soon as we zoom in on something that plays the object role in its fos, we will be able to see it as involved in a bunch of objects. Of every object many things are true. The object as reference point (as that of which many things are true) binds the truths together. In this way, we find it in the Fregean object or, rather, the reference slot. What binds the truths together is a focal point of many senses that point to it.

And this is where I now locate *ontological nonsense:* Objects have to appear to us (and to each other) as different from their fos in order to have a position, a place in their respective fos. And this functional onto-logical difference requires the existence of nonsense as a kind of force that bundles senses into local objects. Objects cannot be dissolved into their senses, as they are rightly invoked in order to halt the looming re-gress we trigger when we realize that we cannot think of an object without somehow describing it, with the result that the object in itself either has no descriptive content (and, thus, turns into a brute, unintelli-gible presence) or is too easily involved in a proliferation of sense.

What I have in mind here can be illustrated with a familiar line of thought. Let the paradigmatic form of informative and non-contradictory, i.e., interesting, identity statements be that $S_1(a) = S_2(a)$, for example, the evening star = the morning star. According to this standard proposal, the two senses cannot be straightforwardly identical, of course, because they precisely differ by representing the same object, e.g., a (= Venus), in different ways. Claiming that the evening star is the morning star is both a recognition of difference (the two senses differ) and a statement of iden-tity concerning the aboutness of the two senses. "The evening star" is as much about Venus as is "the morning star."

But what about Venus itself? "Venus" is certainly not meaningless: in this paragraph we ought to ascribe it, at least, the meaning of "that which is the identical object presented to us as evening star in the evening and as morning star in the morning." In this paragraph, I did not just point to Venus or silently acknowledge its existence. I described a scenario in which Venus is the target of different modes of presentation. This means that we can draw Venus into the equation and assert that "the evening star = the morning star = Venus."

However, if the form of informative non-contradictory identity statements is $S_i(x) = S_j(x)$ such that S designates a function-slot and x an object-slot (with sense = function-slot and *Bedeutung* = object-slot), then Venus (the object) cannot be identical to Venus (the sense used in the extended equation). Hence, the need for the concept of an object that binds senses together without itself being one of them.

We can now think of objects that bind senses together without being identical to any of the senses thus unified *a parte rei*. Without these objects, the object-slot in our thinking would not make sense, which does not mean that the objects themselves make sense. On the contrary, we need to reckon with a layer of reality that is conceptually opaque and ontologically dense or thick, as it were. In contemporary French philosophy (at the latest since Lacan), this layer is called "le réel" (not to be confused with "la réalité"). This opaque layer of objects requires them to be in part opposed to the business of sense. They must be nonsensical.

Notice that the next stage in the argument is not merely a wordplay. For we now move from the recognition of objects that cannot be in the business of being senses (as they are bound by sense-functions without being more sense-functions) to the idea that they constitute ontological nonsense and, thus, maximally local confusions. By binding senses together without belonging to them, objects attract our attention. They have an attentional pull through which they can radiate into conscious minds. In so doing, they constitute field confusion, as they connect subjective and objective sense at the interface of our sensory encounter with objects.

In light of these considerations, I would like to answer one of Graham Harman's questions recently addressed to FOS.[71] Harman reminds me of my earlier commitment to "ontological descriptivism" and the associated assertion that "there are no objects below the threshold of senses."[72] He then asks me if this does not ensnarl me in what he calls the "modern onto-taxonomy" according to which "object-object relations" are never "on the same philosophical footing as those between subject and object."[73]

Since *Fields of Sense,* I have begun to change my mind about nonsense in that I began to recognize that ontological descriptivism does not and must not rule out the phenomenon of confusion. If reality is at bottom confusing (in virtue of its hypercomplexity), then the kinds of things that are, as it were, attractors of attention (and, thus, grounds for inserting something in the regress-halting object-slot of thinking) must be added to the ontology. Calling those things "objects" is all right as long as one has room for a distinction between the way they appear in their fos and their opacity, which is what amounts to the presence of ontological nonsense. Still, that does not mean that there are objects which somehow actively withdraw from our grasp so that their essence (if any) is as such inaccessible to human thinking. What it means is that the kinds of things we think about by inserting nametags for them in the object-slot of thinking are messy, in that they transgress the bounds of sense. If they did not, they could not serve the function of stopping the regress of senses.

Venus itself (not just the name) is a messy affair. No description of it in strictly physical terms ever comes close to exhausting its actual properties and fully predicting its future outlook in detail (which contains much more information than that encoded in information about its position on a calculable trajectory). The same holds for everything that can be an object and, thus, exist (in virtue of appearing in a fos).

I am aware that this (like many other formulations in the expression of FOS) sounds like music to the metaphysician's ears—as if I were finally making (synthetic a priori) claims about absolutely all objects. But that is just a misunderstanding of the structure of FOS. All objects are messy in different ways: the details depend on the actual fos. The ontological concepts used in the articulation of FOS as a theory are precisely not metaphysical concepts under which absolutely everything falls just in virtue of being anything whatsoever. Ontological nonsense is at least as intrinsically manifold as sense.

Notice that metaphysics is based on a particular conception of generality, according to which replacing the maximal variable x in ontology means that we think of all objects as falling under a concept. But from mathematics we should know that there are rules concerning the replacement of variables by constants, rules that should not be confused with the notion that a given object (expressed as a constant) falls under a concept. Falling under a concept usually requires conceptual determinacy, i.e., it should be in principle clear what objects fall under a given concept. Conceptual determinacy is important, and yet there is no concept of all concepts such that the relation of falling under it can be clarified by drawing the boundaries of the concept of all concepts. And replacing a variable by a constant with recourse to a rulebook is not a judgment that brings an object together with a concept under which it falls; x is not a concept, and replacing x with a suitable a is neither a judgment nor a proposition.

In particular, no attempt to think of existence (or being an object, for that matter) as the concept of concepts will allow us to think of absolutely all objects, at least in their broadest contours. That is a consequence of ontological pluralism: The specific instantiations of the form "x_i appears in fos$_i$" will differ from each other in ways that cannot be grasped in synthetic a priori propositions with metaphysical scope. What it is for numbers to exist (if this is even an adequate level on which to discuss the issue: numbers might be too variegated to be part of a single fos, but this is another topic) differs from what it is for witches to exist (in fictional fos) and from what it is for the Higgs field to exist. The fact that in all these cases something appears in some fos concerns a statement made within FOS: in the fos of FOS, we can think of objects in terms of a certain function within a framework of manifold appearing. On this level, I have now argued that objects turn out to be messy in that they are constitutively involved in ontological nonsense. We cannot free the objects from the nonsense that results from the fact that they appear in a fos which, in turn, appears in a fos etc. At their known borders, objects peter out—which explains the phenomenon of withdrawal that the Heideggerian tradition (from Heidegger to Ferraris and Harman) associate with their thick notion of an object as a *Ding*.[74] But none of this entails that we could ever hope to split objects into two sides, as it were, by drawing a distinction between a dimension in which they reveal themselves to us (and to each other, as per Harman) and a dimension which withdraws from our grasp. While such a distinction admittedly makes sense from an epistemic perspective, as we can distinguish what we know about an object and what we don't, there is no line in reality that splits the object-phenomenon into object and *Ding* (where "das Ding" withdraws while the object reveals itself).

The innovation within FOS presented in this chapter consists in a full recognition of the existence of nonsense. *Ontological nonsense* is the phenomenon of field confusion in which objects are involved insofar as they are bound to have a relative messiness. Their messiness is relative to the parameters of the fos under investigation, and it will only show itself in a fine-grained description of the object in its involvement in manifold fos which fuse around the object, as it were.

SENSE, NONSENSE, AND SUBJECTIVITY

Let us look at a prominent example that can serve to illustrate the power of the idea of ontological nonsense. A given object, say, my left hand, both appears in the fos of my vision (I just saw it) and as an object of physics. Yet, qua object of physics, my left hand loses many of the properties it has in the fos of my vision. Physics is constituted by senses that differ from the senses of ordinary exercises of our visual capacities. This then raises the question of the many hands (think of Eddington's two tables here[75]): Is there a hand in the fos of my vision and another one in physics, or are these two completely different objects?

Now the idea of ontological nonsense enters the picture, and it thinks of my left hand as slowly fusing into the objects of physics. In an ideal, yet completely unattainable (i.e., actually impossible!) epistemic position, we could think of the hand without having its visual appearance in mind simply by describing and explaining the complex system of the coordinated behavior of physical elements located where my hand is right now. But that formulation already reveals the nonsense: As long as I need to think of my hand as occupying a given spatial position individuated from my point of view, I have not succeeded in moving it fully to the realm of physics. In physics there are no three-dimensional hands, just as in visual reality there are no elementary particles. They are literally in different spaces with different dimensions, which is something we can infer from both everyday experience and physics, whose mathematical apparatus draws on spaces that are dimensionally and structurally different from those of our everyday experience.

In light of this consideration, we can think of strong emergence as a form of ontological nonsense that is not constitutively tied to the presence of thinkers who are confused about an otherwise stable reality. Given that we are entitled to reject a metaphysical interpretation of our scientific knowledge, we have reasons to assume that nature has real scales or levels of emergence, meaning that both my hand as an organic, biological, and meaningful formation and its biochemical constituents are real without being reducible to some most fundamental layer. There really are layers of complexity such that they fuse into overlapping structures that do not make sense from within just one of them. This causal overlap, producing novel structures in the unfolding of nature, is a form of ontological nonsense—which explains why natural science, responding in its own way to complexity, finds it objectively confusing.[76]

120

Physics only in part explains what is going on in visual reality. Of course, the contours of visual reality significantly overlap with the fos of physical objects populated by processes involving electromagnetic fields and their ilk. For this reason, we can truly say that we humans only perceive a fragment of the radiation in which we are immersed on the level of phenomenal consciousness. Yet, putting it like this is already speaking nonsense. We are led to nonsense as soon as we begin to wonder how it is that we can only perceive a part of physical reality while the rest is hidden from our direct perceptual system. This picture of our organic blindness to physical reality presupposes the strict ontological commensurability of objects in the fos of visual appearance and objects in the fos of physics, which is precisely not given. Literally speaking, we do not perceive physical objects at all. Enjoying a sunset is not a visual fragment of a larger physical scene of which we only see a tiny part. However, our perceptual involvement in a sunset can and should be part of the evidence base of physical knowledge acquisition, as we are in part embedded in nature that is in part open to physical explanation and analysis.

This means that it is indeed nonsensical to think of my hand as both an object of visual perception and as a bunch of physical objects that look to me as if they formed a hand. To think of hands as "elementary particles arranged hand-wise" is a confusion of two fos that overlap but cannot be blended into each other in that way. And yet, there is a causal or some other constitutive relation between my hand and physical particles, a real relation that is involved in objectively existing confusion in the form of emergence.

Having said that, such a concept of strong emergence as ontological nonsense does not lead to metaphysics. For, fundamentally, the model—one object (the hand), manifold appearances (relative to a respective fos: the hand-as-particles or the hand-as-organic)—fails. FOS's ontological pluralism precisely does not assume that there is an overall stock of objects that are mapped onto one of the manifold domains by way of their local furnishing functions (their senses).[77]

FOS cashes this out in terms of *ontological relativity:* The furnishing functions never draw on a stock of pure objects, but always only on objects specified under prior ontological conditions. If objects are mapped from one fos to another, the mapping takes all possible shapes—a structure of facticity known from the mathematical investigation into the

SENSE, NONSENSE, AND SUBJECTIVITY

architecture of functions. Just as in mathematics there is a gigantic, unlimited array of functions that fall into manifold categories (injective, bijective, surjective, trigonometric, non-monotonic, etc.), in FOS there is an unlimited variety of senses (only some of which are mathematical).

Coming back to the problem of hands. My left hand is an object in my visual field. There, it appears in (and therefore is) a certain way. The objects with which my hand can rightfully and truthfully be associated in the fos of physical objects do not reveal a deeper, more objective, or more real nature such that it would even begin to make sense to, say, reduce truths about my hand to truths about elementary particles. The actual relationship between my left hand and physics is as rich, complicated, and complex as the relationship between the manifold fos that intersect at the level at which my hand makes its appearance. These fos cannot be reduced to natural fos (described by physics, chemistry, and biology), on the one hand, and some other mental or cultural field on the other hand, as such a description grossly underestimates the fine-grained multiplicity of conceptually unreduced reality—which is in the target system of FOS.

The notion of ontological nonsense is a key to recognizing the thickness of reality, an important point regularly brought to my attention by my fellow New Realist travelers Jocelyn Benoist and Maurizio Ferraris. However, this thickness of reality has a conceptual dimension as well. It, too, should not be identified with the presence of physical objects in our encounter with reality. Reality is also thick where we are not dealing with objects qua "obstacles to free passage,"[78] to use a felicitous phrase due to Charles Travis.

Any serious student of actual mathematical physics (as well as pure mathematics) has had the experience of dealing with a rich conceptual reality that is as thick and objective as it gets, despite the fact that we access it under astonishingly sharp conditions of conceptual control (via definitions, algorithms, operations, etc.). The "hardness of the mathematical must,"[79] to vary Wittgenstein's phrase, cannot be reduced to the pressure exercised on us by others who train us in mathematics. Rather, it belongs to the objects we are dealing with in mathematics even independently of the fact that mathematics in its application to the universe yields constants and structures that are thick in virtue of being tied to our measurements.

The fact that we never inhabit an epistemic or cognitive situation where absolutely everything is so clear that we can actually carry out a complete analysis of a given object into the bundle of truths that hold good of it (the facts) manifests itself in the form of a remaining confusion. However clearheadedly we navigate a given conceptual territory (and be it in pure mathematics or logics), the landscape will be conceptually foggy and messy around the edges.

In this section, I have argued that this is not just a blind spot generated by the presence of subjectivity but an ontological fact that holds even in the absence of subjectivity. Objects are involved in innumerably many fos without there being an overall mapping of a stock of pure objects onto the manifold fos. Reality, therefore, is characterized by an unsurpassable incompleteness that does not merely come out in the extreme case of global metaphysical confusion.

Therefore, it is misguided to try to overcome nonsense by reducing it to a semantic or epistemic phenomenon somehow generated by natural or ordinary language so that we "just" have to rid ourselves of our linguistically grounded subjectivity to "see the world aright."[80] In particular, nonsense is not just a phenomenon that bewitches philosophers and lures us away from otherwise clearheaded common sense. Rather, nonsense arises from the inevitable fact of ontological confusion to which both objects and subjects are equally subject.

Carman's Challenge: Nonsense between the Lines

Nonsense can take as many shapes as sense, i.e., innumerably many. Reality is as intelligible as it is unintelligible, as propositional as it is non-propositional. Sense and nonsense are both operative at the ontological level: they concern existence itself and, therefore, implicate objects and fields alike.

This is an appropriate place to counter two related sets of objections to FOS and to some of the opening moves of New Realism's theory of subjectivity (called "neo-existentialism") formulated by Taylor Carman from his distinctive contemporary, neo-Heideggerian perspective.[81] In particular, Carman charges me with different kinds of "conflations," most notably "of entities and descriptions" and "true descriptions with facts."[82] In his view, these conflations are supposed to result from my "desire to subvert all traditional dualisms of subject and object, mind and world, and so on."[83] Moreover, he charges me with "forgetting of being"—without quite telling me what exactly this means apart from his recourse to the distinction between *essentia* and *existentia*.

Before I go into some of details of Carman's worry that will shed light on the account of ontological nonsense presented in this chapter, let it be noted in passing that *pace* Carman Heidegger's "Seyn" must certainly not be confused with "mere *that*-being or *existentia* as such,"[84] as if that phrase were especially intelligible. On the contrary, the distinction between *essentia* (as something that can be accessed by way of descriptions, senses, thoughts, propositions) and *existentia* (as pure conceptually primitive, meaningless facticity) is a paradigm of metaphysics in the sense to which Heidegger was opposed. The reason is precisely that this turns reality into a "standing-reserve (*Bestand*),"[85] or a mere presence in front of us, and leads exactly to the kind of dualism of in-itself and for-itself characteristic of Sartrean metaphysics, but utterly alien to Heideggerian "Seyn." The problem for Heidegger is not the "privileging of entities (*das Seiende*) over being (*das Sein*)" but the very stage-setting of that ontological difference that his new form of thinking (designed to articulate "Seyn") sets out to replace by some entirely different mode of doing philosophy, or rather of thinking, full stop.[86]

Here, it is also important to point out the abyss that separates Wittgenstein's idea that we can somehow *show* the thatness of the world without *saying* it and Heidegger's elaborate prose written in a language designed to say all sorts of things in an arena of thought and discourse in which Wittgenstein wanted to remain silent. If one reads Heidegger charitably, he cannot be engaged in the business of indirectly communicating a metaphysical message while in a certain sense recognizing that one cannot say it directly. Rather, he invents a new manner of speaking and writing about how sense and nonsense interfere in reality's appearance to thinkers depending upon their position in reality's self-manifestation.

For this and other reasons, there are parts of Heidegger's diagnosis of what is wrong with metaphysics that I share and that lead me to regard him as an ally (though certainly not in any political or ethical sense). In particular, Heidegger saw that there is such a thing as "poetic thinking," to use Amir Eshel's notion, i.e., thinking between the lines of propositional articulation.[87]

Before we get to that, in this section I will address Carman's worry that I underestimate unintelligibility, nonsense, and facticity and that my realism collapses into "Hegelian absolute idealism"[88] from a different angle. The opening paragraphs of one of his articles correctly describe the upshot of the no-world-view by summarizing an important premise thus: "The very idea of a complete description of anything seems to be ruled out by the fact that a description of anything constitutes a further fact about that thing, whose complete description would then in turn require a further description, and so on ad infinitum."[89] In this passage, he realizes that the no-world-view has local applications in that it undermines the idea of complete descriptions of anything. However, Carman goes on to charge me with absolute idealism, which is explicitly based on the idea of a "necessary and complete"[90] description. Evidently, he misses the crucial connection between incompleteness (or open-endedness), ontological descriptivism, and realism: the no-world-view straightforwardly entails local incompleteness and, therefore, is capable of accounting for unintelligibility and ontological nonsense without recourse to an unspeakable thatness that is inaccessible to theorizing.

What is worse, Carman immediately loses track of his understanding of FOS when he summarizes ontological descriptivism as follows: "The world itself is nothing other than the contents of all the true descriptions of it."[91] What a stunning misconstrual of FOS, a misconstrual without which Carman could not approximate my view to Hegel's.

I would not mention any of this here if—despite the hermeneutic incoherence of his article, which contradicts itself on the first two pages by ascribing beliefs to me that, even according to his reading of FOS, I obviously cannot hold—Carman did not raise an important point. The important point is that existence is associated with a degree of unintelligibility. Yet, unintelligibility need not be reduced to an act of mere gesturing at existence as both actual thatness and as "a primitive notion for which there is not and cannot be any further analysis. If that is so, then there is something perverse in the very idea of advancing a theory of existence."[92] This shows how Carman wants to have his cake (pure thatness) and eat it too (by proposing a notion of existence without having a theory of it). But that raises exactly the question he should be grappling with,

125

namely the question concerning the relationship between a notion of existence and existence itself.

Contrary to his self-portrait as anti-rationalist, Carman draws on an intellectual intuition of an identity of thought and being which reveals itself in his knowledge claim that there is a notion of existence (about which he is not willing to say anything apart from his gesturing at it) which corresponds to existence itself. Reminding me of being (which I am supposed to have forgotten) for him consists in advancing his own theory of existence. He writes that there is something "which remains both distinct from and irreducible to the *what* content of propositional thought, namely the primitive (non-propositionally structured) 'fact' *that* anything *is*,"[93] a passage quite revealing if one looks at the use of quotation marks and emphases, which are gestures at whatever it is he wants to convey about existence without advancing a theory.

Carman puts forward "the idea that existence is recalcitrant to reason, that being is not coincident or identical with thought or intelligibility."[94] While I agree with the idea that being and thought are not identical, this does not entail that being as such, or existence, is unintelligible or unthinkable. Rather, existence is exactly what we grasp when successfully thinking about anything at all, which rules out that "existence and nonexistence (especially our own) are essentially enigmatic."[95]

What Carman misses is important, because it is precisely that to which he believes himself to be committed, namely the non-propositional dimension of existence. In the previous section I have introduced the notion of ontological nonsense as a feature of objects as regress stoppers. While objects within their fos are bundles of senses, the fact that objects can change according to a fusion of fos and, thus, of senses, generates the effects of a Fregean referent. Yet, these effects are reducible neither to semantic nor to other dimensions of the realm of propositional sense. They take place in the interstices of propositional sense.

This is what I already had in mind when introducing both the notion of a field and that of appearing in a way that can indeed be illustrated by the figure-ground schema: For something to exist is for it to make its appearance, to stand out, from a context populated by objects of a similar enough kind for them to interact in the same domain, which thereby constitutes a field.

In general, the concept of a field is sufficiently similar to the concept of a field in physics for us to draw a comparison. If advancing a theory of existence in terms of fields and objects is perverse, then physics, too, is perverse in that it does exactly that (limited to one particular kind of object, namely the category of physical objects, however exactly one delimits that, which is another story). Now, in physics, the concept of a field is the concept of a structure where each point in a space (including space-time) can be assigned a value of an observable (which can both be a scalar, i.e., roughly a number, or a vector thanks to which we can model forces). In a fos, the field is populated by objects which occupy their position within the field in virtue of their difference from other objects and from their properties (where vectors would stand for the direction of sense)—including the field itself, which is an object in some other fos (bracketing for the moment fos that appear within themselves).[96] None of this requires the presence of thinkers or *Dasein* (as Heidegger famously calls subjects, insofar as they are capable of understanding themselves and their position with respect to being) for it to hold good of how things are. *Pace* Carman, Heidegger constantly insists that we precisely do not create the appearances—for instance, by way of transcendental imposition or by drawing geometrical figures in the mental space of pure forms of intuition and so forth.[97]

In order to show what is wrong with Carman's anti-realism (or rather: anti-rationalism) about sense, let us imagine how things would look if "to appear" were "to appear to someone." If all appearances were appearances to someone, then nothing would appear if no one were there. We would thus have to think of reality in the way Carman wants us to think of it: as utterly unintelligible, because we have constructed a notion of reality that is defined by its negation of the presence of intelligibility. But this is not a demonstration of the "fact" that reality in itself is utterly sense-, meaning-, and intelligibility-free but a *reductio ad absurdum* of the "view" for the simple reason that Carman at the same time ought to maintain that reality in its appearing to someone has to be revealed to us in the way it is. If he denied that sort of elementary phenomenological realism, he would not be seen as following in the footsteps of Husserl, Heidegger, Sartre, and Merleau-Ponty at all. Thus, the best he can do is to commit to what Meillassoux has called "strong correlationism," i.e., the view that within the correlation of subject and object, reality manifests itself while having an inscrutable thing in itself at its core to which we can, at best, brutely refer.

In this context, the idea of "brute reference" marks the polar extreme of good old descriptivism that—I assume rightly—argued that there is no reference (not even of singular terms such as proper names designed, say, to refer to exactly one entity) without some descriptive content or other.[98] We cannot name anything whatsoever without thinking of it in some way. But this does not mean that we have drawn ontological nonsense—the confusing, dynamic, changing, unpredictable nature of reality in its manifold appearing—into the realm of sense.

It is important to bear in mind that in the context of our practices of sensemaking, nonsense does precisely not amount to meaninglessness at all, contrary to what Carnap and Wittgenstein believed, in their fervor for cleansing language of its poetical dimension in order to create a world-picture according to which the world is made up of facts qua constellations of objects—a world-picture Carman inexplicably ascribes to me too.[99]

The origin of my notion that nonsense takes place in the interstices of fos without thereby being hidden is tied to poetic thinking.[100] Recently, Hans Ulrich Gumbrecht's and Marisa Galvez's work on the Occitan troubadours has convinced me of the point that we cannot understand poetry without distinguishing between nonsense and meaninglessness. One of their examples is the term "noigandres," which is a hapax legomenon: the word "appears only once in the Occitan language, in Arnaut's canso, and is apparently a neologism."[101] Beyond the fact that this quote provides sufficient linguistic evidence for one of the many actual usages of "appear" without the implication of "to appear to someone," the context is very illuminating. For the famous Brazilian Noigandres group of concrete poets (inspired by Ezra Pound's reintroduction of the mysterious, untranslatable Occitan term into modern poetry), the word plays the role of a mysterious signifier whose nature is not to refer to anything in particular or maybe simply not to refer. However, it only seems to be meaningless nonsense as long as one assumes that language-based sensemaking is essentially in the business of either straightforwardly referring to objects within given fos or of contributing to the conditions of propositional articulation of truth-apt thought and discourse.

In general, an important function of poetry is to create nonsense that is not meaningless. Interestingly, even the Occitan editors of Arnaut

NONSENSE

Daniel's canso had problems with translating the word, and their translations include proposals such as "relief from boredom" and "nutmeg."[102] However, that does not mean that "noigandres" is meaningless nonsense, even though we cannot make sense of it in any of the ways that are characteristic of a program, such as Quine's, to associate linguistic meaning with our ways of dealing with objects and facts in the "external world," as if this activity were constitutive of meaning.[103]

That poetry has the capacity of "signifying nothing"[104] is not a discovery of modernity (let alone romanticism). Remarkably, a song by the troubadour William IX, Count of Poitiers and Duke of Aquitaine (1071–1127), i.e., from roughly the same context that produced "noigandres," is quite explicit about this in a way that would generate straightforward paradox in a propositional, fact-stating setting.

> I'll do a song about nothing at all;
> It won't be about me nor about others,
> It won't be about love nor about happiness (or youthfulness)
> Nor about anything else,
> For it was composed earlier while (I was) sleeping
> On a horse.[105]

If we thought of the verses of this stanza in propositional terms of sense-making, they would amount to paradox. From a propositional ("literal") perspective, the song is about all sorts of things, including things it claims not to be about (the author / lyrical I, other, love, happiness, and the rest of it). But the point of the verses is that the conditions of aboutness we associate with "literal" meaning are absent in the context of the poem.

Here we encounter the truth in both Heidegger's and Wittgenstein's conversion to poetic thinking. Heidegger's case is familiar, while it often goes unnoticed that Wittgenstein, too, at some point started to think of the nonsense that creeps up in the very context of putting an end to it, as poetic and not as meaningless: "philosophy ought really to be written as a form of poetic composition."[106]

Having said that, recognizing the possibility of poetic thinking between the lines of propositional articulation and reference to objects need not require us "to call into question the sharp line between sense and nonsense that philosophers like Carnap wanted to draw."[107] Why should

SENSE, NONSENSE, AND SUBJECTIVITY

there not be a sharp enough line between sense and nonsense? Sense and nonsense, after all, are not the same. To be an actual thinker is to constantly traverse boundaries of fos, to be on a "voyage through the infinite," as I put it elsewhere.[108] In every instance of our conscious lives, we are confronted with objects that are embedded in field confusion and, therefore, manifest themselves both in sense and in nonsense.

This does not mean that in addition to fields of sense, there are also fields of nonsense. Nonsense does not precisely map objects onto a field, but rather blurs the outlines of fos and destabilizes propositional, factual reality. This manifests itself in the form of time and becoming, which we cannot get a complete hold of at all by, say, reducing time to a parameter t. Of course, there is time as thought of by physics, that is to say, there is such a thing as what t refers to. But physical time t differs from ontological time or becoming in many ways; t at best captures the relational terms "earlier" and "later" and is void of tenses such as past, present, and future. Other than our own lifetimes, t has no privileged moment, no central presence of our existence. Within FOS the most obvious difference between time in general and t is that ontological time implicates objects and fields which are not physical—which matters more than the complicated issue of whether t has a direction associated with entropy to which our experience of time somehow corresponds.[109]

Nonsense takes place between the lines, as it were: in transitioning from one fos to another, objects change the local architecture of the fos in which they are involved. Poetry's use of lines that separate verses, its ways of leaving things out in order to create musical structures, provides a platform for the manifestation of nonsense as such, which is not a critique of poetry by any means. On the contrary, it is a way to understand poetry's crucial difference from the precision-oriented propositional language whose nature it is to make explicit everything it is designed to communicate.

Having said that, one might still wonder how this welcoming gesture with respect to nonsense is compatible with ontological descriptivism, for nonsense arises under conditions of confusion that are paradigmatically temporal. To many commentators, FOS seems to be committed to an Eleatic stance with respect to reality, in particular, concerning the identity riddle.[110] If objects are identical to description bundles, i.e., if they do not differ from the facts in which they are embedded but hold them together

NONSENSE

as their glue, how can there possibly be change? Is the concept of change not tied to the idea that an object has one set of properties at one time and some other set of properties at another time so that nothing really changes (because the object is just the bundle of all of the facts in which it is involved)? Moreover, the actualism built into the modal structure of FOS (which equates existence with being actual) seems to amount to a form of necessitarianism according to which it is impossible for an object to be identical across modal variations.[111]

However, these worries arise from a wrongheaded metaphysical reading of FOS. They assume that the theory quantifies over absolutely everything in such a way that it proclaims a whole series of synthetic a priori truths concerning the architecture of FOS and objects embedded in it. Yet any such reading is incompatible with the no-world-view. It underestimates the crucial dimensionality of ontological relativity: what exists appears in some fos. Given that there is no fos of all fos, we cannot think of necessity in terms of truths that hold good of any object whatsoever and, thus, postulate necessary facts (facts that obtain in absolutely every fos). Necessitarianism in this quantitative (reductive) form is incompatible with FOS.

For change to be possible is for it to occur. Possibility in FOS is an abstraction from the actual. Successful abstraction generates new objects which are actual in some other fos. Grasping a possibility is grasping modal facts concerning a given populated field and identifying modal patterns which lead to other fos. Given that there is change and paradigmatic confusion in the shape of consciousness, FOS has to account for this facticity. And it does so by adding the concept of ontological nonsense to its vocabulary, a concept designed to reckon with unintelligibility and confusion.

Herein lies the clue to my response to the charge of speaking Wittgensteinian nonsense when expressing the no-world-view.[112] In *Fields of Sense* I wrote: "For me, saying anything about the world is plain nonsense, like saying the following: 'XCEANNRs12*' or the following: ''. As Frank Ramsey said in a similar context about Wittgensteinian nonsense: 'But what we can't say, we can't say, and we cannot whistle it either.'"[113] This invites the straightforward objection that the meaning of "the world does not exist" is plain nonsense, so that the phrase "the world does not exist" is semantically indistinguishable from "XCEANNRs12" or at least from

"XCEANNRs12 does not exist." And that potentially threatens to undermine the intelligibility of FOS and create serious issues for the no-world-view (the no-XCEANNRs12-view).

My response to this is that many (though by no means all) expressions on the formal level of the ontology of fos deal with ontological nonsense that is grounded in pre-ontological experience. Otherwise put, there is a whole psychology of the desire to fuse with absolutely everything, or to become a subject that is opposed to an external world, and so forth. There are metaphysical experiences. Yet, these experiences should precisely not be read as claims about anything, let alone about absolutely everything, the world.

In a recent statement of an expressibility objection against the no-world-view, James Hill maintains that my arguments at most demonstrate that an extensionalistic type of metaphysics fails.[114] According to his analysis, this leaves ample space for "the possibility of intensional access to the absolute" that, he claims, "has been passed over in silence by Gabriel's empiricist pluralism."[115] Hill wants to allow me to produce a rule of disjunctiveness in order to articulate the claim that "the series of fields of sense is indefinitely extensible *in the right way*"[116] without thereby referring to a given domain. While his article provides some interesting resources for thinking of the vocabulary of FOS in terms of a maximal generality, he does not show why this would lead me to accept the existence of the world. At most, he has shown that my view is expressible in a somewhat ordinary manner without thereby having to refer to a domain whose ontological constitution is discrete in the sense to which I have been objecting.

Hill is still in the grip of what I have been calling first-order metaphysics. Despite his welcome distinction between "generality and quantification,"[117] which captures the spirit of FOS, he himself falls prey to the metaphysical illusion that we can somehow move from an insight into the generality of a given discourse to there being something in particular that provides the referential substrate or object of the discourse.

Hill points out that the expressive resources of the functional concepts that make up the core vocabulary of FOS do not necessarily lead FOS into an untenable "Wittgensteinian" position where the entire architecture of the positive ontology of FOS breaks down—as if throwing away the ladder was always the same as burning all bridges behind oneself. FOS is perfectly expressible—in functional terms. Instead of thinking of the concepts "thing," "object," "existence," "field of sense," "necessity," etc. in terms of maximal or even absolute generality, FOS asks for specific application conditions tied to a given fos. The concepts themselves are incompatible with setting up a fos of all fos (which is the conclusion of the demonstration of the no-world-view).

The no-world-view claims that the metaphysician gets entangled in global and local nonsense as soon as he begins to articulate an actual worldview that goes beyond an expression of a desire to have one. The introduction of the concept of ontological nonsense into FOS now allows me to explain the origin of metaphysical nonsense in terms of our pre-ontological relationship to reality. Reality's confusion—which, among other things, manifests itself in the shapes of the stream of consciousness—can easily be mistaken for the presence of an all-encompassing domain or absolute object of which absolutely everything (possibly including itself) is a proper part.

But if this maneuver saves the no-world-view from collapsing into nonsense as straightforward meaninglessness, it also threatens it by opening up the possibility of practicing metaphysics in a poetic key. To be sure, many so-called analytic metaphysicians would not be content to learn that, at best, they are poetic thinkers who speak in exactly the same nonsensical, logical tone of voice as the late Heidegger. But why would we accept in the first place that metaphysics has to be like physics, only more fundamental? The idea that metaphysics latches onto how reality really is, that it carves nature at joints and so on, is misguided in too many ways for it to be the standard based on a metaphysical "knee-jerk realism."[118]

With "the world (really) well lost"[119] by thinking of it as nonsense, FOS therefore threatens to collapse into poetic metaphysics, as it suddenly has room for a positive use of the term "the world." We therefore apparently generate an antinomy whereby the world both does and does not exist (according to one's poetic preference).

Yet, the point in the nonsense passage from *Fields of Sense* is quite different from what this reading suggests. If speaking about the world generates nonsense and if "the world does not exist" is not nonsensical, it simply cannot be a statement *about* the world. This provides ample space for a poetic use of the term "the world" even in a context with metaphysical ambitions, say, Schopenhauer's *The World as Will and Representation*.[120]

SENSE, NONSENSE, AND SUBJECTIVITY

In a surprising sense, then, Nietzsche was quite right to conclude from a reading of that text that "only as an *aesthetic phenomenon* is existence and the world eternally *justified.*"[121] "The world" can capture our imagination; we can begin to think that there is such a thing as a worldly totality to which we belong or with which we fuse. But, as Nietzsche insists in the context in which he professes this famous statement:

> Our highest dignity lies in our significance as works of art—for only as an *aesthetic phenomenon* is existence and the world eternally *justified*—although, of course, our awareness of our significance in this respect hardly differs from the awareness which painted soldiers have of the battle depicted on the same canvas. Thus our whole knowledge of art is at bottom entirely illusory, because, as knowing creatures, we are not one and identical with the essential being which gives itself eternal pleasure as the creator and spectator of that comedy of art. Only insofar as the genius, during the act of artistic procreation, merges fully with that original artist of the world does he know anything of the eternal essence of art; for in this condition he resembles, miraculously, that uncanny image of fairy-tale which can turn its eyes around and look at itself; now he is at one and the same time subject and object, simultaneously poet, actor, and spectator.[122]

The world, then, is an illusion for Nietzsche too. There is no way for us to think of it as an object without creating the problem of fusion and confusion that is at the heart of the no-world-view.

Poetic discourse involving the term "the world" and our metaphysical experiences—which, on closer inspection, are not about anything at all except for the confusion that they articulate—does not undermine the no-world-view. All I am saying is that there is a poetical use of language that allows us to understand both what it would mean for the world to exist and that it does not, as the extraordinary requirements for its existence (absolute totality plus subjectivity appearing within totality as a locus of its manifestation) simply are not met.

What poetry and poetology teach us, then, is that we ought to divorce nonsense from meaninglessness. Ontological nonsense is not meaningless, even if meaninglessness is a form of nonsense. Poetry, therefore, can meaningfully speak in terms that allow us to express metaphysical experience without thereby ontologically committing to a referential use of "the world," as this is exactly poetry's semantic hallmark: To detach sense from reference and to free us from the illusion that to speak is to create a framework of sensemaking grounded in reference, as if language were primordially a tool for designation or a kind of pointing at mind-independent reality.

Language is not grounded in any one of its manifold functions and, therefore, can rightly serve as an illustration of ontological incompleteness. In light of this, Carman is perfectly right when he draws on Wittgenstein's famous comparison of language with a city:

> Don't let it bother you that languages (2) and (8) consist only of orders. If you want to say that they are therefore incomplete, ask yourself whether our own language is complete—whether it was so before the symbolism of chemistry and the notation of the infinitesimal calculus were incorporated in to it; for these are, so to speak, suburbs of our language. (And how many houses or streets does it take before a town begins to be a town?) Our language can be regarded as an ancient city: a maze of little streets and squares, of old and new houses, of houses with extensions from various periods, and all this surrounded by a multitude of new suburbs with straight and regular streets and uniform houses.[123]

This should, of course, not mislead us into believing that in reality (or in the world) there aren't any cities.[124] Rather, we can do indefinitely many things with our words. Language does not have a tighter ontological architecture than non-linguistic reality.

Here, Derrida had a point in his famous polemical exchange with Searle about Austin:[125] Poetic language is not somehow abnormal or parasitic upon some normal use.[126] It is just one of the many forms that language takes. Language is not primarily an instrument to get a hold of objects "out there" so as to then communicate about them by anchoring our language use in mind-independent, purely designated (not itself designating) reality.

SENSE, NONSENSE, AND SUBJECTIVITY

Having said that, *pace* the postmodern and poststructural twists of the linguistic turn in Derrida, Rorty, and others, this insight should not be misconstrued as a denial or even a problematization of the referential use of language. Of course, there is reference. But reference is not a relationship between a sign and an object such that we have to draw a sharp Fregean distinction between the sense of a sign and the object that we encounter at the end of the semantic vector, as it were.

Nonsense as the Subject's Ontological Signature

As subjects we have an inexorable desire to grasp reality as it is. Being in touch with how things are is literally a question of life and death. Propositional thought articulates objective sense in ways accessible to a subject. However, due to its inevitable focus on a given fos to the detriment of others, propositional thought is constitutively blind to the non-propositional. It can only recognize it in the form of nonsense. At the same time, this recognition is blocked by the confusion of nonsense and meaninglessness. Propositional thought cannot see the meaning in nonsense and, therefore, misses out on ontological nonsense. But ontological nonsense, too, is part of what there is.

Reducing reality to measurable, elementary forms of propositional judgment that aim to represent accurately or even fuse with the facts, is a concrete, real way of being wrong. Reality is not entirely propositional, which is not to say that it is unintelligible or in some other way resists conceptualization. Reality is precisely that which we only grasp partially in propositional terms and do not thereby fully exhaust—it includes the non-propositional (nonsense included) without thereby forming a whole.

At second glance, Wittgenstein's account of the subject in the *Tractatus* might be on the right track. In one of the much-discussed closing remarks of the *Tractatus* he brings in subjectivity.

> My propositions serve as elucidations in the following way: anyone who understands me, in the end recognizes them as nonsensical, when he climbed out through them—on them— over them. (He must so to speak throw away the ladder, after he has climbed up on it.)

He must overcome these propositions, then he sees the
world aright.[127]

Wittgenstein's propositions are not merely in the fact-stating business of
claiming the truth, as they are recognizable as nonsensical once we understand *him.* The recognition of nonsense is a form of understanding. What
matters is that we understand *Wittgenstein,* not his propositions. Understanding Wittgenstein consists in transcending the propositions in order
to see the world aright.

None of this entails that Wittgenstein maintains that at least some
or all of the propositions (including 6.54, the very proposition we are
reading here) of the *Tractatus* are nonsensical. Rather, their nonsense
resides between the lines, which is where we encounter subjectivity.
Recognizing his propositions as nonsensical means realizing that there
are gaps between the steps of the ladder. This often goes unnoticed, but
Wittgenstein asks us to imagine that someone climbs through the propositions in order to transcend them. Climbing a ladder presupposes that
there are not just steps but also empty spaces between them. And I read
6.54 as pointing to those empty spaces, to what lies in between the steps
of the ladder. And that is not nothing but the subject's signature, which
allows us to understand Wittgenstein by grasping the elucidatory nature
of *his* propositions.

Let us look at Wittgenstein's propositions about the subject (in particular, *Tractatus* 5.631–5.641), which seem to be contradictory. On the one
hand, we read that "the thinking, representing subject does not exist."[128]
On the other hand, he tells us that the "subject does not belong to the world,
but it is a limit of the world."[129] To be sure, this can be read as the claim that
to exist is to belong to the world, and that is not the case for the subject.
This is one way of making sense of the apparent contradiction in that series
of propositions. If we accept that reading, then we encounter the subject
between the lines of the propositional grid of what Wittgenstein calls "the
world," i.e., a totality that can be depicted in propositional terms.

If speaking about something requires propositional, logical form,
then indeed we cannot speak of the subject and, thus, must be silent about
it. This is not a normative claim or a recommendation to avoid nonsense
in favor of propositional thought but, if anything, a claim that language directed at the subject is not directed at anything in the world, does not

SENSE, NONSENSE, AND SUBJECTIVITY

capture an object of any kind and, thus, violates the basic condition of aboutness. We cannot speak *about* the subject in that sense.

To which one might be tempted to respond by pointing out that we can easily deflate the notion of aboutness so as to think of ourselves as subjects without identifying ourselves with an object in the propositional order (Wittgenstein's world). But this in turn underestimates the presence of the subject as that which can get things right or wrong; for being able to get things right is as much a capacity of Wittgenstein's "metaphysical subject" as the ontological signature of subjectivity. Subjectivity is an objectively existing illusion, a form of distortion that is part of any reality we can possibly grasp.

That does not mean that there is no mind-independent reality or that we are stuck with a correlation of subject and object without ever being able to transcend our inner sphere so as to arrive at the object. It is perfectly straightforward to think of an object, a fact, or an event as taking place in the absence of subjectivity. Yet, the situation, the fos, within which the operation of grasping such mind-independent aspects of what there is, is, of course, not itself mind-independent. The subject is present even where it successfully (truthfully) directs its attention to how things are. Trivially, the thought that p is *my* thought when I successfully claim to know that p. When p is known, it is known by someone. But no one ever gets absolutely everything right, not even about a single object that we have in clear view (be it in literal vision or in some methodologically controlled setting, such as a mathematical proof that explores the formal properties of an object, such as the value of a function at a well-defined point). Thus, the factive mental state of knowing that p is in one way or another soaked in falsity, illusion, one-sidedness, error, bias, noise, and many other forms of flawed judgment.

Being right and being wrong are inextricably interwoven in our actual mental lives. There is no such thing as getting absolutely everything right about a given object. But there is also no such thing as getting absolutely everything wrong about a given object. Being wrong about a given object presupposes that one has gotten enough things right about it, even though some other facts about it are essentially obscured. In thought, there is no absolute falsity, if by "absolute falsity" we refer to the idea that we could be entirely detached from the object about which we are in some kind of error.

NONSENSE

To be sure, there is a clear enough conceptual distinction between truth (which has been extensively studied by philosophical logic) and falsity (which is irresponsibly undertheorized). Minimally, truth is some kind of opposite of falsity. I am not arguing that we should abandon the distinction between truth and falsity or that between sense and nonsense. Yet, the conceptual fact that these are different notions and the empirical fact that we often enough get things right in propositional terms does nothing to show that we ever fuse with reality. Even in actual true thought we remain at a deontological distance from reality that manifests itself in the fact that our mental life never contains only truths. Knowing that p is always at the same time being wrong about some constituent or other of the proposition known. For instance, I know that I am writing this sentence in an office at Stanford. I know this full well; no skeptical or mundane doubt creeps in and makes me hesitant.[130] Yet, I know that there are indefinitely many things I do not know about this office and Stanford. If asked enough questions, it will turn out that I actually have some false beliefs about this office and Stanford, which will be true for everybody who is capable of knowing that they are in that office at Stanford.

The fact that knowing that p involves a host of forms of not-knowing, and being wrong about some of the constituents of the known proposition does nothing to undermine knowledge. We can know p without exhausting its logical, inferential environment. Knowledge is and remains finite in that sense without therefore being impossible.[131]

Subjectivity is a paradigmatic form of ontological incompleteness. It is paradigmatic in virtue of the fact that we are never in a position to think of reality without thereby at some point or other also providing an account of our presence in it. We are indispensable for our understanding of reality, which does not mean that reality is somehow mind-dependent. Yet the reality we know is, of course, in part mind-, language-, culture-, consciousness-, and theory-dependent, as we are part of it.

To be sure, that does precisely not mean that we are an obstacle or a kind of screen that separates us from what there is. Our proneness to error is a manifestation of our belonging to the manifestation of reality on the level we know as subjectivity in virtue of our capacity for self-knowledge. Philosophy is a paradigmatic exercise of self-knowledge through which we calibrate our sense of what there is, which is grounded in the pre-ontological experience of "being here," as I called it in earlier work.[132]

SENSE, NONSENSE, AND SUBJECTIVITY

Pre-ontological experience is the target-system of philosophy insofar as it does not aim to step entirely outside of the subject's skin. Pre-ontological experience reveals reality as a temporal unfolding of manifold appearing, a fact that documents not only a mind-independent reality but, at the same time, our own irreducible existence as knowers, thinkers, agents—in short, as subjects who sometimes get it right and sometimes are wrong. With this in mind, we now turn to subjectivity.

3

SUBJECTIVITY

THIS CHAPTER IS dedicated to subjectivity. Its main thesis is that being a subject is constitutively tied to being wrong. Subjects are not only *capable* of getting it wrong, but they also essentially get something or other wrong even if their mistakes only make sense if they get things right in some other respects. The subject of knowledge claims, the S in "S knows that p," as such is always involved in some kind of actual error, mistake, misperception, distortion, misrepresentation, simplification, ignorance, false belief, etc. Subjectivity is, thus, not defined by the self-conscious, incorrigible grasp of one's own thinking. I reject this Cartesian paradigm and argue that we should replace it with an approach that sets out from insight into the manifold modes in which we are wrong. These modes make us who we are, turning us into individual thinkers who make myriad knowledge claims, some successful, but many of them not.

Subjects are essentially fallible. This does not, of course, mean that subjects never get anything right. There are full-blown cases of knowledge, even knowledge knowing itself as knowledge. However, these cases are embedded in a subject's mental life. They cannot be isolated from subjectivity as it actually unfolds. This does not imply in any way that actual knowledge cannot be shared. Yet, sharing knowledge, transmitting information, and, thus, our practices of gaining knowledge by testimony, hearsay, and socially orchestrated training presuppose social conditions in which fallible subjects mutually correct each other's flaws in judgment so as to lift society up. Such is the idea and the promise of modern knowledge societies.

Some contemporary theories of specific modes of being wrong (such as biases, perceptual illusions, socially systemic illusions, etc.) have demonstrated that there is no single epistemological or scientific position from which we could distinguish between truth and falsity by way of specifying a priori criteria for how to use our conceptual capacities. In this way, these theories (grounded in empirical research in psychology, behavioral economics, cognitive science, and so forth) can be used as a guide to subjectivity.[1]

Having said that, we need to go beyond an empirical, evidential approach to subjectivity and focus on its essence. In this context, I will argue that the essence of subjectivity manifests itself in an open-ended proliferation of different modes of being wrong. These modes of being wrong cannot be brought under a single simple concept of falsity as not-truth. For their reality is the unfolding of our mental lives whose structure cannot be reduced to a list of conceptual capacities (such as cognition/thinking on the one hand and perception/sensing on the other hand) whose misfiring would explain error, confusion, illusion, delusion, false thought, and so forth.

In a recent discussion of his book on noise as a source of error, Daniel Kahneman—one of the most influential scientists in the field of research on systemic flaws in judgment—was asked if we could begin to domesticate noisy behavior in judgment by way of cultivating epistemic virtues.[2] In this context, "noise" is a technical term designed to designate an "undesirable variability in judgments of the same problem,"[3] such as idiosyncratic and largely random variation in sentencing behavior in court by the same judge at different times of the day. In the cases investigated by Kahneman and his coauthors, such variability in judgment wears its undesirability on its sleeve. Hardly anyone could defend the idea that it is good when physicians, judges, or police officers pass incompatible judgments in the same type of cases based upon idiosyncratic features of the person or occasion (such as being a more lenient judge in the morning or being a doctor who, facing the same symptoms, prescribes opioids rather than antibiotics in the evening).[4]

SUBJECTIVITY

Kahneman's response to the question of whether we could cultivate epistemic virtues that are directed at the source of noise was quite remarkable and, I take it, entirely correct: we cannot domesticate noise in anything like a systematic, epistemological way because there is no "single interesting source of noise," as he put it.

This leads me to the linchpin of this chapter: noise, like other flaws in human judgment, is an effect of subjectivity and, thus, of our irredeemably fallible position within a hypercomplex environment. A source of error, a mode of being wrong, is not an epistemic bottleneck through which information passes according to some alethic criteria. Rather, it consists in a complex web of mental states and actions that manifest themselves in patterns of mistakes lacking a single unified origin—such as a unified transcendental subject that sometimes gets reality right and sometimes gets it wrong. Subjectivity is not grounded in a single, unified source. The subject's reality is as manifold as the hypercomplex environment within which it takes place. Subjectivity is, therefore, not opposed to a world of objects. It is part and parcel of any scenario we can make sense of—which is not to say that the presence of subjectivity erects an obstacle to knowledge of mind-independent reality. Subjectivity makes objectivity possible and does not undermine it.

Given that, as thinkers, judges, agents—in short, as subjects—we are part of fos, it should not come as a surprise that hypercomplexity (meaning the transfinite proliferation of fos) also manifests itself at the heart of judgment. The empirical, psychological fact that there is no single interesting source of noise should thus not come as a surprise. Just as reality cannot be synthesized into an all-encompassing whole (i.e., the world), our manifold mental states are not grounded in a subject in such a way that we could more or less easily identify a bunch of sources of judgment (such as thinking and sensing) in order to specify a readily surveyable list of epistemic or other virtues that can become theoretical guides for systematic epistemological hygiene and practical guides for behavioral change.[5]

Being wrong (and being right for that matter) describe a subject's relation to what there is. In this regard, they differ from the logical notion of truth and its underdefined antipode, falsity. While it makes perfect sense to think of truth as a property of utterances or propositions, utterances and propositions do not get it right or wrong. Errors, mistakes,

143

SENSE, NONSENSE, AND SUBJECTIVITY

misrepresentations, delusions, and epistemic vices that lead us astray by "getting in the way of knowledge"[6] characterize parts of reality in which subjectivity is constitutively involved.

This chapter will develop a theory of subjectivity based on these negative phenomena. It thereby establishes a countercurrent to the widespread idea (often associated with Descartes) that to be a subject is to be a self-conscious, self-knowing self—a status whose epistemological advantages ideally could serve as a foundation for the entire enterprise of knowledge.

Since at least Plato's *Theaetetus* and *Sophist,* the question of the epistemology and ontology of being wrong (ψεῦδος) has set out from the following overall problem. If to be wrong about something presupposes that one has the right object in mind while obscuring some of its features in such a way that one can attribute something to it that does not belong to it, one can never be entirely wrong about anything. To be wrong about some feature or other of London, say, presupposes that one is sufficiently in contact with London to make that particular kind of mistake. But this means that one is not directly wrong about London, as it were, but rather about one of its features, by attaching the wrong feature to it. Yet, how is this possible if we have both London and the (wrong) feature in view while we ascribe it to London? Is being wrong, ultimately, just believing a false proposition about the right object, and if so, what role, if any, does the form of our belief and its formation play for the explanation of the mistake?

In this context, it is tempting to think of truths as tied to the facts (to being, ὄν/ἐόν, as the Greeks would say) in such a way that in true thought the subject's relevance for the account of its grasping how things are vanishes. In true thought (paradigmatically in knowledge as non-accidentally justified true belief) the subject either completely disappears or it fuses with the part of reality it effectively grasps in the form of being right about it. By contrast, in false thought there seems to be a distance from reality that cannot be accounted for by reference to reality alone; the subject seems to be needed as the relevant explanation of the distance from reality built into the concept of being wrong. While this classical line of thinking is on the right track, it owes us both a conception of the sources of the multifaceted variety of being wrong and of the role of subjectivity in the good case of knowledge.

144

SUBJECTIVITY

Philosophy studies our mental cartography through the lens of rational reconstruction. Here, *rational reconstruction* means that philosophy not only draws doxastic and epistemic maps of regions of the human mind but does so with respect to a set of normative goals that guide its investigation.[7] While a perfectly rational mind that tries to eliminate all mistakes and replace them by insights cannot be achieved by actual subjects, we nevertheless know that there is a type of reflexive insight—such as the one just articulated—that cannot itself be subject to the type of mistake worth replacing. Thus, there is a gap between our capacity for epistemological self-knowledge and our actual first-order knowledge of reality. To the extent that our epistemological self-knowledge is aware of itself as knowledge, it serves as a paradigm to guide our philosophical investigations. Compared to this paradigm, our first-order knowledge falls short in manifold ways. Hence, philosophy's perennial struggle with a recognition of first-order knowledge's involvement in illusion.

There is a normative gap between our reflexive insights into epistemic achievements and our actual practices of knowledge acquisition. Let us call this gap (which has manifold ramifications in different regions of thought and action) the *deontological difference.*[8] A subject cannot overcome the deontological difference by knowing how things are. Someone's actual knowledge that p is part of her mental life in such a way that the subject cannot fully disappear in the achievement of a knowledge claim.

Ever since the Platonic revolution of using insight into the existence of the deontological difference to fuel critique of the epistemological, ethical, aesthetic, and political status quo, philosophy has rightly pointed out that we can do better, that we can be more rational by way of reducing the gap between the space of reasons and the space of objective occurrences that flow from our actions. However, this methodological position easily lures philosophers into confusing the reflexively available norms of getting it right (the true, the good, the beautiful) with pure states of our mind, as if there were an absolute subjectivity, a subjectivity as such that is the core or essence of our finite, fallible minds. A contemporary avatar of this perennial temptation is the notion that knowers are essentially in possession of conceptual capacities that they actualize in exercises triggered by their integration into an environment ("the world").

What exactly would it take to identify those conceptual capacities so as to arrive at an updated version of a table of categories? Unlike in the

SENSE, NONSENSE, AND SUBJECTIVITY

heyday of Kantian and post-Kantian attempts to actually produce a table of categories and demonstrate its being "necessary and complete,"[9] the contemporary landscape of transcendental theorizing, for the most part, contents itself with abbreviated demonstrations of the existence of absolute subjectivity and, thus, with the broad idea that there just has to be some set or other of fundamental conceptual capacities that support our mind's success conditions in the doxastic, epistemic, and practical realms.[10]

Against this trend, in what follows I will argue that the deontological difference should not be misconstrued as a relationship between our pure conceptual capacities that aim at the true, the good, and the beautiful on the one hand and their earthly, embodied, empirical distortions that somehow stray from the natural course of knowledge acquisition on the other. I thereby reject the picture of the human mind as essentially in touch with how things really are, which leads to the wrongheaded self-conception of knowers as transcendental egos or representatives of absolute subjectivity. As soon as it seems to us as if we were two subjects—one transcendental, the other empirical—we miss out on the fact that our empirical subjectivity is responsible for both the good and the bad case of knowing and acting.

In order to account for the essential, ineradicable existence of negative epistemological and practical phenomena at the core of subjectivity, in what follows I will approach the theory of fallibility from a novel angle. To repeat, the key claim is the notion that to be a subject, to be someone responsible for one's thoughts and actions, is to be wrong about certain things. Subjectivity, then, is not a *source* of possible illusions, mistakes, errors, and falsity, but the *actuality* of these phenomena of theoretical and practical negativity.

The theory of subjectivity offered here rejects the assumption that the success case of knowledge and good action is the paradigm of subjectivity and argues that the actuality of being wrong about many things is a constitutive hallmark of it as well. There is no such thing as a really existing architecture of unactualized capacities to be judged in light of their past, present, and future actual performances. There is no category structure of the mind. While thoughts arrived at in the form of the good case are indeed essentially shareable and in that sense objective, they are not exercises of a capacity whose misfiring would explain the bad case.

An influential trend in contemporary philosophy sets out from the now-famous McDowellian slogan that successful thought "does not stop short of the fact."[11] Similarly, successful action (ideally, ethically good deeds) cannot be subject to further evaluative concerns. What is good is good, as much as what is true is true. Knowledge and morally good action seem to fade into reality, as it were: they put us immediately in touch with how things are in knowledge, and we realize what ought to be the case through good action.

Against this background, contemporary philosophers following McDowell maintain that the good case scenario is constitutive for understanding our theoretical and practical capacities and, thereby, ourselves as rational animals, as subjects.[12] On this basis, some adopt a Neo-Aristotelian framework and believe that there is a teleology inherent in the normative constitution of thought and action such that successful instances of the actualization of our capacities somehow realize the capacity better than our shortcomings.[13]

Good case scenarios are rightly deemed successful because they meet the norms of truth and goodness, for example, and thereby turn out to be essentially shareable. A true thought can be transmitted, which is why knowledge itself can be turned into a public good and need not be restricted to anything like a series of subjective mental states. Similarly, good action is paradigmatic in virtue of the fact that it recommends itself universally. Doing the ethically right thing for the morally correct reasons is a paradigm of an action form others are invited to imitate. The good recommends itself not as an exception but as a standard for all action. The bad case, on the contrary, individualizes us, which underlies the widespread intuition—epitomized by the Kantian tradition—that there is a relationship between forms of egotism and evil. The subjective standpoint emerges from our false assumptions and misguided actions. To be someone is thus to remain at a distance from the highest goals of human thought and action.[14] Having said that, the fact that knowledge and morally good action are by their very nature as achievements laudable does not entail that there could be a subject whose mental life could unfold as a pure epistemic and ethical success story. On the contrary, I will argue that no one could be both a subject of knowledge claims and ethical norms while being essentially infallible.

SENSE, NONSENSE, AND SUBJECTIVITY

This chapter approaches subjectivity in three steps. First, it discusses *theoretical subjectivity,* i.e., our epistemic relationship to what there is, in light of the overall assumption that to be a subjective thinker is to be wrong about some things.

Second, it makes use of the results from Chapters 1 and 2 in the context of a *philosophy of nature* that finds a place for sense and nonsense in nature while circumventing the metaphysical source of much confusion in the philosophy of mind according to which there has to be some clear-cut distinction between consciousness and nature, mind and matter, consciousness and brain, or what have you, such that consciousness' very existence turns into a kind of mystery when compared to physical observables, i.e., to facts discoverable by physical science.

Third, it focuses on *practical subjectivity* and argues that we are essentially prone to ideology, manipulation, propaganda, and so on, because we cannot avoid diverging from the highest norm of practical subjectivity, the morally good. One of the reasons for this is that our social, economic, and technological conditions for action coordination are complex, so we simply cannot avoid making moral mistakes. This is not an excuse for bad (whether epistemic, moral, political, or economic) behavior, but rather a call for a realistic form of improvement—what I have taken to calling "moral progress in dark times."[15]

PART ONE:
SUBJECTIVITY AND FALLIBILITY

The guiding thread of the first part of this chapter is encapsulated in the famous opening line of Aristotle's *Metaphysics:* "All humans by nature desire to know [πάντες οἱ ἄνθρωποι τοῦ εἰδέναι ὀρέγονται φύσει]."[16] The terms "intention" and "intentionality" derive from the Greek verb ὀρέγεσθαι, which, like its Latin translation *"intendere,"* means to stretch out. The Greeks—most prominently Aristotle at the beginning of the *Metaphysics* and throughout his work—used the term to characterize desire as a stretching out for something, a kind of longing.

SUBJECTIVITY

The desire to know is an expression of our subjectivity. The issue of knowledge, thus, cannot be reduced to *objective* knowledge in the sense of a shareable factive mental state, let alone its pure content. If someone, *S,* knows that *p,* that *they* know it is an expression of an achievement such that we need to understand how both the achievement and the failure are possible. And we cannot understand how the achievement and the failure are possible by providing an analysis or description of the good case alone.

In this part of the chapter, I will argue that our fallibility is constitutive of theoretical subjectivity. To be someone is not just to be the mental owner of one's beliefs, some of which happen to be false. Rather, to be someone is to be the subject of one's actual beliefs, which means that the very idea of cleaning one's doxastic and epistemic slate in order to arrive at the *tabula rasa* of pure, subjectless consciousness is misguided, a particular form of second-order illusion about our epistemic endowment.

I will proceed in four steps. First, I argue that our fallibility cannot be reduced to the presence of sometimes unactualized capacities that make up our minds. Rather, the bearer of epistemic responsibility is the subject of knowledge claims, a fallible human being and, thus, a specifically minded animal who constitutively gets something wrong.

Second, I will spell out the *subjectivity assumption* according to which being a fallible thinker means being subject to a constitutive and often wide-ranging ignorance as to which of our beliefs are actually true and which false.

Third, I will argue that our practices of justification are ways of limiting the impact of subjectivity and its modes of being wrong on our successful knowledge claims.

Fourth, I will return to the issue of consciousness and try to show that it is an objectively existing illusion—a part of reality that constitutively confuses us in such a way that we inevitably run into ontological nonsense in our attempts to clarify both the notion of consciousness and its presumed relationship to nature.

Our Fallibility

We hold beliefs. Some of them are true, some of them false. As we hold them, we cannot both take them to be true and suspect them of being

SENSE, NONSENSE, AND SUBJECTIVITY

possibly false. Our knowledge that some of our beliefs are false does not undermine them unless we have specific reasons to hone a part of our belief system in light of some incoming critical evidence.

Not only do we know that some of our beliefs are false while not ever being able to replace all our false beliefs by true ones to set our doxastic record straight, we also know that we have contradictory beliefs that are sufficiently isolated from each other in our mental lives for them not to constantly occur together within the scope of our epistemological attention.

Thus, we know that if we were able to draw a full map of someone's beliefs, it would show us a dynamic system with local patterns of coherent thoughts that is inconsistent and incoherent as a whole (if it can actually be thought of as a single dynamic whole). Moreover, the content of two belief systems associated with two thinkers will significantly differ in detail. Each of us holds different beliefs.

Let us call a representation of a given belief system (however comprehensive) a *doxastic mental map*. There are different practices of doxastic cartography, some of which amount to forms of scientific investigation, to the extent that they have developed tools and methods for understanding human mindedness in its diversity across time and space.[17]

Human (and other) conscious minds are characterized by the central presence of a subject. Here a subject is someone who holds beliefs. Subjects take their beliefs to be true, while being in a position to correct themselves. Correcting oneself means either replacing some false beliefs with recognizably true ones or suspending one's beliefs in light of incoming evidence that they might not be true. Beliefs do not merely co-occur in a place. They are not like raindrops or other purely natural occurrences. Beliefs belong to someone. To be someone, to hold or have beliefs, is to be in a fallible position. We know that everyone has true and false beliefs. Subjects are and remain fallible. This is what it is for them to be around.

The starting point of epistemology is the assumption that there are some things we know. Minimally, this means that the concept of knowledge is sometimes instantiated. Hence, there is some subject, S, who knows something about something. The proposition that S knows that p is sometimes true.

In setting up any more specific agenda for epistemology, many contemporary epistemologists regrettably neglect to pause at this point and

SUBJECTIVITY

reflect on the crucial fact that they have helped themselves to an important piece of knowledge. They claim to know something about knowledge when they claim to know the proposition that it is sometimes true that S knows that p.

What they claim to know about knowledge essentially involves the subject. For it is precisely a subject, S, who is supposed to know something, for example, that p. For this reason, epistemology not only borders on the theory of subjectivity (and thereby, among other things, the philosophy of mind) but constitutively relies on results from other fields of philosophy as well as on inquiry from other disciplines.

Subjectivity is the target system of the social sciences, the humanities, and some of the natural sciences. They too have to provide an account of the position of the knower within the larger frameworks of reality they set out to study by breaking reality down into domains of inquiry (fields of sense) for which suitable methods are available.

In light of this simple consideration, it should be clear that it would be a mistake to practice epistemology as if it were primarily or even exclusively in the business of providing an account of the subject's grounding in a mind-independent reality—as if the *external* world were identical with the set (or some other structure) of all true, knowable propositions. Rather, epistemology is first and foremost about the relationship between subjectivity and the type of objectivity achieved by the paradigmatic, epistemically demanding concept of knowledge.

The constitutive self-knowledge of which the epistemologist necessarily has to avail herself in order to specify her more specific agenda is motivated by a confrontation with skepticism.[18] Here, *skepticism* is an array of conceptual puzzles concerning the concept of knowledge, which in the worst case amounts to an argument to the effect that no one knows anything. Given that the skeptic as epistemologist both relies on her self-knowledge and impugns its existence by way of an argument whose premises and conclusion have to be known, skepticism is a looming threat both to the second-level project of epistemology and to first-level knowledge. This threat has to be overcome.

In order to circumvent skepticism, epistemologists have been in the business of constructing theories of knowledge that cling to the evident fact that we know something. In so doing, a prominent strategy in epistemology associated with the theory label "disjunctivism" sets out

SENSE, NONSENSE, AND SUBJECTIVITY

from the assumption of facticity, according to which "*S* knows that *p*" entails *p*.[19] Given that it is impossible to know something that is false, an actual piece of propositional knowledge cannot be fallible. The propositional attitude we call "knowledge" guarantees the truth of the proposition known. This is, in a nutshell, the view of *infallibilism about knowledge*.[20]

Despite its obvious virtue of defending knowledge against skeptical threats, I now want to repudiate infallibilism about knowledge by showing that it rests on a sort of category mistake: it confuses the fact of facticity, i.e., that actual propositional knowledge entails the truth of the proposition known, with the actualization of someone's capacity to know something. Objective knowledge in the sense required to infer that *p* from the fact that someone knows that *p* is neither fallible nor infallible: only actualizations of someone's capacity to know something are candidates for evaluation in light of the norms that constitute getting it right or being wrong. And only those norms are suitable for praising someone as infallible or blaming them for having become victims of their fallibility. But that means that knowledge cannot be infallible, not because it is fallible after all, but rather because it is not the bearer of epistemic responsibility. The bearer of epistemic responsibility is *S,* the subject who can make knowledge claims, and that subject is never infallible.

Getting it right and being wrong must not be confused with the truth or falsity of a known proposition. They consist in aspects of someone's epistemic mental states. What makes those central epistemic states mental is the same factor as the one that makes them someone's states. The "mineness" of the central epistemic mental states of getting it right and being wrong consists in their integration into someone's overall mental state. Now, everybody's overall mental state continuously changes. It is, as I have argued in Chapter 2, an objectively real confusion of fos, ontological nonsense. Its objective reality does not, of course, conflict with the subjectivity of the states. For them to belong to objective reality just is for them to be knowable both by the subject who "owns" them, as the saying goes, and by someone with whom those states are shared by being avowed or to whom those states are epistemically accessible in some other suitable (e.g., empirical) way.

Actual exercises of epistemic capacities that contribute to knowledge acquisition are not subject to the demand of facticity. They can misfire in various ways and thereby give rise to mistakes, error, ignorance, manipu-

SUBJECTIVITY

lation, illusion, delusion, etc. Let us call the class of these different forms of failure *negative epistemological phenomena*. Negative epistemological phenomena are the elements in the target system of epistemology that account for the fact that we deviate from the best cases of our satisfaction of epistemic norms. We invoke them in explaining an important part of the contrast class of knowledge, namely the manifold cases in which we are wrong.

The theory of subjectivity or subjecthood, i.e., the theory that reflexively deals with the question of our status as fallible knowers, is the key to being wrong. This theory is designed to put us in the position of understanding the existence of a deviation from the truth without having to invoke false facts.

The problem of false facts is known from discussions of the unity and disunity of the proposition.[21] It arises in a context where one assumes that (1) there are propositions (2) whose nature it is to be determinately true or false and (3) to which we bear a mental, subjective relation of judgment. In this constellation, it is straightforward to think of the true propositions as being graspable in a judgment, whereas the false propositions are due to a shortcoming in the judgment. One could worry that the alternative to this family of construals would have to admit that there are false propositions that we grasp in false judgment. The problem with the notion of false facts is that we have to assume that a reality that does not contain the notion of a judging subject can find itself at a logically relevant distance from how things are. But how could a reality we grasp as being a certain way (in this case: false) deviate from reality? How can there be false facts or "false objectives," as they were called in the heyday of the classical Meinong-Russell exchanges?[22]

The problem dissolves once we overcome the tendency to think of "reality" as essentially mind-independent. If reality fully includes thinkers (which, of course, does not entail that we reduce reality to its thinkability or some other modally more or less strong relationship to subjects occurring within it), then the negative epistemological phenomena that characterize many of the socially orchestrated affairs of shareable judgments can easily be seen as legitimate (though somewhat undesirable) parts of reality.

Our theoretical access to the concept of falsity presupposes our acquaintance with being wrong. We derive our understanding of falsity from

SENSE, NONSENSE, AND SUBJECTIVITY

having been wrong and having been corrected by others who made us aware of an epistemically significant difference between our relationship to a given part of reality and that reality.

Falsity is derivable from being wrong just like the concept of a fact is derivable from that of getting it right. Falsity, therefore, cannot just be the contrast of truth, its privation or negation. Falsity is more than not-truth in a classical, two-valued logics. Falsity is a negative epistemological phenomenon essentially tied to getting it wrong and not a logical status of a proposition (*mutatis mutandis* for truth).

To be sure, in the wake of early Wittgenstein one could try to argue that falsity is logical by virtue of being derivable from the concept of nec-essarily false propositions, i.e., contradictions. However, this not only begs the question against the widely recognized claim that there are perfectly coherent forms of non-classical logics.[23] What is worse, it does not teach us what falsity is apart from pointing out that some falsities might be nec-essary due to some logical form of a mistake, such as contradiction in a classical formal system. In any event, by itself this does nothing to account for falsity as such; at most it offers a formal criterion of identifying flaws in inference patterns on the level of logical form.

Neither truth nor falsity as such are purely logical. The logical theory of truth—paradigmatically carried out in the Tarskian tradition—neither yields an account of falsity nor explains how a thinker can grasp a truth without thereby changing the nature of truth from a logical pattern to a relation between a thinker and a part of reality. Tarski-style semantic the-ories of truth cannot exhaust the norm of truth to which an empirical thinker is wedded in her attempts to figure out how things are and to com-municate them by way of knowledge claims.

A *fact* is a truth: in a fact something is true of something. If it is true of a logical subject a that it is such and so, it is a fact that a is such and so. Here, being true of something indeed coincides with a's being such and so, which is the rationale of the redundancy and identity theo-ries of truth. Getting it right is being in touch with a fact in such a way that one can be thought of as being in a state whose epistemic outlines can be modeled in terms of true judgment, where the "truth" compo-nent differs from the judgment component. Reality *contributes* truth to the judgment, which evidently need not mean that judgment *corresponds* to the truth.

SUBJECTIVITY

Truth cannot be correspondence between a judgment and reality if we think of the relevant part of reality as already true and, thus, providing us with an architecture of facts. If true judgment were implicated in the business of correspondence, this would mean that a true judgment is not merely one that corresponds with reality, but rather a judgment that somehow hangs together with a judgment that corresponds to reality. For truth would be a relation between reality and judgment such that it did not make sense to attribute that relation as a property to a judgment. If "truth" were correspondence between reality and judgment, there simply could not be a true judgment without a pile of infinitely many judgments, each of which corresponds with a judgment without ever making it to the first-order reality originally envisaged by a knowledge claim.

Therefore, it is possible to assume that truth is factual and not identical to a relationship between judgment and fact. The facts are self-sufficiently true in virtue of just being the way they are. However, that need not mean that truth is an irreducible aspect of reality whereas falsity is a more complicated matter involving subjects that disrupt the desirable epistemic silence of the Eleatic unity of truth and reality. Quietism betrays a desire to be in that scenario, where subjects bear the burden of sin in wanting to distance themselves from reality's cold, crystalline splendor. Quietism is the desire to eliminate the subject.[24]

The theory of subjectivity deals with the notions of getting it right and being wrong. Reflexive investigation into these notions is what provides us with concepts of truth and falsity and, thus, with insight into the kind of facts that bind subject and object together (the interface, as I called it in Chapter 1). Here, facts indeed play the role of accounting for an important part of the epistemological success we attribute to getting it right. Yet, this neither means that there is an utter absence of facts in being wrong nor that, in addition to the true facts, we have to posit false facts that are grasped by the states we classify as being wrong. What it takes to think of reality as being a certain way, on the one hand, and of knowers, in terms of agents, who sometimes get it right and sometimes not, on the other, is for us to think of ourselves as subjects whose epistemic mental states are episodes in a flow of consciousness that is an objectively existing illusion.

Actual knowers are by their very nature prone to mistakes: in order for them to be actual knowers, they have to have made mistakes. There is no actually infallible knower. Yet, this does not compel us to accept fallibilism

SENSE, NONSENSE, AND SUBJECTIVITY

about *knowledge*. Rather, the right neighborhood for an acceptable view is fallibilism about *knowers*.[25]

Knowledge is neither fallible nor infallible. It is an actual state of reality that can be shared across subjects. Let us call this *objective knowledge*. According to this conception of objective knowledge, it is essentially shareable (objective) because it is not tied to the specificities of the exercises of any mental capacities actualized by a given subject. While any given human knower and any community of knowers are intelligible only if we take their specific capacities into account, what they know has to be sufficiently detached from their individual and communal practices of giving and asking for reasons designed to keep the social network of mutual, epistemic attitude adjustment up and running. Hence, objectivity matters.

However, objectivity is not the opposite of subjectivity. The objectivity of factual, objective knowledge is not identical with *p,* not even with *p's* mind-independence, because there are evident cases of self-knowledge where *p* essentially involves a subject. Paradigmatically, this is the case for epistemological knowledge, which is knowledge about knowledge and, therefore, essentially involves the subject. The epistemological paradigm of knowledge cannot be knowledge of the so-called external, mind-independent world, as this knowledge is individuated by a highly specific set of deviation conditions that account for the case of failure, namely the partial independence of the domain from our conception of it.[26] Given that this type of independence does not hold in the epistemological paradigm case of self-knowledge, we must always be wary of confusing objectivity with thought directed at thoughtless nature.

This line of thought reveals a tension in our self-conception as knowers: On the one hand, we are entitled to be certain that we know something. On the other hand, we are entitled to be certain that the epistemic capacities on which we draw in acquiring knowledge sometimes misfire. This means that there is a crooked dividing line in reality, which runs through the epistemic realm of finite, fallible knowers like us. That line separates actual knowledge from an indefinitely variegated array of forms of non-knowledge. The problem is that we cannot draw that line in general and thereby—by some magical act of transcendental self-knowledge—isolate the presence of objective knowledge in our epistemic

SUBJECTIVITY

lives from our ignorance concerning indefinitely many potentially life-saving facts.

Both fallibilist and infallibilist epistemology misconstrue the nature of our subjectivity. Qua subjects we are not only in a fallible position. Rather, there are many things we know and many things we miss in highly specific ways due to an indefinitely large class of sources of error that beset the human subject. There is no specific set of a priori conditions (such as transcendental categories of the mind) that determinately either put us in touch with how things are (an idea motivating infallibilist accounts) or somehow isolate us from reality (as the skeptic argues).

We lack a sufficient vocabulary for making sense of the sources of error. The more scientific knowledge we accumulate, the better we understand that the abyss of ignorance over which the knowledge enterprise is built is shockingly deep.[27] For instance, it turned out that psychoanalysis's attempt to delimit the sources of error by categorizing the kinds of mistakes to which humans are subject in light of the therapeutic situation in the talking cure draws on misguided assumptions about the normalcy conditions for subjects. Digging deeper into the structure of the human psyche as well as into the specific embodiment of human knowers endowed with a complex nervous system showed that our mental life is ridden with illusions on all levels of knowledge acquisition, from sensation to perception, from scientific discourse to the use of technology based on the latest scientific discovery. Yet, once again, we cannot make sense of this picture of ourselves as immersed in the realm of ignorance and illusion without at the same time relying on a huge background of shared, objective knowledge that makes our ignorance available to us. Subjectivity and objectivity are intertwined in our fallibility.[28]

The Paradox of Self-Consciousness and the Subjectivity Assumption

Each of us can begin to list their current conscious mental states so as to identify some of them as sources of knowledge. Right now, I see the screen of my computer, my hands, etc. I gently feel how some parts of my body are in touch with the objects that physically support my posture. I feel the

SENSE, NONSENSE, AND SUBJECTIVITY

floor, my chair, etc. Each of those perceptual sources of knowledge represents things from a certain perspective. What I thus consciously represent is broadcasted to me with strong ties to selection functions (senses) that together make up my constantly shifting "egocentric index," as Tyler Burge has called this.[29] If you ask me in this situation what I know on the basis of my current conscious mental states, I am in a position to provide you with objective knowledge, knowledge that abstracts from my egocentric index by drawing on details of the overall scene that we cohabit. I can inform you that I see my screen and tell you something about its makeup. The information I transmit in thus replying to your inquiry concerning my mental states is coded in a propositional form available to us as subjects. Yet, the modes of presentation by which I acquire the information I transmit to you as pieces of objective knowledge are not themselves thus known. However successfully I enlarge my range of objective knowledge about my subjective states, it can never replace them. Knowing that such and such physiological processes are correlated with the subjective experience I am undergoing as I am thinking about that subjective experience does not alter the fact that I am undergoing subjective experience. What changes when I articulate objective knowledge about my subjective states is the content of my overall subjective state, as I now identify elements in my mental life that correlate with objective knowledge in such a way that I can tell you how it is that *I* know that such and such is the case.

To be sure, that endeavor is less stable than it might seem at first glance. For there are many things I know without knowing how it is that *I* know them. My mental life thus consists of an array of epistemic elements of varying complexity, including straightforward first-order knowledge of reality acquired in the form of conscious perception, second-order knowledge about how *I* come to know certain things (e.g., by conscious perception), as well as higher-order knowledge of my ignorance concerning the pedigree of some of my best-established and most cherished knowledge claims.

This leads me to an important rung of the ladder on the way to a motivated theory of subjectivity, namely, *the paradox of self-consciousness*.[30] Different versions of it can be found in Western and Eastern, ancient and modern philosophy, from the writings of the Buddha to Plato, Aristotle, Plotinus, the German Idealists, and beyond. It also plays a crucial role in various paradoxes of self-reference in the foundations of mathematics,

SUBJECTIVITY

theoretical computer science, artificial intelligence research, and contemporary philosophy of mind and semantics. Here is my version of it.

(1) Consciousness is consciousness of an overall mental state.

(2) An overall mental state consists of an individual arrangement of contents.

(3) The consciousness of a given individual arrangement of contents is either part of its contents (a) or a separate reality (b).

    (a) The Fichte paradigm.

(4) If the consciousness of a given individual arrangement of contents is part of its contents, there has to be a consciousness of the overall mental state, including the very consciousness of that same overall mental state.

(5) But that raises the question of whether there is a consciousness of the consciousness of the overall mental state.

(6) If there is no consciousness of the consciousness of the overall mental state, we cannot ever be in a position to formulate the premises thus far articulated.

(7) There is a consciousness of the consciousness of the overall mental state, a self-consciousness.

(8) Given (4), self-consciousness and consciousness are one and the same.

(9) However, if consciousness figures among its contents as simply more content, we multiply the contents of consciousness *ad infinitum*.[31]

(10) Thus, consciousness is not part of its contents. We are not in this way conscious of consciousness.

    (b) The Frege paradigm. It remains to be seen what happens if we assume that consciousness is a reality separate from its contents. Now we face me, the conscious subject, and my objective contents.

(11) If consciousness is a reality that is separate from its contents, the conscious subject at best *grasps* the contents as they present themselves.

SENSE, NONSENSE, AND SUBJECTIVITY

But that raises the question as to how the conscious subject can grasp its own grasping; how can it catch itself *in flagranti?*

(12) If the subject cannot grasp its own grasping, it cannot become conscious of itself as conscious.

(13) We are conscious of ourselves as conscious and are evidently in a position to grasp our own grasping (we just did it).

(14) In grasping our own grasping, we are not separated from the contents of our grasping.

(15) Consciousness cannot be separated from its contents. We are thrown back to the Fichte paradigm.

(∴1) Consciousness is neither part of its own contents nor is it a separate reality.

(16) What there is, is either part of consciousness's contents or a separate reality. *Tertium non datur.*

(∴2) There is no consciousness.

In the context of the paradox, (∴2) is evidently paradoxical insofar as it is inacceptable to believe both that the kinds of things there are, are either within the range of a conscious subject's grasp or not and that there is no such thing as consciousness. For this reason, we cannot content ourselves with happily endorsing (∴2). *Consciousness denialism* is not a solution to the paradox, which is easy to see if we compare our situation to other paradoxes, such as Zeno's paradoxes of movement: Zeno should not convince us that nothing moves but invite us to find the odd guy out in the inferentially ordered structure of premises and conclusions that constitute the paradox. After all, that is the decisive difference between a valid argument and a paradox: In the case of a paradox, we know that either some premise or other has to be false or some rule of inference or other has to be faulty, simply by virtue of knowing that the conclusion is false or otherwise unacceptable.

What might be special about the paradox of self-consciousness and its many variations is that we know the conclusion has to be false because its truth entails that we cannot make sense of the premises that entail it. We cannot meaningfully come to know that there is no such thing as a conscious subject in virtue of exercises of our capacity to reflect about ourselves qua conscious subjects.

SUBJECTIVITY

Let us pause here and look at the problem from a slightly different perspective. Once more, take the overall mental state that I am currently in. I feel a certain way, I have certain thoughts, I am trying to answer certain questions, I have been looking at my mental history, and I am weighing reasons that speak in favor of what I believe (as well as against it) so that I can get a reasonable point of view on my own point of view. I practice philosophy. As I do this, I change my overall mental state by virtue of thinking about it. If I am conscious of consciousness, if I am consciously thinking about thinking, I change the state that I am targeting because my overall mental state is now different, featuring a second-level conscious relation to my conscious dealings with reality. I might use yet another third-level state in order to think about me thinking about thinking, but this makes things more complicated and does not help me to get outside the skin of my thought, as it were.

There is an associated linguistic problem that is often overlooked in contemporary philosophy of mind and other mind sciences. If you look at the history of literature in the twentieth century, Hugo von Hofmannsthal's "Letter to Lord Chandos" can be read as making the following point.[32] When we state our self-conception in any kind of linguistic or technical code (such as a scientific model) by describing ourselves as a "conscious," "rational," or whatever kind of thinking animal, the competent use of language does not guarantee all by itself that anything in physical, biological, or any other kind of reality corresponds to the concepts attached to the meaning of those words. How do we know that we are conscious without knowing that the English word "consciousness" picks out something in a reality that is not made of words (but say of neurons or whatever it is that correlates with your use of words designed to articulate your alleged capacity to catch yourself in the act of thinking)?

In light of this somewhat more intuitive version of the paradox of self-consciousness, we can formulate what I have taken to calling *the hardest problem of consciousness* or *the Lord Chandos problem*.[33] Whether consciousness poses an easy or a hard problem is supposed to depend on the availability of a neurophysiological, functional account of the neural correlates of consciousness. If a complete causal model of the correlation between consciousness and its neural correlates leaves nothing further to explain, consciousness would be an easy problem for a futuristic cognitive neuroscience; if not, it is a hard problem, because there is something about

SENSE, NONSENSE, AND SUBJECTIVITY

the nature of consciousness that eludes the grasp of scientific, causal explanation.

Yet, before we face this kind of choice familiar from the landscape of contemporary philosophy of mind, many decisions have already been made that are even more debatable than the nature of consciousness. For one thing, we must know what the word "consciousness" means in order to determine by way of experiment and theory how to identify the neural correlates of consciousness thus or so understood. But that is exactly the problem, because the word "consciousness" has many perfectly ordinary meanings for which it would be meaningless or wrong in other ways to so much as search for a neural correlate. Paradigmatically, the term "consciousness" refers to a part of an intentional state or process, such as perception, that puts us in contact with how things are in our environment. Consciousness in that sense (intentional or access consciousness) cannot have a neural correlate, as it consists of episodes taking place within the confines of an organism and its environment. The whole bunch of episodes contains much more than neural patterns of any kind of complexity, meaning it is simply misguided to search for a neural correlate of that whole state. Hence, if anything, consciousness must be a part of the state of perception, the part that does not involve the environment (phenomenal consciousness, as it is usually called).

Thus, in order to so much as wonder what the neural correlate of consciousness might be, we must have chosen the right kind of meaning from among the meanings available to us in the context of a linguistic description of the choices to be made between different meanings of the word "consciousness." Yet, in making our choice and motivating it via large-scale cooperative efforts between linguistics, psychology, cognitive neuroscience, artificial intelligence research, and philosophy, say, we cannot rule out that the phenomenon we would like to get a hold on is not well captured by any of the currently available meanings of the English word "consciousness."

At this point, one might object that the Lord Chandos problem could be a premature form of defeatism and that it takes more to show that there is no single family of phenomena underpinning the issue of consciousness.[34] But in what sense are "intentional," "access," and "phenomenal consciousness" all forms of "consciousness"? One might reply that there could be something in common between different states of what-it-is-like-

SUBJECTIVITY

ness, but that does not show how and why phenomenal consciousness (to the extent that the concept is sufficiently unified after all, which it is not really when one considers the range of literatures across different languages) is the fundamental notion. In short, even if one admits that there is a common core of a range of mental states we refer to as tokens of "phenomenal consciousness," this does not amount to the idea that there is an actual form of pure phenomenal consciousness. Actual conscious states will always involve more than this postulated level of what-it-is-like-ness. This then leads back to the Lord Chandos problem, as it is unclear how our actual overall mental ("conscious") states could be reconstructed in terms of a variety of "conscious" states that are nested within each other, grounded in some primary form of consciousness.

It does not help to transcend the monolingualism of the mainstream of Anglophone philosophy of mind. We cannot fix the Lord Chandos problem by expanding our mentalistic vocabulary and by bringing more linguistic meanings of "consciousness" across languages and traditions to the table. However broad our access to mentalistic vocabularies and histories of ideas concerning our subjectivity might be, we still cannot guarantee that our linguistic code suffices to pick out any causally relevant parts of reality. Therefore, any account of the neural correlates of consciousness might ultimately be deluded, even though it can do some clinical job or other, such as help to identify some form of consciousness in patients who are in coma-like states and incapable of manifesting their conscious states to us in any of the usual ways.

In sum, the clinical success of a candidate theory of the neural correlates of consciousness is no evidence of the correctness of a conceptual choice to prefer a given meaning of "consciousness" to any of the other currently available meanings in our mentalistic portfolio. Ultimately, this argument from the Lord Chandos problem is designed to demonstrate that the very idea of figuring out whether consciousness poses an easy or a hard problem is profoundly misguided, because it cannot answer the million-dollar question: What is it that you are even looking for?

So far, we have been dealing with ourselves as conscious subjects, and we have encountered some potentially profound problems of self-consciousness, in particular the paradox of self-consciousness and the Lord Chandos problem. It does not seem possible to grasp ourselves as grasping ourselves while grasping any more specific mental contents. For

163

SENSE, NONSENSE, AND SUBJECTIVITY

this reason, we cannot even hope to find the neural correlates of consciousness without first resolving our conundrum.

Now, I want to argue that the paradox of self-consciousness builds on a transparency conjecture that turns out to be false. If this is correct, we are entitled to change perspective in the theory of subjectivity and move ahead. The *transparency conjecture* is the notion that there is a unified, individual arrangement of contents somehow associated with consciousness. A prominent and intuitive way of motivating this notion relies on Ernst Mach's famous drawing of his visual perspective,[35] which clearly does not contain his consciousness of the snippet of reality directly available to him. Mach's subjective visual field is not itself part of Mach's subjective visual field—a fact that got him and us into trouble. Yet, trouble or not, what remains stable in Mach's picture are the neatly individuated contents that make up the subjective visual field represented by Mach's drawing. But therein lies the problem. Consciousness is not a series of snippets of reality; it is nothing like a film that ultimately consists of a series of snapshots ordered in sequence.[36]

Rather, at any moment, indefinitely many parts of my overall mental state can at most be dimly represented, whether pictorially or linguistically. To the extent that we are conscious, we are in the dark concerning the crucial, life-and-death questions regarding the details of the dark regions of our own minds. To put it less emphatically, there are indefinitely many truths concerning what we do not know about ourselves as subjects of conscious experience: we do not even know whether we are making progress with respect to the endeavor of philosophical and scientific self-knowledge. The models we deploy in our time and age to determine the range of our ignorance concerning our own thinking and doing are themselves subject to the kind of investigation that motivates the worries we are addressing here. For instance, in the wake of Kahneman's prominent contributions to the theory of biases, we are aware of the fact that we do not think and act as rationally as some earlier economic and psychological models had assumed. Similar results abound in behavioral economics and associated disciplines.[37]

But how do we know that Kahneman and Kandel rather than Nietzsche and Freud got the phenomena right? Well, the reply will typically invoke a highly specific notion of science and scientific progress, which notes how Kahneman and Kandel, unlike Nietzsche and Freud, ran controlled experiments based on established models. Yet, this seemingly reassuring reply simply shifts the bump in the rug. For how do Kahneman and Kandel know that controlled experiments based on established models are the right kind of instrument for peeping into the dark corners of the soul? As a matter of fact, it can rather count as an advantage for Nietzsche and Freud that they explicitly repudiate the idea that we can make sense of our ignorance about ourselves in terms of a highly specific and historically parochial model of scientific knowledge acquisition that makes use of quantitative models and reproducible experiments—all of which ultimately still leads back to the overall paradox of self-consciousness and the Lord Chandos problem.

Against this background, we are entitled to try out another path of reflection. My starting point is a rejection of the transparency conjecture that, despite appearances, underlies much contemporary babble about alleged natural-scientific or economic discoveries of the quantitative details of our ignorance.

Instead of an implicit or explicit reliance on a transparency conjecture, we should endorse the following *subjectivity assumption:* To be a fallible thinker means being subject to a constitutive and often wide-ranging ignorance as to which of our beliefs are actually true and which false. To be a subject is to be wrong about some things without ever being in a position to settle once and for all which of our beliefs are non-accidentally true (and thereby constitute knowledge). Who we are as subjects is thus best characterized in view of the limits of our current individual and shared objective knowledge. The theory of subjectivity thereby reconnects with epistemology in order to fill the important gap in our concept of knowledge that separates fallible knowledge claims from non-fallible objective knowledge.

Apologies: The Justificatory Gap

According to the picture of human knowledge I have been drawing so far, the overall theory of subjectivity reconnects with epistemology in order to fill out the important gap in our concept of knowledge that separates fallible knowledge claims from non-fallible objective knowledge. Modifying a much-discussed proposal in the theory of phenomenal consciousness, let

SENSE, NONSENSE, AND SUBJECTIVITY

us call this gap *the justificatory gap*.[38] The main motivation for recognizing such a gap is the conceptual distinction between holding something to be true, i.e., believing it, and its being true. We need a concept that connects belief and truth in such a way that the two do not at best merely coincide.

Being true is conceptually available to creatures who sometimes get it wrong. What we come to grasp by understanding this fundamental distinction is the difference between two possible mental states, namely being wrong and getting it right. But what exactly is the difference between them apart from the obvious difference in truth value?

Traditionally and, I hasten to add, rightly, the difference can be traced back to the existence of justification. For this reason, we should cheerfully follow in Plato's footsteps and understand "knowledge" as non-accidentally justified true belief, i.e., getting it right for the appropriate reasons.[39] The appropriate reasons constitute our justification in the context of knowledge acquisition. Justification is a bridge from holding true and being true to knowledge. The concept of justification thereby provides the epistemologist with insight into how belief and truth are connected in the best case scenario of transparently justified knowledge.

At this point, I want to reintroduce another crucial aspect of Plato's canonical discussion of knowledge as ἀληθὴς δόξα μετὰ λόγου (non-accidentally justified true belief).[40] In the *Theaetetus* Plato asks us to imagine someone who is trying to get hold of a certain kind of dove swirling around in a dovecote among other doves. The doves are moving targets and hard to hold onto. The idea here is to compare knowledge claims to acts of trying to get hold of the right kind of bird, namely a true belief. Grasping the right kind of bird would amount to having the appropriate reasons, the logos, as Plato calls it. However, how can we know which kinds of birds are in the aviary if answering this question already presupposes a firm grip on the paradigm bird? And what if their movement is so dynamic that trying to grasp the bird is a hopelessly chaotic activity, much more like groping in the dark than like picking the right kind of object from two clearly identifiable options?

In this context, Plato discusses and arguably rejects the idea that the gap between an attempt to catch the right bird (a knowledge-claim) and the success of being in possession of the right bird (knowing) can be bridged with recourse to the idea of epistemic capacities that might or might not be actualized. The problem with this idea of the knowing human

SUBJECTIVITY

mind is that it portrays it as an arrangement of epistemic capacities that have to be actualized from time to time so as to be assessable in light of the truth. According to this line of thought, which I would like to call *the epistemic capacities approach,* we happen to be endowed with a bunch of epistemic capacities that allow us to make knowledge claims, such that some knowledge claims actually turn out to be true in virtue of their non-accidentality. But what exactly does it mean for a true belief to be non-accidentally true, i.e., to be justified by the appropriate reasons? If all it means is that the true belief amounts to knowledge, the theorist merely stomps her feet in order to insist that knowledge differs from mere knowledge claims by the magical ingredient of non-accidental justification. Thus, the capacities approach maintains that the difference consists in the right kind of actualization of our epistemic capacities, where the right kind of actualization is one that provides us with infallible, truth-guaranteeing reasons to believe that *p*. Yet, at this stage of the dialectic, as Plato already pointed out, recourse to the notion of truth-guaranteeing reasons is no better than or at least dangerously analogous to the idea that we can catch the right kind of bird by tying it to our hand. But you can only tie a dove to your hand if you already have a grip on it; this strategy therefore fails, because it stipulates the kind of success that it wants to explain with recourse to the idea of a very firm grip on reality. If the actualization of an epistemic capacity is what is supposed to bridge the gap between a knowledge-claim and actual knowing, we run the risk of merely repeating the same problem twice: first, we have the problem of having to justify our knowledge-claim; second, we have to show that the activation of our epistemic capacities turned out to be the right one.

Another fundamental problem in the capacities approach—be it of the fallibilist or infallibilist variety—has already been identified by no lesser thinkers than Plato himself, Aristotle, Hegel, and Nietzsche: Postulating the existence of a "bag full of faculties [Sack voll Vermögen]"[41] does not get you anywhere unless you postulate some unmoved mover of your mental life, the subject, that has the second-level capacity of actualizing her first-level activities in an appropriate manner. But this merely relocates the problem of the dovecote to the inner arena of the human mind where the subject has to perform the feat of actualizing the right kind of capacity for a given job. Therefore, populating the human mind with epistemic capacities designed to render our successful knowledge claims

SENSE, NONSENSE, AND SUBJECTIVITY

intelligible makes recourse to. second-level knowledge claims (including those of the epistemologist), which repeats the problem all over again. If we cannot solve the problem of knowledge on the first level, why would we manage to solve it one level up, by splitting up a thinker's many epistemic capacities to get it right or wrong? To make a long story short, the capacities approach sooner or later faces the familiar second-level problems of ancient skepticism (West and East/Sextus Empiricus and Nāgārjuna): the idea of truth-guaranteeing reasons threatens to be either viciously circular, merely hypothetical, viciously infinitist, or question-begging in one way or another.[42]

Be that as it may, there is a kernel of truth in the capacities approach, which allows us to make significant progress. This kernel of truth consists in the idea that any given mental state is intrinsically structured. By "intrinsically structured," I am referring to the idea that any given mental state has a rich structure; it is a highly specific, individual unity of different aspects of reality. The unity of our mental states is a synthetic unity, to borrow Kant's famous term for this state of affairs, where a "synthetic unity" is not only a whole that is somehow prior to its parts, but rather a whole that cannot be dissolved into its parts without thereby producing another state of affairs with its own synthetic unity.[43] The elements unified in terms of this specific synthetic unity are mental contents that cannot be separated from the way in which they happen to hang together without transforming their reality.

At this stage, the capacities approach wrongly thinks of the human mind as presenting us with a bunch of faculties that are somehow activated both by some sort of stimuli and by internal mental actions performed by a subject, maybe even a so-called transcendental subject affecting itself. The mistake in this line of thought is that mental contents are bound not to faculties that need to be activated, but rather to parts of reality itself. It is impossible, or rather nonsensical, to believe that our mind is decked out with invisible faculties or conceptual capacities that philosophical reflection could bring to light by a special meta-faculty activated in philosophical thought. For, even if that were the case, the faculties would have to appear in the arena of philosophical thought and thereby be transformed into ordinary, first-level mental content; the problem would then repeat itself on the metalevel introduced to circumvent it.

The intrinsic structure of a given arrangement of mental content is such that there is no position from which anyone could observe and botanize it. Thus, there is an important sense in which the mind is mind-dependent, i.e., a sense that goes beyond the trivial idea that the mind depends on itself simply in virtue of its self-identity. Mind's mind-dependence consists in the fact that the mind is indispensable in its attempt to grasp itself. However, this does not entail that it is thereby ever in a position to provide a complete account of what it is. Mind's grasp of its own reality remains forever incomplete.

For this reason, it is hopeless to carry out the kind of "transcendental deduction" required to make sense of the very idea of the mind as a structured bunch of conceptual capacities. Any attempt to actually carry out the ambitious project of a transcendental deduction of the mind's conceptual furniture fails due to the inevitable phenomenon of incompleteness.

We are now at the heart of the matter, because I maintain that we should identify subject-hood with this phenomenon of mental incompleteness. The subject is not some kind of invisible, transcendent, or transcendental unity of apperception, entirely outside of the realm of objects, but rather subject-hood is due to the fact that our mental states form unstable unities that unfold in complex ways that are never completely archivable.

The explanatory function of a theory of subjectivity in this sense consists in its contribution to making sense of our fallibility. Fallibility resides not in the gap between a faculty's dispositional state and its activation conditions, but rather in the complexity of the arrangement of mental content that makes it impossible for anyone to monitor the activity of knowledge acquisition by way of a perfect, absolute method.

Let me break this down in terms of the distinction between knowledge claims and knowledge. A knowledge-claim can go right or wrong. It is subject to an epistemic assessment in light of the norm of truth. Knowledge cannot thus go wrong, because it is our title for the success case. This led us to the notion that we need a concept that accounts for the transition from a knowledge-claim to its success, a concept that cannot be identical to that of truth. The idea was that justification could do the trick, where "justification" needs to come apart from the concept of being in possession of the truth. Yet, this picture is insufficient as long as it lacks the resources to provide the theorist with *implementation*

SENSE, NONSENSE, AND SUBJECTIVITY

conditions of the desired conceptual architecture. Here, the capacities approach has the huge advantage of making a claim about the modal structure of mental content designed to make sense of fallibility, i.e., of the possibility of getting it right or wrong. We can get it right or wrong, because our minds are equipped with two-way capacities, as Neo-Aristotelians sometimes put it.

The problem with this notion, though, is that our minds do not contain any unactualized capacities that might or might not misfire. They are nowhere to be found. Thus, the question became whether we could identify some actual structure in the architecture of mental content that accounts for our fallibility. And my answer to this question has been that mental content comes in incomplete yet highly specific bundles of synthetic unity that cannot be surveyed by the subject as an innocent bystander, so to speak. The subject is heavily involved in her mental activity to such an extent that she cannot get hold of the entirety of her operations *in ipso actu operandi*.[44]

The weakness of the capacities approach lies in the idea that we need a bridging principle that leads us from knowledge claims to knowledge. The very idea of conceptual capacities or mental faculties is designed to fill this gap. However, there cannot be such a gap because our mental states are as much part of reality as anything they might present us with on the level of consciously available mental content. Claiming knowledge only makes sense within already-established confines of reality, including the structure of conscious subjectivity and its constitutive integration into a community of knowers, who differ from each other by occupying different perspectives. Knowledge claims take place within reality; they do not approach it from the outside. Failed knowledge claims—illusions, mistakes, error, and ignorance—do not set us apart from how things are. Rather, they change reality by modifying our status as knowers.

Our desire to know is a source of error, ignorance, and many other forms of mistake, simply because we cannot know anything without correcting the flow of illusions that constitutes our actual conscious mental and epistemic life. Remarkably, the correction itself does not typically come to consciousness. True judgment constantly takes place without being noticed. True judgment is a largely non-conscious activity of the mind. If I am right, there is a deep philosophical reason for the unconsciousness of true judgment. In true judgment we nearly merge with reality;

SUBJECTIVITY

here, being and thought seem to coincide. True judgment strikes us as a selfless encounter with how things are.

But that is exactly why we can never hope to become identical to this level of our minds. He whose thoughts are all non-accidentally true in virtue of fusing with how things really are disappears. He is no one. For this reason, true judgment only ever makes its appearance in the midst of the realm of illusion. We are not the subject of true judgment, but rather the maximally specific, individual series of mental events that constitute the mental life we experience as our perspective.

Consciousness as an Objectively Existing Illusion

We can resolve the paradox of self-consciousness and the Lord Chandos problem by letting go of the transparency conjecture. Subjectivity is, to some extent, opaque to itself: consciousness is never in any position to fully get hold of itself. The infrastructure of subjectivity is thus an embodiment of fallibility, i.e., a complex meshwork of true and false beliefs that cannot be surveyed from an all-encompassing position. Being fallible, therefore, is not a property of a single state or process, such as claiming to know that p. Rather, our fallibility resides in the form of subjectivity as such, the reality of which is multifariously dynamic.

Our mental and, thus, epistemic life does not contain any unactualized capacities. On the level of our self-knowledge as knowledgeable rational animals, we find a series of non-conscious and conscious actual attempts to be in touch with how things are. Some mental contents are conscious, some aren't. If this is true, consciousness (be it phenomenal, intentional, or some hybrid of both dimensions associated with the term) cannot be the mark of the mental, as Freud already pointed out.[45] I will now argue that, if anything, subjectivity (and not "consciousness," whatever we mean by the term) is the mark of the mental.

In what follows, it is important to bear in mind that an illusion is not by itself a mistake. Being presented with two lines that appear to be of a different length, while in fact being roughly equally long, is a paradigm case of a perceptual illusion (known as the Müller-Lyer-illusion).[46] However, being presented with those two lines in that species-relative way is not, as such, any kind of mistake, because we can easily correct the false thought that the two lines are of a different length by measuring them. Illusions, therefore, can be the ground of successful knowledge claims concerning reality without thereby going away.

In general, our conscious mental life is full of illusions. Conscious mental content presents us with profiles, as first-wave, Husserlian phenomenology has taught us. The fact that I can only ever see at most three sides of a cube (without using mirrors or other tricks) from a given visual perspective does not mislead me into thinking that there aren't any cubes—*mutatis mutandis* for profiles in any of the other sensory modalities.

Mental contents are never free-floating episodes in reality. They bear the mark of subjectivity in virtue of being someone's states, yours or mine. As soon as we find them, we possess them in the peculiar way that they appear *to us*. There is an important truth in the much-repeated Cartesian adage that as far as consciousness is concerned, its appearance coincides with its being. Yet, it is equally true that we can be wrong about consciousness. The true thought that consciousness is self-attesting differs from the thought that we know that and how we are conscious. Contrary to a powerful Cartesian strand in epistemology and philosophy of mind, consciousness is nothing like a self-transparent form of pure evidence—quite the opposite.

Consciousness has a phenomenal side to it; it comes in many shades, associated with a host of different sensory modalities. The many shades of consciousness are so many sensory modalities, each articulated in indefinitely many ways. No one knows how to put a limit on the manifestations of consciousness in its many modes. Currently, we do not know how many sensory modalities we human beings have, to say nothing of the varieties in which they manifest themselves.[47] This is one of the many reasons why it is nonsensical to quibble about the neural correlate of consciousness.

The physicist Harald Atmanspacher recently pointed out the following to me.[48] Let "ψ" signify some known conscious mental state and "φ" be some neuronal state such that we know (by way of appropriate measurement) that they are correlated. Now, the fact of correlation does not mean that there is a one-to-one relation between the mental and the neural token. Actually, the following cases are all instantiated:

SUBJECTIVITY

(1) The one φ-to-one-ψ correlation.

(2) The many φ-to-many-ψ correlation.

(3) The many φ-to-one-ψ correlation.

(4) The one φ-to-many-ψ correlation.[49]

As a metanalysis by Michael Anderson shows, the generic case is (2)—the combination of (3) and (4)—so that the kind of neo-phrenology (one mental state = one specific neural object) that still populates the cognitive neuro-science literature has to be abandoned.[50] One may even entertain the possibility that there might be conscious mental states without correlated brain states or that (very plausibly) there are brain states that do not correlate with any conscious mental states. This leads to an asymmetry between mental and brain states, such that there are brain states un-correlated with conscious mental states but no conscious mental states uncorrelated with brain states. Such an asymmetry stands in need of explanation.[51]

Notoriously, philosophy of mind, in tandem with empirically oriented and mathematically driven mind sciences, has been arguing that there is a pattern of efficient causation manifested in the form of mind–brain correlation, expressing itself in nonsensical jargon like "brain activity causes mental states." However, the very asymmetry that is needed to make that case is mysterious. Why should there be brain states without correlated conscious mental states, but no conscious mental states without correlated brain states? To be sure, if it could be shown that there are four types of causation underlying the four types of correlation between φ-tokens and ψ-tokens, we could cover quite a range in conceptual and empirical space. Yet, we would still not have come to know that there really is the relevant kind of asymmetry between φ-tokens and ψ-tokens to the effect that only one of them can be free-floating, i.e., uncoupled from psychological manifestations.

A possible way out is the stipulation of non-conscious mental states all the way down. According to this stipulation, which arguably is the conceptual origin of Freudian psychoanalysis, the ψ-tokens that are not correlated with any φ-tokens are correlated with α-tokens where an α-token is a non-conscious mental state correlated with appropriate ψ-tokens.

SENSE, NONSENSE, AND SUBJECTIVITY

Be that as it may, it raises a specific version of the question concerning the mark of the mental. If consciousness need not be the mark of the mental, because there are good reasons to assume that there are non-conscious mental states, what is the mark of the conscious states? And here the subjectivity assumption kicks in on the level of the ontology of the mind, because we have opened up the possibility that the mark of our conscious mental states consists in the fact that they are illusions on the basis of which we can get it right or wrong. The illusions themselves are neither right nor wrong; they merely are what they are. Their being and their appearance coincide. Yet, this does not make us immune from error vis-à-vis the conscious mental states in question. On the contrary: if they are illusions, they are both our vehicles of acquaintance with how things are and obstacles on the path to knowledge. Thus, the same type of state, an objectively existing illusion, can lead to two epistemically separate realities, one where we know and the other where we don't.

To be sure, isolated conscious mental states are very rare, if they occur at all. Our mental life is typically rich and highly dynamic. It is subject to variations and modifications that take place in temporal dimensions, only some of which can be consciously experienced. In short, our mental and epistemic life is a meshwork of conscious and non-conscious mental states that are not subject to an overall, invariant pattern that specifies something like a priori rules of a partition that would allow us to nicely separate the a priori from the a posteriori. This is one more reason to argue against the infallibilist trend in contemporary epistemology, which maintains that knowledge and consciousness are associated in such a way that the facticity of knowledge is manifested in the form of consciousness.

In this first part of this chapter, I have argued that it is actually the other way around. Consciousness bears the mark of subjectivity—we only have it, or rather *are* it—in virtue of the fact that there is something we get wrong. For this reason, consciousness stands in constant need of correction. As soon as we are conscious of something, it already begins to fade out. Our minds wander, almost never standing still; when they do, they lose consciousness and get transformed into some non-conscious state or other.

Whatever one's philosophy of mind or account of consciousness, one should not deny that mental states, at the very least, are tightly correlated with non-mental physiological and physical structures. We are embodied, and our bodies are parts of a larger natural environment with its natural (evolutionary) history. New Realism's recognition of the irreducible existence of subjectivity and its relation to the realm of sense, therefore, has to provide an account of the relationship between subjectivity and its integration into natural, non-mental reality. This is not to say that nature is identical to the non-mental. However, nature certainly has parts that do not in any significant way depend on the mind's presence. These parts do not stand in metaphysical opposition to subjectivity but are mereologically interwoven with our modes of grasping them.

PART TWO:
SUBJECTIVITY'S PLACE IN NATURE

As subjects, we take part in ontological confusion. Being wrong involves a specific kind of distance from reality. That distance is part of what there is and does not allow us to locate ourselves in a kind of transcendent realm of nonsense. Distance is a form of difference or non-identity. Let us take mistakes as an example. Here, "mistake" refers to the simple idea that a fallible subject mistakes a given object of her thought for another object by attributing some property to it that it does not have. Mistaking Jules for Jim consists in thinking of Jules as having properties that Jim has and, thereby, confusing them.

Any mistake presupposes that the subject has a prior grip on the object that requires her to have some true thought concerning the object. A mistake is not just an absolutely false thought. In order to be mistaken about something, one has to be right about it in some other respect. This is one important way for being wrong and falsity to come apart: being wrong cannot be reduced to grasping an absolutely false thought, where an "absolutely false thought" is one that is false on all levels. For instance, the thought that Donald Trump actually won the 2020 election is false, but it is not absolutely false insofar as it involves the true thought that he was a serious candidate for the position of president of the United States. There is a difference between the thought that Donald Trump won the

175

SENSE, NONSENSE, AND SUBJECTIVITY

2020 election and the thought that Markus Gabriel won the 2020 election, and that difference is, of course, not their shared property of having the truth value false. Rather, the falsity of the thought that Trump won the 2020 election is essentially involved in a whole series of (unfortunately) true thoughts such as the thought that Donald Trump had a really good chance of being reelected, whereas I am not even eligible to become a candidate for the US presidency.

Mistaking Donald Trump for Joe Biden—i.e., confusing the actual loser of the election contest with the actual winner—presupposes a partial distance from the facts. To be sure, that partial distance is part of the facts. For this reason, it can, in principle, be explained in social-scientific or some other terms why so many people are wrong about the actual outcome of the 2020 election. And in order for the wrong belief to be part of reality it requires some kind of alethic grip on how things are. There is an indefinite array of modes of epistemic distance, an idea not exhausted by our alethic concepts designed to carve out a clear (usually binary) difference between true and false simpliciter.

In this second part of the chapter, I want to draw the outlines of a realist philosophy of nature according to which nature is the space of our potential (and actual) deviation from the facts. Nature is the dimension of reality that we do not necessarily grasp on its own terms. Otherwise put, nature is the in-itself.[52]

This does not mean that "nature loves to hide," as Heraclitus mused.[53] Nor does it entail that nature, after all, tends to reveal itself, say in the mathematically rigorous models of natural science. Rather, nature is the dimension of reality that holds a potential divergence between how things are and how they seem to be. Nature is both the way things are and the way things seem to be. Due to the fact that these aspects can come apart, nature plays an important role in being wrong.

In what follows, I will explore one direction of a multifaceted, multidirectional mereology. While nature, in one mereology, is part of the realm of sense, even of thinking (as articulated in Chapter 1), in another direction—the one I will focus on here—sense and thinking are part of nature. They have a place in nature.

That nature is part of the realm of sense can easily be shown by considering our epistemic successes in grasping nature, i.e., the in-itself. Our most impressive epistemic achievement is our cumulative and sometimes

SUBJECTIVITY

revolutionary extension of mathematical models that break the spatiotemporal unfolding of nature down into points located on curves such that we can, in principle, calculate the logico-mathematical position of every given point in our model. To the extent that nature and our model overlap, this allows us to predict nature's unfolding and to describe it in the most precise mathematical terms of modern physics.

From this standpoint of epistemic achievement, physicalism seems to border on an a priori insight. In this context, *physicalism* would be the view that there is nothing in measurable reality that could not be mapped onto a field such that every point in a given space is completely defined in virtue of occupying a point-like position. To many with sophisticated mathematical skills, it seems preposterous to assume that there could be something in measurable (physical) reality that could not, in principle, be thought of in terms of points and their position on curves.[54]

At this point, a distinction between the *universe* and *nature* comes into play.[55] Let *the universe* refer to those parts of natural reality that we can effectively model in terms of mathematical physics as we know it. Given that nature is the official maximal target system of physics, the parts of nature that we actually grasp in terms of mathematical physics can be thought of as being exactly the way we successfully take them to be. The universe is the knowable part of nature.

At the same time, one thing we know about nature and our relationship to it is that we do not know absolutely everything about it. There exists a known difference between the universe and the hitherto unknown parts of nature. What is more, thanks to modern physics we even know that there are parts of nature we cannot know due to the inherent limitations given by our position as observers within nature. We have figured out that the universe is at least in that sense finite, as it is smaller than nature.

But how can sense find a place in nature without thereby being naturalized in an objectionable manner? This is an issue because we know that there has to be a place for sense in the universe. If the universe were utterly senseless, we could not produce astonishingly accurate mathematical descriptions of it that allow us not only to measure it but to connect the dots and to form a picture of how things really are in known nature. That we can rotate a given figure in space around various axes and that the rotation together with other parameters allows us to

SENSE, NONSENSE, AND SUBJECTIVITY

predict the future behavior of a rotating system means that the matrices we identify in characterizing the intrinsic structure of the rotating system must latch onto the system as it actually is. Physical reality contains events that are, at the very least, vector-like, meaning that we cannot always easily draw a distinction between a vector and what is going on in nature as the in-itself.

The idea that mathematical physics is just a toolbox for describing something that is of an entirely different nature than the structures deployed in the characterization is utterly implausible in the face of the precision of contemporary science. The relationship between given structures and coordinate systems by way of which we can identify every point of the structures as being located somewhere (i.e., the very concept of a space) is a manifestation of a sense that is already there, ready to be found in the structures themselves. Considerations of methodological elegance, simplicity, etc. are roads to reality and not just projections of human mind maps onto a reality that is categorially different from our best mathematical descriptions.

In this part of the chapter, I will first argue that fictionalism in the philosophy of science can be interpreted as a form of realism. It shows how sense and nonsense can overlap in scientific models without this amounting to any obstacle to our knowledge of the universe.

Then I will return to consciousness as ontological nonsense (or rather, objectively existing illusion) and locate it with respect to the universe-nature distinction. In this context, I will offer a topic-neutral notion of both sense and nonsense, which covers natural and non-natural phenomena alike without thereby grounding one in the other.

Fictionalism as a Form of Realism

In contemporary philosophy, fictionalism about a truth-apt region of thought and discourse typically maintains the following:

(1) Propositional utterances concerning the domain of thought and discourse are to be taken literally. The utterer ought to mean what she says, for instance, when she says that $F = ma$, or that Anna Karenina is a divorcee.

SUBJECTIVITY

(2) The utterances, thus taken literally, are recognizably false (or incorrect in some other significant respect).

(3) At the same time, the utterances are useful. They are pragmatic reasons for not changing the thought and discourse in question.

(4) Narrative patterns (or other patterns familiar from officially recognized fictional discourse in the aesthetic sense of "the fictional") play a constitutive role in the region of thought and discourse.[56]

The major source of motivation and inspiration for views of this form is Hans Vaihinger's influential formulation of a general fictionalist framework in his *Philosophy of the As If*.[57] The motive leading to fictionalism is familiar from the following basic thought about the relationship between reality—as it is given to our everyday, to some extent pre-theoretical experience—and our scientific modes of identifying patterns: objects involved in events with which we are in perceptual touch (and, thus, in which we are ourselves involved as objects) behave in ways that can be spoken about in scientific terms, such as in differential equations. At the same time, these types of objects sometimes do not behave in exactly the way we would expect them to behave according to our theories, as some other aspect of our theory or even aspects of nature not yet theorized interfere with a clear execution of our predictive modeling rule. Feathers and cannonballs do not fall with the same perceivable speed if we drop them from the top of the Eiffel Tower, while we know that they would have fallen with the same perceivable speed if the event took place in a vacuum.

In short, scientific thinking in the form of models contains idealizations. The very idea of an idealization entails that idealizations, while sometimes literally true, are sometimes false, as some other force interferes with the purity of the conditions of the unrestricted application of a modeling proposition.

Moreover, there are prima facie mysterious operations and terms in the mathematical apparatus of scientific models whose referential standing is dubious. To this category belongs, for instance, ∞ or the complex numbers.[58] Without ∞, we could not formulate the rules of calculus and, thus, would never have won our epistemic way through to modern physics. Without complex numbers, we would not be where we are right

SENSE, NONSENSE, AND SUBJECTIVITY

now in physics, engineering, and so forth. Formulations containing ∞ and instances of $a + bi$ are used to calculate real results (also in the mathematical sense of results not containing any complex numbers that still contain an occurrence of i). Expressions containing them are obvious candidates for a fictionalist understanding, as are the average household income or, more influentially, GDP.[59]

While Vaihinger and many other fictionalists move the further articulation of this line of thinking in an antirealist direction, the formulation of commitments with which we opened makes it clear that fictionalism is fully compatible with almost any form of scientific realism. The simple reason for this statement is that the candidate expressions for a fictionalist construal are seen as "false when taken literally." Hence, they are truth-apt, but fail to accord with the reality envisaged by the thinker in some clearly recognizable way. Fictionalists compare a reality they must have grasped as it actually is with parts of a given model in order to come to the conclusion that there is something wrong with the model. However, what is wrong with the model is no reason for a full-blown revision. ∞ and $\mathbb{C}$ are too useful for the algorithmic architecture of our scientific thinking to be eliminated.

To be sure, this should not mislead one into an all-out error theory of the region of discourse in question. The fact that some mathematical concepts or other types of seemingly referring expressions do not refer to the reality in question in a literal way does not entail that the entire discourse is in principle false.

Hence, fictionalism can be seen to commit to the idea that the region of discourse for which it is suitable contains both literally true and literally false propositions. Physics, as a whole, then, is by its very nature a hybrid of true and false thought expressed in the language (if it is a language) of mathematics.

Language itself (in the concrete forms of the natural languages actually spoken) is the most obvious candidate for fictionalism. Everybody should be a fictionalist about language itself, as any speech community says things they do not literally take to be true while the utterances have a propositional form that, in a given case, turns out to be both false and too useful to revise and replace.

Given this elementary exercise in articulating fictionalism, I would now like to shift our attention to the realist dimension of fictionalism as

SUBJECTIVITY

an obvious truth about some region of thinking of discourse (minimally about language itself as the maximal discourse).

It is part and parcel of the motivation of fictionalism that some propositions are (taken literally) false. This is relevant because they can, more or less, easily be compared with pre-theoretical reality. Let "basic first-order pre-theoretical reality" refer to a set of target systems of scientific discourse; this notion is important in that it incorporates the very idea of mind-independence that too easily leads into an overgeneralization when applied to the realism debate.[60] Basic first-order pre-theoretical reality, for instance, contains all the objects and structures in nature with which no thinker has ever tinkered. Notice that science's target systems are, of course, not exhausted by this category, i.e., the category of target systems that can be thought of as suitably thought-, mind-, language-, and theory-independent (let's simplify this into the usual formula of "mind-independence").[61] While water and, thus, H_2O molecules are largely in that category, the water in the Rhine, which has long been affected by human business, is not. Many things that are true about mind-independent H_2O continue to be true about it in a scientific investigation of the Rhine. But the exact location of a given H_2O molecule in the Rhine right now could not be specified without ultimately bringing minds into the best explanation of why that molecule is where we find it. The reason for this is simply that the structure of the Rhine's riverbed, as we know it today, is partially a result of human planning and engineering activity. Reality, as we find it, cannot be meaningfully reduced to events in the set of mind-independent target systems. For any reality we find, on some level or other, involves us as subjects relating to it.

There is nothing unnatural about artificial molecules, i.e., molecules produced by human industry based on scientific research. The overall composition of our atmosphere is full of intentional products and non-intentional byproducts of molecules that would not have existed had there been no minds. For this simple reason, science cannot exclusively be understood as an investigation into basic first-order pre-theoretical reality. Physics is not (at least primarily) about mind-independent reality.

The set of target systems of science is, therefore, larger than the set of mind-independent target systems. Given that this applies to natural science, too, whose overall target system is nature, we can safely maintain that nature is not, as such or on the whole, mind-independent. But if nature is not mind-independent, mind is part of nature too. Thus, sense has a place in nature.

If sense has a place in nature, why reduce natural sense to systems that correlate with mental representations of mind-independent target systems? The desire to reduce sense to mental representation and mental representation to its "more natural" correlates is part of the various strategies designed to naturalize intentionality, i.e., to explain away the existence of non-natural affairs within nature and contribute to what many self-declared naturalists consider to be the only decent understanding of reality. However, this desire is driven by the misguided notion that science represents the maximal epistemic success in virtue of its privileged access to mind-independent reality as nature. But this characterizes, at best, a proper part of the deep methodology of science and of its meta-physics.

Here, "the deep methodology of science" or "meta-physics" refers to the idea that science itself cannot exhaustively account for its successful relation to reality. Indeed, the analysis of its ontological commitments, let alone an answer to the question of why mathematics is so much as apt to latch onto physical reality, is not within the reach of physics alone.[62] Meta-physics cannot succeed without physics, but it cannot succeed without philosophy either. To the extent that meta-physical operations are carried out in the progress of science, there cannot be progress in science without concomitant progress in philosophy.

According to the neo-realist account of fallibility defended in this book, fallibility is the property of knowers, i.e., of knowledgeable subjects who always get something wrong even in a context where they get something right. Getting it right and being wrong are inextricably interwoven in the dynamic fabric of individual thought and collectively orchestrated knowledge acquisition.

Now, fictionalism identifies an interesting structure in fallible thought. For some stretches of fallible thought and its articulation (such as no lesser system than language itself) are clearly in fictionalist shape. We often enough say things that—taken literally—are recognizably false, mean them (literally), and know that things are not (quite) like that. To be a fictionalist about anything, one cannot be a fictionalist about everything, not even about everything contained in the larger region of discourse and thought under fictionalist consideration.

182

SUBJECTIVITY

Let a discourse-theory be an account of the shape of truth (and, thus, reality) conditions for a given fos that is at least in part thinkable. Fos that are for some reason or other inaccessible to specifiable, concrete thought do not contain a discourse-theory. Fictionalism is a discourse-theory that is based on a comparison of thoughts belonging to a model whose parts deviate from elements in that thought's target system. According to fictionalism, reality is not (at least not quite) like the way it is portrayed by the model level of the discourse under scrutiny.

At this point, a version of the argument from facticity kicks in.[63] This version has it that, in the case of natural science, the unavoidable layer of facticity has to be something that can deviate from the best model we can possibly produce on our end of the epistemic relationship between intentional thought (model) and reality. That does not mean that the best models are destined to get it wrong, but rather that the best scientific model of reality cannot guarantee that it exhausts its target system, nature, in such a way that the universe and nature coincide.

Fictionalism is a plausible contribution to the philosophy of science, as it postulates a structure for scientific discourse-theory that makes sense of the fallibility inherent in scientific progress. Scientific progress consists in shifting the proportions of true and recognizably false thought within science, sometimes resulting in a situation where a fictionalist proposition can be replaced by a literally true one (just think of the replacement of Greek atoms, which were fictional in the sense under discussion here by elementary particles, a concept that still contains idealizations and fictions, but different ones).

Somewhat surprisingly, then, fictionalism as a discourse-theory supports a dynamic form of realism by offering us an account of the integration of the fallible knower into a dynamically shifting landscape of thinkable events of which she is a part. Fictionalism allows us to find sense and nonsense in our models of nature without which we could not translate the universe into mathematical code.

Universe, Nature, Consciousness

Another, traditional way of drawing a distinction between what I have been calling "universe" and "nature," respectively, would be to draw a distinction between *natura naturata* and *natura naturans*. In our context, *natura naturata* is the universe, described by a sophisticated mathematical architecture that allows the theoretician (1) to identify a given measurement with an event (entry) in an event space and (2) to reidentify the events at some other position in the event space. The point's movement can then be seen as a trajectory through the event space whose structure is articulated by means of the sophisticated choice of coordinates that allows the theoretician to think of time (t) as parameterizing the difference between an event's positions in the event space, a difference that is mathematically accessible in terms of calculus. Thus, *natura naturata* is thoroughly characterized by the notion that there is no barrier in principle to thinking of time as t, which physicists often somewhat aptly symbolize as a pointwise represented parameter in a function $f(t)$ describing movement along a trajectory. It is not a coincidence that pointwise meta-physics and calculus were discovered in the aftermath of the ingenious Cartesian idea of an overall mathematical representation of movement.[64]

In contradistinction to the universe as *natura naturata, natura naturans* is the part of nature that is not adequately captured or not even captured at all within the scope of the idea that the target system of natural science contains point-like events that generate patterns by moving along a trajectory whose form they determine by their sheer movement. Otherwise put, *natura naturans* is the part of nature that is not geometrical at all.

However, the neo-realist version of the distinction between universe and nature does not amount to a form of neat meta-physical dualism according to which natural reality is split into two clearly separate parts. For that which is accessible to mathematical modeling in any desirable sense is precisely a part of nature and not something that somehow deviates from it. This is a crucial departure from the Schopenhauerian-Nietzschean invocation of nature as something that is not geometrical at all—a concept of nature that figures in so many prominent philosophical critiques of the "unnaturalness" of science. Nature is not the irrational, anti-geometrical, anti-logical other of mathematically rigorous concept formation, because the universe as *natura naturata* is precisely a part of nature whose properties are adequately articulated by natural science. Just as in any other case of epistemically and alethically successful thought, in the success case, thought does not metaphysically deviate from the facts but grasps them as

SUBJECTIVITY

they really are. Nature is, therefore, not as such hidden behind a veil of theory, nor is it located on the dark side of the universe, as it were.

The difference between the universe and nature is not stable, but dynamic. After all, the universe cannot be a mathematical given, i.e., something that could in principle be derived by identifying the proper subset of mathematical structures that figure in a complete account of physics. This is due not just to the epistemic limitations of working scientists who are fallible, finite creatures within nature. Even an idealized thinker could not derive the proper subset of mathematical structures that figure in physics, because the target system of physics, nature, changes in certain ways for which we do not have a geometry.

A straightforward argument for this point begins by reminding us of the condition that mathematics (and, thus, geometry) cannot be an all-encompassing fos, because there cannot be such a thing in the first place. This, by itself, does not entail that physicalism is wrong about nature, where *physicalism about nature* would be the view that nature can be exhausted by mathematical modeling (meaning that nature is fully captured at the idealized end of inquiry). In order to get there, we have to realize that any scientific account of nature has to be part of nature. The only way of identifying the proper subset of mathematical structures that have a physical meaning is by way of intervening in natural reality.[65] Intervention—such as measurement—takes place *in* nature, and it cannot be circumvented by merely inspecting the logical space of mathematical options. Simply put, physics is essentially an empirical science supported by vertiginously ingenious mathematical maneuvers in theoretical physics. Theoretical physics' *demonstratio more geometrica* is bound to have an empirical grounding; not even a God could circumnavigate it.

That line of thought presupposes that the physicist essentially belongs to nature without being reducible to a more or less complicated trajectory in a suitable subset of the relevant event space. Thus, the physicist essentially belongs both to nature and to fos that are outside of the reach of mathematical modeling conducive to physics. Hence, even if God were the type of omniscient knower who gets absolutely everything there is to know right in the most demanding sense of the term, he would not think of the knower in her entirety as an object within the fos of physics.

The ontological difference between universe and nature, therefore, runs through the physicist. The physicist experiences the ontological difference as the quality that seems to resist the calculation, i.e., as consciousness.

At this point, it is useful to return to what might be one of the birthplaces of the contemporary conscious qualia debate, namely, Emil Heinrich Du Bois-Reymond's famous 1872 speech "The Limits of Knowledge of Nature."[66] In this speech, Du Bois-Reymond argues that there are two limits of our knowledge of nature, one "forevermore determining our incapacity to comprehend matter and force, the other determining our inability to understand mental facts from their material conditions."[67] The second limit is associated with "consciousness," which he uses in order to refer to "the fact of an intellectual phenomenon, of any kind whatsoever, even of the lowest grade."[68] He illustrates the constitutive elusiveness of consciousness thus understood by way of the fiction of an idealized thinker (here, Laplace's demon):

> Even the Mind imagined by Laplace, with its universal formula, would, in its efforts to overstep these limits, be like an aëronaut essaying to reach the moon. In its world of mobile atoms, the cerebral atoms are in motion indeed, but it is a dumb show. This Mind views their hosts, and sees them crossing each other's course, but does not understand their pantomime; they think not for him, and hence, as we have already seen, the world of this Mind is still meaningless.[69]

To be sure, Du Bois-Reymond does not offer any additional argument for the existence of the second limit. The first limit is derived via the claim that no identification of a fundamentally elementary ("atomic") layer of physical reality would ever add up to an explanation of itself, meaning that the very existence of an elementary layer will always elude explanation due to its status as brute facticity. The second limit's existence could be supported by different arguments familiar from the subsequent qualia debate, which was thoroughly underdeveloped in the 1870s. What matters in our context are not the details of the space of rationally acceptable positions vis-à-vis the existence (or non-existence) of qualia in an otherwise quality-free universe. Rather, my concern is with Du Bois-Reymond's recourse to "consciousness" as a placeholder for those parts of the universe the physicist can constitutively not get into view.[70]

SUBJECTIVITY

Hence, I do not wish to claim that consciousness (whatever that is) is an objectively existing mystery that both is and is not really an object of natural science. While this is the letter of Du Bois-Reymond's *ignorabimus thesis,* it need not be its spirit. He does not say that we are incapable of understanding the mind: he merely commits to an "inability to understand mental facts from their material conditions."[71]

In Du Bois-Reymond's discussion, as well as in much of the contemporary literature on consciousness and its relation to non-conscious nature, "consciousness" figures as a title for a minimal limiting concept. It refers to those aspects of the physicist's involvement in nature that cannot be understood by observing non-mental nature. The observation of non-mental nature takes place within a fos that treats all physical objects alike by not trying to understand their behavior with recourse to mentalistic vocabulary. The concepts of physics are subject to furnishing functions that exclude access to the vagaries of the mind.

Du Bois-Reymond, like his knowing and unknowing followers, at this point, makes the mistake of searching for "consciousness" in the universe where we can, indeed, never find it, because it is ontological nonsense that does not lend itself to the type of mathematical fine-grained resolution that is capable of articulating the behavior of non-mental physical reality in terms of space trajectories. The events of consciousness just cannot be represented pointwise.

This easily gets obscured by the usual additional confusion associated with the failed attempt to pinpoint neural correlates for as many clearly conscious states as possible with the goal of generating a one-to-one mapping that would exhaust our mentalistic vocabulary—as if there existed an isomorphism connecting the concepts (and, thus, sets) of consciousness and brain. The idea that consciousness in all of its guises (from raw feels to the intellectual joy of solving differential equations) is a kind of trajectory connecting the dots (the individual neurons) of pointwise representation of coordinated behavior is a paradigmatic case of local confusion. It mistakes a wide, utterly disunified array of mental phenomena with a single type of phenomenon ("consciousness") that both does and does not take place in nature. It is supposed to take place in nature due to its allegedly one-to-one correlation with obviously natural events (such as the coordinated firing of individual neurons), while at the same time acknowledging that the observation of the pointwise representation of

SENSE, NONSENSE, AND SUBJECTIVITY

elements in that part of the target system gets us nowhere in explaining consciousness as such.

That such a mystery is generated should not mislead us into believing that there is something wrong with nature. On closer inspection, the mystery of consciousness boils down to a mystery of "consciousness," i.e., to a confusion of fos that overlap in dynamic ways in the self-conscious life of the theoretician. Physicists know that they undergo a series of mental states in their actual articulation of physical thought. There are material, socioeconomic, neural, animal, historical, etc. conditions for the emergence of any given successful physical thought that arises within nature. Some of the conditions can be turned into the object of physical science. Physics has a self-reflexive dimension that allows it to produce engineering applications based on its results that in turn allow it to produce new results. It not only intervenes in nature but intervenes in nature in light of its epistemic goals. Such is the origin of CERN, the James Webb Space Telescope, and many less impressive instruments that enhance our cognitive observation of nature.

Yet, physics is not self-reflexive to such an extent that it can grasp the various logical and mental conditions under which it takes place, as these conditions stretch out into those parts of nature that physics itself identifies as currently, or even "forevermore," outside of its cognitive reach.

To be sure, there are at least two broad options at this juncture, which I would like to call *fos-dualism* and *fos-confusion,* respectively. *Fos-dualism* is the view that the most relevant part of the events we experience and rightly identify as "conscious" or "mental" take place in fos that are essentially non-natural and, thus, meta-physical. For instance, ∞ and $\mathbb{C}$ are objects (and contain objects) that do not occur in nature (at the very least they do not appear in the observable object domain of the universe).[72] If mindedness essentially appeared in meta-physical fos, we would be dealing with a full-blown version of dualism, which need not be a disaster, as this would occur under novel theory conditions. These novel theory conditions must not be prematurely and wrongly identified with Cartesian dualism, for the potential fact of mind's belonging to non-physical fos does not commit one to the notion that mind is a substance that metaphysically differs from the extended substance of physical reality. Not all ontological distinctions result in objectionable dichotomies.[73]

SUBJECTIVITY

Having said that, *fos-confusion* is the more interesting candidate view for characterizing the relationships between mind and matter. Here "fos-confusion" refers to an architecture that allows for the mutual mereological inclusion of mind and matter in a third fos. The third fos would be neutral with respect to mind and matter, i.e., neither mind nor matter. For instance, the neutral fos could consist in a bidirectional mereology according to which mind has parts that appear in material nature and material nature has parts that appear in mind. The fos of their mutual appearance would be neutral in that it is defined by a furnishing function that differs from those of the fos of mind and matter. The broad category of views of this form can then impose further structure on the various relationships between mind, matter, and the neutral—relationships that range from mere overlap to a more fine-grained mereology or even to a full-blown theory of mind's and matter's entanglement in a knowable type of neutral fos.[74]

Yet, on its own, a bidirectional mereology connecting the neutral on the one hand with mind and with matter on the other does not force one into this model. Due to a threat of accepting too many assumptions that threaten to throw us back to a (sophisticated) form of dualism (mediated by a third term), FOS, rather, brings in confusion as a way of *rejecting* an overall version of the mind-matter relationship: there is a sheer, unsurveyable multiplicity of fields dynamically interacting in unsurveyably manifold ways, with subjectivity—mindedness—being the locus of the attempt to unify them and, thus, a site of confusion.[75]

At this point, the thesis that discussions of "consciousness" ultimately are discussions of sense (becoming aware of itself on indefinitely many levels) allows us to further clarify the situation. Sense is a mode of presentation of objects (sometimes on the level of sense and sometimes on the level of reference which leads to nonsense, as I argued in Chapter 2). In addition to straightforward modes of presentation of objects, there are also modes of presentation of such modes. Sense does not come into existence in the aftermath of the epistemically cold, opaque phases of the universe. Sense has to be operative at any stage of the development of the universe, even on a cosmological scale—which can take the form of mathematical constraints on how the universe unfolds. These constraints are clearly an ineliminable aspect of our best cosmological explanations and,

SENSE, NONSENSE, AND SUBJECTIVITY

thus, causal in some sense, for instance, in the sense of metaphysically harmless *causae formales*. Sense is certainly part of the universe, which is why the universe is mathematically describable, explainable, and predictable. Thereby, sense becomes a part of a part of nature.

Now, what about the other part of nature, the vastness of *natura naturans* not yet transformed into structures in the universe? Given that nature as a whole, comprising both *natura naturata* and *natura naturans,* is the target system of natural science, elements from *naturans* sometimes show up in the format of *naturata* that is a form of scientific progress. The logic of discovery that applies here must not be regarded as another somewhat failed attempt at bridging a metaphysical gap between nature in itself and our model-like representations that at most approximate the ultimate truth. Rather, the universe is exactly as we find it to be in our successful mapping of its scientifically accessed dimensions. This means that nature has to be a place for sense, regardless of the presence (if any) of thinking animals that grasp structures of the universe. Such is realism about sense applied to the discussion at hand.

Mutatis mutandis for ontological nonsense: Confusion is mind-independent, too, in that fos fuse with each other regardless of the additional fact that we take note of it. Reality is not a conceptually tidy place before we enter the stage and bring conceptual chaos, incoherence, contradiction, weakness of the will, error, mistakes—in short, subjectivity—to the fore.

Sense and nonsense are topic-neutral. They are ontological categories, belonging to the conceptual apparatus of FOS, which articulates a series of concepts that are functionally, but not substantially, universal or transversal. Some have wondered how the ontology of fos can maintain things such as "to exist is to appear in a fos" without thereby making direct or indirect metaphysical claims about absolutely everything.[76] However, the thrust of this line of argument to the effect that metaphysics again turns out to be inevitable relies on the core idea that philosophical concepts such as object, fos, existence, being, and concept are not only topic-neutral but refer to a set of categorial concepts under which everything that we can think and speak about falls. According to that powerful idea, everything by its very nature is an object, exists, has being, and falls under concepts that at some point or other fall under the concept of concepts.

SUBJECTIVITY

If this were the case, ontology and metaphysics would at least partly overlap and there could not be a non-metaphysical ontology.

Logics, too, would be drawn into the vortex of this argument to the extent that logical concepts exhibit patterns of topic-neutrality. Thus, logics and ontology would return to their traditional place within metaphysics. However, the no-world-view blocks this road to metaphysics. Even if there were a concept of concepts such that all concepts (including itself) fell under it in virtue of partaking in the nature of the concept, the no-world-view would entail that there is, therefore, something or other that does not fall under a concept.

In general, the no-world-view's basic constraint is satisfied by any view that does not collect absolutely everything into a single fos. Notice that this excludes dualism or any other form of *n*-alism that maintains that there is a specifiable number of fos that jointly exhaust everything there is. For *n*-alism posits a fos within which the *n* fos appear and is thus a form of metaphysics. FOS as a form of ontological pluralism must therefore not be interpreted as an instance of *n*-alism. Ontological pluralism is not a metaphysical view.

It is correct that the articulation of FOS requires conceptual resources that are sufficiently topic-neutral in order to border on views that lend themselves to metaphysical modeling. However, FOS itself does not commit the theorist to a metaphysic, nor are metaphysical interpretations somehow inevitable on pain of a looming threat of self-defeating generality.

The simple way out of the conundrum is a distinction between different ways of conceiving of generality or falling under a concept. If everything we can direct our attention at with any minimal conceptual structure in mind—such as merely thinking of it as being in the set of things we can direct our attention at—fell under an appropriate concept of being an object, this would show, at most, that the concept of an object is topic-neutral. It would not guarantee that we had found a metaphysical property that all objects share regardless of how we take them to be.

Sense and nonsense are both topic-neutral. It does not matter for them whether the objects and events within the reach of sense-making concepts and the experience of nonsense put a thinker in touch with a

SENSE, NONSENSE, AND SUBJECTIVITY

particular kind of object, such as physical objects. Realism about sense and nonsense are not as such views about language or nature (to name two dimensions in which they apply).

While I typically emphasize the non-natural, non-physical dimensions of sense and nonsense, this does not mean that nature is the other of sense, outside of sense altogether. There are no bounds of sense separating us from nature, and there are some that relate us to it. Nature is an important part of the explanation of being wrong. It is a paradigm for what we can be wrong about in that it characterizes facticity as an in-itself that does not care about our epistemic interests. It neither reveals itself to thought out of a metaphysical generosity nor does it like to hide itself. It merely is.

Its mere being, however, does not exclude that it is thus and so, i.e., embedded in the realm of sense. Nature is structured, although we do not really know how its structures arise in general (nature ultimately does not offer itself "carved at its joints"). For this reason, the universe can be a part of nature—which need not mean that nature is a closed atemporal whole. Nature, like the universe, can be expanding and changing in hitherto unknown ways.

That sense has a place in nature can easily be read off the epistemic success of mathematizing physics. In mathematics we encounter a pure form of sense. In its applied, physical dimension, it contains reference points that put the mathematical thinkers in touch with how things are in nature. These glimpses of physical realities can be translated into mathematical structures and even into numerical values—measurements— that relate to each other. In simple cases, these connections can be articulated in terms of transformations of given values. None of this would be possible if nature were senseless, a chaotic mess of metaphysically random events.[77]

Yet, this does not mean that nature could ever coincide with the universe. There is a gap between nature as we know it and the parts of nature we do not and cannot know. These parts of nature differ from the universe in non-metaphysical ways. This difference is not spatiotemporal. It pertains to ontology, not to mathematics. *Natura naturata* is not elsewhere, such as beyond the event horizon of the universe or in some tiny dimension of the universe, such as on a string or brane level.[78]

SUBJECTIVITY

For this reason, non-mathematizable nature also differs from dark matter and dark energy whose existence and amount (currently thought to add up to 96 percent of the matter-energy content of the universe) follow from our contemporary models. In contradistinction to dark matter and dark energy, *natura naturata* stands in no quantifiable relationship to the universe. And yet, the universe also extends into *natura naturata* by way of our knowledge accumulation.

Consequently, there are two different types of expansions of the universe. First, the familiar cosmological one we have come to know about in the twentieth century in terms of physical discoveries concerning the theory of relativity and its consequences. Second, an expansion in terms of our epistemic penetration of nature that makes it thinkable to us.

Sense is topic-neutral. By its very nature it therefore covers both physical and non-physical fos. *Mutatis mutandis* for nonsense. It occurs both within nature and in non-natural domains. Our experience of nonsense in the form of the flow of consciousness is a manifestation of both natural and non-natural nonsense, because "consciousness" refers both to natural and non-natural events. There just is no overarching theory that unifies these two dimensions of "consciousness" into a single fos that finds its proper place in nature, let alone the universe. All theories that postulate a measurable, at-bottom mathematical relationship between consciousness and its natural (neural) correlate fail in virtue of their basic assumption that there is a clear line that distinguishes the natural and non-natural parts of the relationship between mind and matter.

The fact that consciousness, in its manifold meanings, is (1) involved in ontological nonsense (as field confusion) and (2) that there this no a priori conceptual, let alone natural, border separating the natural and non-natural parts of consciousness (in any of its more specific meanings) thus allows us to see how we can overcome the problem(s) of consciousness—ranging from the hard problem via the paradox of self-consciousness to the Lord Chandos problem. Consciousness's intrinsically manifold reality and its complex mereological integration into natural fos (only some of which are knowable by us, from the standpoint of reflexive minds grasping themselves as parts of nature) is the key to a dissolution of the aura of mystery surrounding the confusing reality of being a specifically minded animal.

PART THREE:
PRACTICAL SUBJECTIVITY

Theoretical subjectivity is evaluable in specific normative terms, ranging from the low-level veridicality and minimal objectivity of sensory registration to the highest norms of reflexive knowledge claims concerning knowledge and its constituent concepts, such as truth, justification, evidence, etc. As subjects we always also assess our performances in light of standards set by practical achievements. In this context, concepts such as good, permissible, morally neutral, evil, just, fair, legal, legitimate, and their manifold ramifications, through which we think of our actions as subject to a specific type of normative evaluation, have their proper home. Again, we encounter a complex mereology of circular constitution: On the one hand, the activities describable in terms of theoretical subjectivity (such as thinking, perceiving, and making knowledge claims) are actions as well and, therefore, are part of practical subjectivity. On the other hand, practical subjectivity is involved in activities that cannot be characterized without bringing notions such as facts, knowledge, ignorance, delusion, etc. into the picture, whose content depends on our conception of theoretical subjectivity.

In this concluding part of this chapter, I will explore dimensions of practical subjectivity. Here, "subjectivity" is, of course, used in the sense specified throughout this book. It refers to the conditions of the subjectivity assumption according to which no subject, that is to say no agent, could ever be in a position of meeting all standards of practical achievement. There is no "holy will" or "moral saint," to borrow Kant's and Susan Wolf's language.[79]

One of the reasons why moral perfection is impossible for anyone subject to normative assessment is the complexity of our agency. It is impossible for us not only to predict or control the consequences of our action but also to fully grasp the conditions of realization of a given action, because any action is involved in a complex system of social facts that no one fully grasps. These social facts in turn are embedded in natural facts such that social and natural complexity are interwoven, nested within each other in the reality of our agency as human animals.

Society is complex: it is a dynamic, changing whole of interrelated transactions among agents and groups of agents. A transaction is the

SUBJECTIVITY

product of an implicit or explicit attitude adjustment of a multiplicity of agents. In the case of human societies, the agents are typically other humans. However, humans would not be what they are (including animals of a certain kind) if they were not enmeshed in non-human environments, some of which contain agents capable of attitude adjustment, such as other, non-human animals.

A fact is social if it is produced as a consequence of the attitude adjustment of a multiplicity of agents.[80] Social facts make up societies, which bind transactions together by way of producing social facts within which further social facts are embedded. Societies proceed in virtue of a constant integration of social facts into practices designed to maintain social stability and social change.

Social stability is a complex measure of conditions of repeated creation, maintenance, and reform of social facts with which individual agents and collectives are presented as matters of fact. It is desirable because it provides agents with norms, some of which are sufficiently explicit so as to allow for adjudication between conflicting courses of action. Neverending social turmoil (which is the fate of many societies) is hard to stabilize, because there is indeed nothing outside of society that, by itself, recommends a specific course of action. We cannot read the form of ideal institutions off the script of nature, which is why the old conundrum of the transition from the state of nature to a social contract is unsolvable and, thus, ill-formulated.

Despite all that, humans still aspire to find social norms in nonhuman nature. In the contemporary moment, there seems to be a particular urgency for grounding society in nature due to the fact that modern society turns out to be a gigantic array of conditions of industrialized destruction of the parts of our environment without which we cannot even survive. To many, the ecological crisis, which has clearly turned into a series of manifest catastrophes, seems to be sufficient evidence for the need to take highly specific courses of action. But no reference to nature (or science) suffices to close the deontological gap. The fact that society and non-social nature are nested in each other in both socially and naturally complex ways does not deconstruct the deontological difference between these two fos.

In what follows, I will first argue that our practical self-determination, our understanding as agents, is as fallible as our theoretical grasp of

195

ourselves in terms of our mentalistic vocabularies. Then I will present an outline of a conception of ethics as grounded in facts concerning a specific type of obligation, of rights and duties, that we have simply in virtue of our shared humanity. This leads me to postulating an important link between ethics and anthropology in the sense of any type of investigation into human being or human co-becoming, as I will say with reference to a proposal by Takahiro Nakajima.[81] Last but not least, I will focus on some prominent contemporary societal phenomena, discussing ideology, propaganda, and ignorance with a view on our digital modernity. This will be a place to connect the theme of our contemporary epistemic crisis (often discussed under the heading of "post-truth," "the death of expertise," or "science skepticism") with practical subjectivity.

Fallible Self-Determination

Like many other living beings, human animals are social. Here, the term "social" refers to practices of mutual attitude adjustment. Human social agents, practical subjects, do what they do not only in light of their individual self-conception as agents. For their individual self-conception as agents is always also a function of their relationship to other agents who first teach them how to establish minimal conditions of agency, such as how to use one's senses to distinguish objects, events, etc. in their environment from their internal states.

We experience society in the form of what Lucy O'Brien has called "ordinary self-consciousness."[82] Ordinary self-consciousness is a fundamental way by which we become aware of other subjects and their evaluation of ourselves through which they recognize us. As she puts this, it is "an affective sensitivity to the evaluative attention of others: it is consciousness of oneself as up for evaluation." In this context, "recognition" is a term for the type of cognition of others as subjects that differs from the perception of the presence of their bodies in our surroundings.[83] O'Brien supposes that "the evolved purpose of our capacity for ordinary self-consciousness is to allow for a conduit through which the evaluation of another of me is taken up in my relation to myself—in order to secure coordination and co-operation with my con-specifics."[84] While this hypothesis is certainly a plausible account of a link between the evolution of

SUBJECTIVITY

our organic survival form as prosocial mammals and the exercises of higher forms of self-consciousness (such as the ones required to do philosophy), it does not exhaust the varieties of social self-consciousness, as O'Brien herself points out. For we respond to portraits, self-portraits, and other imaginary and, thus, fictional modes of potential recognition by exercising the very same recognitional capacities that bind society together. Otherwise put, some social facts are produced due to an interaction between a single individual and a fictional, imaginary presence of the evaluative gaze of another.

While the evolutionary grounding of ordinary self-consciousness explains the causal trigger of the phenomenon, it cannot exhaust it due to the emancipation of self-consciousness from its purely objective, non-self environment. This leads her to the following insight, which is crucial for understanding the emergence of socially orchestrated epistemological negative phenomena (modes of being wrong) on which I will focus in this part of our investigation:

> Acknowledging this extension to our capacity to feel self-conscious, and with it the multiplication of occasions of feeling self-conscious, is vital if we are to get a proper sense of what it [is] like to live as a self-conscious animal in a world, as ours is, of image replication—either through mirrors, or photographs. A capacity that no doubt evolved in order that we could incorporate the views of others into our view of ourselves, is now operative in a way that we also use it—often—and to incorporate our view of ourselves, as we see ourselves from the outside, into [ourselves].

In this regard, I have been speaking of the human self-portrait as constitutive of subject-hood.[85] To be someone is to live life in light of a self-conception through which we articulate a self-portrait, i.e., imaginary positions from which we experience ourselves as objects of evaluative recognition as subjects.

Self-consciousness is a form of self-determination. Self-determination means that some facts obtain in virtue of the circumstance that any explanation of the facts in question essentially invokes the presence of a self.[86] If Romeo gives flowers to Juliet, any explanation of the event will

SENSE, NONSENSE, AND SUBJECTIVITY

have to mention some intention or other. No full explanation of the event that mentions only anonymous, self-less causal processes (be they physical, deterministic, or quantum processes; class struggle; hormonal flows; neural firing patterns; or all of those together) will ever do the job of getting the event into view. At least, we cannot concoct a theoretical setup that would allow us to explain all social facts without ever mentioning a self and, thus, subjects as participants in social transactions. These participants cannot all be produced as side effects of the relational transaction. Self-determination precedes social self-consciousness.

Our epistemic relation to self-determination (be it as an object of sociological investigation or in the shape of self-conscious self-determination) is fallible and, thus, subjective. Turning oneself into an agent of a particular kind by conceiving of oneself as that type of agent does not suffice to make it the case that one actually is that type of agent. Just imagine someone who believes himself to be a natural born tango dancer. He has watched many videos about tango dancing and practices dancing by himself for many years. Having prepared himself for a glorious entrance on the international scene, he travels to Buenos Aires and shows up at Maldita Milonga to show his skills. Unbeknownst to him, though, his dancing (if dancing it be) does not even remotely resemble tango, and nothing he does on stage can be recognized as tango dancing. Hence, while he conceived of himself as a tango dancer and did many things in light of that self-conception (including buying a ticket to Buenos Aires, dressing up, consuming hours of tango videos, reading books about tango, learning Spanish, etc.), he failed at meeting some of the minimal norms of actually being a tango dancer at all.

Another example of the structure of failure at the heart of self-determining subject-hood is tied to the possibility of nonsense. We think of ourselves as animals. At the same time, we are aware of manifold distinctions that separate us from other animals; we are specifically human animals. But if we share animality with the other animals, if we are animals in exactly the same sense in which Bonobos, snakes, fruit flies, and paramecia are animals, what separates us from the other, non-human animals cannot be derived from our animal nature alone. Hence the question of whether and how we are identical with animals of a given type.

SUBJECTIVITY

Let us call the factor through which we determine ourselves as *human* animals "the specific something."[87] On a fundamental philosophical level, some think of the specific something as akin to an immortal soul. What distinguishes us from non-human animals would be the presence of an immortal soul that becomes conscious of itself in earthly life. Others identify themselves with neural firing patterns, maybe even with a series of activations of the neural mechanism that only correlates with basic self-awareness or consciousness.[88]

Whatever one's preferred position vis-à-vis the relationship between the human mind and its animality / corporeality, every specific position is a form of self-determination that results in action patterns. Thinking of oneself as having an immortal soul leads to religious practices; identifying oneself with a neural firing pattern rules that out and opens up another spectrum of action possibilities depending on one's further metaphysical assumptions about the relationship between animal survival and societal constraints.

Now, whether we have an immortal soul or are identical to neural firing patterns (this list of options is, of course, not exhaustive) is a perfectly factual affair. For we either have or do not have an immortal soul. Determining ourselves in light of our experience as if we had an immortal soul does not suffice to produce one. *Mutatis mutandis,* identifying oneself with neural firing patterns does not destroy one's immortal soul, should we have one.

Insofar as we constitute ourselves by way of fallible self-determination, theoretical mistakes concerning who we are as subjects have immediate practical consequences. Who or what I take myself to be constitutes the framework for my action. Hence, there is a fundamental form of practical error that manifests itself on the level or our action-guiding self-portrait.

However fundamental self-determination might be for subject-hood, the structure of self-determination does not shield the subject from the realm of error. Quite the opposite. For self-determination exhibits content patterns that are suitable for appraisal in terms of various alethic, aesthetic, social, political, and ethical norms. We can get ourselves wrong despite the fact that the best explanation of who someone is who gets himself wrong sometimes refers to acts of self-determination without which the subject in question would not be who he is.

SENSE, NONSENSE, AND SUBJECTIVITY

The sense of society, its glue, is mutual attitude adjustment. Our survival form is profoundly social. Human animals come into being and grow only under conditions of some socially orchestrated division of labor. Our bodies as organic systems are shaped by social facts, including the social conditions of sexual reproduction, the nourishing of a fetus in a human mother before birth, and the caretaking activities without which humans could not ever make it to a stage in life at which they can sustain their own life processes without direct support of others. As human animals, we are thus social through and through.

As self-conscious, self-determining agents, we are social as well. The majority of our most cherished activities presuppose interaction with others and, thus, modes of action, coordination, and cooperation without which the social rules that govern coordinated behavior could not have a grip on individual subjects.

At the same time, our status as subjects, i.e., subject-hood, is not as such socially produced or social. Reality, among other things, is populated by individual subjects who relate to each other through social networks without being entirely produced by them. This irreducibility of subjectivity to social networks must not be confused with a commitment to a naturalistic overreaction according to which everything that is not social has to be natural in the sense of anonymous processes (such as processes on the cellular level of a survival form) that take place regardless of our attitudes toward them.

Given that subjects are real, there is no reason to think of their agency and, thus, of action explanation as somehow less real. Reducing agency or replacing it by some naturalistic surrogate notion not only misses this dimension of reality but threatens to lose sight of the normative vocabulary we need in order to account for our fallible self-determination.

This normative vocabulary evolves in contexts of social practices. These practices are subject to synchronic and diachronic, i.e., historical, variation conditions. Moreover, nobody is in a position to command the entirety of our normative vocabulary; there is no absolute judge of all human affairs. Thus, while there are moral facts, i.e., things that we ought to do or ought not to do on specifically moral grounds, these facts are directed at us. They concern us as fallible, historically situated subjects constitutively involved in social complexity.

SUBJECTIVITY

Ethics and Anthropology

The performances of subjects are judgeable in light of different types of norms. Theoretical subjectivity is paradigmatically tied to the norm of truth, practical subjectivity to that of goodness. Insofar as our subjective performances are judgeable in light of these norms, our performances can count as successes or failures, i.e., as falling into the category of the good or the bad case respectively.

The norm of truth becomes self-transparent on the level of knowledge. We are capable of knowing that we know something and thereby realize that some of our attitudes succeed in grasping how things are. We have some true (propositional) attitudes of a particular form, the form of knowledge.

The norm of goodness is articulated in the form of good actions. An action is good if it accords with demands that we cannot help but recognize as universally binding. Good actions ought to be performed under any circumstances and by everybody who is capable of understanding the circumstances that require certain actions from them. The good is the deontologically necessary.

The theory of practical subjectivity is a crucial part of ethics. By "ethics," I understand the discipline that investigates the nature and scope of moral facts.[89] Here, a *moral fact* is a true answer (if such there be) to the question of what one ought to do in a given situation simply in virtue of the fact that one is a human moral agent. Morality, the system of moral facts, is the target system of ethics. This is one way of addressing the thorny issue of a "definition of morality" in the sense of a conceptual determination of the target system of ethical theorizing. As Bernard Gert puts it in his article on the delineation of the target system of ethics:

> Morality is the one public system that no rational person can quit. The fact that one cannot quit morality means that one can do nothing to escape being legitimately liable to sanction for violating its norms, except by ceasing to be a moral agent. Morality applies to people simply by virtue of their being rational persons who know what morality prohibits, requires, etc., and being able to guide their behavior accordingly.[90]

201

Gert identifies moral agents with "rational persons," and those, in turn, are seen as knowing the demands of morality. They are in touch with the moral facts. Unlike Gert (and Kant, for that matter) who identifies a moral agent with a rational person in general, I propose to think of the moral agent as a human person. A human person might or might not count as rational in some specific sense of "rationality." What matters is not rationality as a particular form of accountability and self-transparent commitment to the demands of morality, but rather the shape of human self-determination.

The shape of human self-determination consists in our exercises of the form of humanity. The form of humanity, being human, is the remarkable capacity to live life in light of a conception of oneself as a human agent, i.e., as someone who differs from all known non-human entities (including other animals) and who shares something with all other humans. Humans grasp themselves as belonging to the same species as other humans; they recognize each other. At the same time, we interpret this fact of our own speciation in different ways, which takes place on a metalevel of responses to the question as to what makes us human as much as on the level of highly individual self-conceptions tied to our social identities. Given that we can only exercise our humanity by providing specific answers to how we want to live as individuals and how we ought to live together as humans, we can think of human being as human co-becoming, to use Nakajima's formula again.[91]

Human beings interpret themselves as human by acting in a certain way. Our actions thereby reveal our self-conception on the most general and on more specific levels down to the level of what makes us individual, i.e., entirely different from all other humans despite our shared humanity.

Practical subjectivity realizes itself between good and evil.[92] It chooses a course of action out of many possibilities that are given to the subject at any moment of their lives. Intentional actions can be classified as falling within either of the following three broad categories: the good, the neutral, and the evil.[93]

The good is the practically necessary. If φ is good and S is in a position to φ, then S ought to φ. If S ought to φ, then S must be capable of doing otherwise. Yet, the capacity to do otherwise does not mean that S could have done otherwise. What S did defines who S is. Our deeds constantly shape our identity. However, we can do otherwise in the future. Being capable of φ-ing does not mean that one automatically φs. Deviating from moral facts requires that one can become aware of the urgency to correct one's course—in the future, not in the past.

Evil is the practically impossible, which does not mean that no one can act evilly. It means that evil is that which no one ought to do under any circumstances. There is no situation that morally justifies an evil act. If we do evil in light of some consideration within a genuinely moral outlook in order to be able to do good elsewhere in our system of actions, we still do evil and have not justified our doing evil in any morally relevant way.

Most everyday actions are neither good nor evil, they are neutral. Neutral actions are subject to non-ethical practical norms of performances. There are many different normative systems that specify the realm of the ethically neutral. The law, aesthetics, social norms, etiquette, habits, rules of games, etc. provide many examples of norms by which we judge performances that are ethically neutral.

To be sure, evil comes in many forms. Here, I use the term "evil" as a title for the broad action category of the morally absolutely prohibited. Evil in that sense should be distinguished from paradigmatic forms of radical or brutal evil.

The good, the neutral, and the evil are grounded in the human life-form. Human animals are the only known animals that are capable of knowing the good for what it is, i.e., as something "we owe to each other" in virtue of a particular ontological status, the status of self-knowing agents who live their lives in light of their self-conception.[94] For this reason, our capacity for good and evil, i.e., the ethical dimension of our practical subjectivity, clearly sets us apart from members of any other species.

This is not to deny zoological knowledge. Other species are capable of acting in prosocial, altruistic ways or creating systems of cooperation that allow their communities to flourish.[95] However, prosocial behavior does not add up to an insight into the morally good. For there to be insight into the morally good and, thus, ethical responsibility, the agent has to realize that the demand on her action holds for everybody who would be in the same situation.

A lion, therefore, is neither good nor evil, while he might regularly exhibit different forms of prosocial, even altruistic, cross-species behavior. However, if a lion, say, refrains from brutally devouring a Gazelle, he does not thereby come to the conclusion that he should consider vegetarianism or develop hunting methods in the future that are less brutal.

SENSE, NONSENSE, AND SUBJECTIVITY

What is special about practical subjectivity, as we know it from our own human case, is precisely that we can come to know that there is something that we ought to do such that everybody else ought to do it too, and for the same reason. This is why moral insight, ethics, cannot be reduced to empathy or any other form of feeling that helps us to refrain from harmful behavior towards other sentient, conscious living beings. While there can certainly be moral feelings and an associated training of our moral sensibility, these feelings (or the lack thereof) are not what makes us moral.

The reality of moral judgment in action is always going to be a complex web of moral feelings, pure practical reasons, conjectures, and delusions. Just like theoretical subjectivity, practical subjectivity cannot be completely purified by transforming us into moral saints. A moral saint would be someone who, out of a necessity of their character, always does the morally good. A moral saint either does good or acts neutrally. However, a moral saint would not be a practical *subject,* as he would be free from mistakes and, thus, incapable of choosing between good and evil. If one knows in theory that "φ is evil" is true but is not capable of φ-ing, one is not a practical subject but, at best, a divine, distant observer of earthly affairs.

It is constitutive of practical subjectivity that we become acquainted with the good by committing evil acts. If the language of good and evil sounds too dramatic, one could also simply say that we become acquainted with what we ought to do on moral grounds by doing what is morally reprehensible. Thus, it is not a coincidence that we teach moral insight to our children on the basis of gently making them aware of their moral mistakes. We teach them, by way of example, not to harm themselves or others, to control their emotional outbursts, to occupy other sentient beings' standpoints, to see themselves as members of social systems in which they occupy roles that other people can also occupy, and so forth. If children never made moral mistakes, they would never come to grasp the nature of the good.

Hence, there would not be any moral insight if there were no moral mistakes. The deplorable existence of evil is both a *ratio cognoscendi* and a *ratio essendi* of the good in human society. For the good would not be what it is if we were not able to recognize it as such. Recognizing the good for what it is requires going through moral mistakes, which is why any stable

SUBJECTIVITY

human society that tries to make moral progress needs practices of moral forgiveness in order to introduce human agents into the "kingdom of ends."[96] The *kingdom of ends* is the community of human moral agents into which we are introduced as soon as we are judgeable in light of the norm of the good.

Humans are the paradigmatic members of the kingdom of ends. For we are the only species of living beings unambiguously known to us whose members are typically capable of grasping the good as such. Grasping the good as such involves articulating linguistically coded normative claims directed at humans. We want ourselves and others to accord with what we recognize as morally good regardless of their specific constitution, unless we have good reasons to believe that they are currently or generally not able to grasp the good as such. For this reason, we do not include non-human animals in the kingdom of ends, which does not mean that we somehow denigrate them. Many living beings (including some humans) who are not capable of grasping the good as such are clearly recipients of ethical attention, of caregiving, respect, and different degrees of dignity, which range from the dignity of being endowed with some form of sentience to full-blown human dignity.

Now, being in a position to recognize the good for what it is involves being wrong and transgressing the boundaries of the good. No epistemic agent (no thinker) ever knows absolutely everything accessible from within her horizon. Otherwise, she would cease to be a subjective thinker and, thus, not know anything at all. A vessel of objective knowledge is not just a thinker, but at most a kind of flawless library. *Mutatis mutandis,* no human moral agent ever only does what she ought to do for moral reasons. In one way or another, in one instance or another, we all deviate from the good—sometimes knowingly, sometimes due to tragic circumstances.

Tragic circumstances are social or other material conditions on individual agency that make it practically impossible for an agent to do the good. If there are ethical dilemmas in the strict sense of contradictory moral demands, they confront an agent with a tragedy, where a *tragedy* is a situation in which the agent both ought to φ and ought not to φ so that both φ-ing and not φ-ing amount to violations of the good.

Having said that, I believe that tragedies are precisely not ethical dilemmas in that they undercut the conditions of responsibility and accountability for an individual human moral agent. If a human moral agent is not capable of doing the good without thereby doing evil, she is not free to do the good and, thus, cannot do the good at all. If she cannot do the good, she cannot do evil either, though she might be forced by the social and material circumstances to harm herself or others in ways that would count as evil if she were appropriately accountable for her actions.

The kingdom of ends is not an ontological island. As human moral agents we are embedded in the hypercomplexity of fos. The good provides an orientation that transcends our actual situation within given fos. Its normativity is future-oriented in that it demands one to do something that has not yet been done and to revise past moral mistakes. Action is part of reality and, thus, implicated in its ontological texture.

The hypercomplexity of fos manifests itself in ethics in the form of our partial individual and collective ignorance concerning what we ought to do in socially or otherwise complex scenarios. Here, an action scenario is complex if the morally relevant aspects of the circumstances remain partially hidden to the agent and if the outcome of the action is strongly uncertain and unpredictable due to morally relevant social parameters that are not within the reach of the action situation. For this reason, as is well known from behavioral economics, psychology, and so forth, complex action situations increase the probability that individual agents deviate from ethical norms. Complex action scenarios disperse responsibility and generate forms of potentially harmful social opacity.

Like in the epistemological case, in ethics we should not be searching for pure capacities, such as the freedom to form intentions that we can then evaluate in light of norms, before we exercise them. What Kant calls "the will" or "pure practical reason," therefore captures practical reality as little as his description of the categorial furniture of the human mind does the full range of our conceptual capacities. There just is no pure reason—a fact that should not be read as a commitment to the idea that all knowledge is empirical or that all agency is impure, guided by the vested interests of the agent.

Kant's and others' idealizations at most manage to get epistemic and ethical normativity in view as a demand on our exercises to reform them in light of recognizable mistakes. This fact about us (our finitude, if you will) is not a deplorable weakness of human nature nor does it deserve to be labeled "radical evil."[97] Being wrong and doing evil are conditions of knowledge and the good: they cannot be eradicated without undermining the normative, desirable goals of getting it right and doing good.

This is not a normative justification of specific mistakes and short-comings, only an ontologically grounded justification of the very existence of mistakes. Mistakes remain what they are, something that ought not to exist and, therefore, a call for epistemological and ethical reform.

CONCLUSION

THROUGHOUT THIS BOOK, I have offered an innovative account of fallibility. According to this account, the subject of fallibility is not a given conceptual capacity instantiated by rational animals, but rather an individual subject who is never in a position to choose between more or less clearly delineated alternatives, as if a knowledge claim would result from a rational choice between endorsing p or $\sim p$. Here, I build upon a form of realism in social ontology I developed elsewhere, according to which human subjectivity is a product of human action coordination and, in that material sense, social.[1]

The sociality of human thought flows from the social production and reproduction conditions of the kinds of animals we are. It does not result from mutual mind reading and recognition between a plurality of self-conscious agents but precedes the realizations of such high-level exercises on the ground floor level of the human. Thus, there is a connection between the depth of sociality, so to speak, and fallibility. We are social prior to the emergence of higher-level performances of our cognitive architecture (such as having a theory of mind, an attitude towards the mental lives of others).[2]

By virtue of primitive, ground-level sociality, we find ourselves in the situation of a literal divergence of sense. Others perceive things differently

CONCLUSION

from us by occupying a different perspective. Sociality and disagreement hang together in such a way that we become acquainted with our subjectivity in light of the fact that we are actually corrected by others.[3]

As long as we are around, as long as we are alive, we make mistakes we can only eliminate piecemeal in the context of historically evolving practices of socially orchestrated mutual correction. Subjects alone can correct themselves only in light of incoming evidence if they have undergone initiation into such practices. Initiation into practices presupposes going through a series of mistakes, ideally controlled by advanced institutions that allow us to avoid past mistakes and to learn how to overcome epistemic and ethical obstacles by way of examples and experiments that do not undermine the conditions of our transmission of accumulated objective knowledge.

The correction of someone's beliefs thereby differs from a mere adaptation to one's environment. If a living system (be it a bacterium, a complex non-human organism, or a part of our nervous system) changes its course due to a subliminal, in-principle non-conscious adjustment to its environment, it does not thereby always correct itself in the sense envisaged here. We do not do everything we do because we are believers. Some of the things we do happen to and with us in manifold ways associated with our status as organic agents. They are not subjective but are objective occurrences that sometimes support and sometimes counteract the higher life-form of our subjectivity.

Practical negativity in the manifold modes of being wrong cannot be adequately accounted for if we think of being wrong merely as a kind of defective exercise (a mere privation) of an otherwise well-functioning capacity or series of capacities. Rather, the human potential for knowledge, which plays such a formative role in the increasingly rapid transformation of the modern public sphere by means of scientific and engineering progress, necessarily leads to an increase in subjectivity and, therefore, a dissemination of ways of being wrong. In this way, the theory of subjectivity offered here promises to address the paradox that scientific and engineering progress in our society constantly creates new ways of being wrong, which are increasingly politically and socioeconomically dangerous and detrimental.

Objective knowledge and moral facts can be obscured by systems of belief formation through which negative epistemological and practical

SENSE, NONSENSE, AND SUBJECTIVITY

phenomena spread. In this concluding part, I want to focus on three of them: ideology, propaganda, and ignorance. These concepts designed to capture sociopolitically salient distortions of reality serve as case studies for a theory of practical negativity based on the account of subjectivity offered in this book.

I will look at practical negativity through the lens of the assumption that our digital age has added novel layers of social complexity to what we call society. In particular, due to hitherto unknown techno-scientific and socioeconomic advances, concepts such as knowledge, reality, moral facts, justification, truth, and belief have come under somewhat paradoxical pressure: Thanks to the rapid accumulation of epistemic and social successes in advanced modern knowledge societies, we were able to broadcast information and data throughout the vast majority of human social formations. What has thus been broadcasted online amplifies human and, thus, subjective judgment for the simple reason that the information and data that are shared are models of human thinking, acting, judging, and self-representation. To the extent that actual episodes of thinking, acting, judging, and self-representing are subjective, they contain prima facie hidden modes of being wrong that are amplified through massive distribution.

In short, the omnipresence of bullshit engines such as ChatGPT and of digital ideology, propaganda, and other "lie machines"[4] in our digital media influences the unfolding of social complexity. Throughout modernity, advanced institutions have generated networks of socioeconomic transactions that no one can oversee, predict, or steer into a single direction. Social complexity undermines the idea of overall control—even in principle. Thus, we cannot even know what an ideal theory of a perfect social contract would look like without bringing in assumptions from our ultimately unfathomable position within the highly dynamic fos of social complexity. There cannot be an ideal blueprint for a society compared to which our social actualities fall short because we cannot even hope to achieve an understanding of those actualities that allows us to see how everything in the social world is connected.

Socially disruptive information technology (most prominently social media) and the digital mapping and transformation of gigantic patterns of socioeconomic transaction were made possible by scientific and technological progress that could not have been anticipated by any previously

CONCLUSION

available account of the human mind. Thus, we need to update our self-portrait as specifically minded, human subjects in the face of such contingent transformations. For this reason, we cannot ever hope to produce a complete and fully systematic list of sources of error. The open-ended taxonomy of modes of being wrong includes illusion, delusion, hallucination, falsity, error, misperception, ideology, propaganda, ignorance, fake news, and contemporary forms of political rhetoric.

Let us focus on ideology, propaganda, and ignorance as social formations of practical negativity consecutively. Like many other modes of being wrong, they share the feature that there is a *pejorative,* a *neutral,* and even a *positive* use of terms referring to them. On the one hand, ideology, propaganda, and ignorance can be seen as social pathologies, distorted representations, forms of false consciousness, the production and reproduction of systemically harmful blind spots. On the other hand, there are neutral and positive uses of these terms. Ideology can be seen as a constitutive element of the public sphere. It can create social cohesion by contributing to the realization of desirable political ends.[5] When we think of propaganda, political uses of propaganda (from Hitler and Mussolini to Putin and Trump) typically come to mind. This is the negative use of propaganda for which Jason Stanley has provided a recent analysis.[6] In this vein, one can think of contemporary propaganda in the wake of Trump, Putin, and others in terms of Harry Frankfurt's influential notion of bullshit, according to which bullshit is a type of discourse for which truth and falsity do not matter at all.[7] Yet, critiquing contemporary propaganda in the negative sense and detecting bullshit (a term that does not have a positive use) should not mislead us into ignoring the positive dimension of modern modes of steering public opinion. Not every form of political rhetoric (for which fact-stating is always only one part of the agenda) is harmful. While the negative use of "propaganda" is currently more widespread, its use in the context of modern advertisement, public relations, and, traditionally, for the spread of (allegedly) truthful religious doctrines still resonates in contemporary usages within propaganda studies, a form of research not yet connected to the philosophical critique of propaganda (in the pernicious sense).[8]

In this conclusion, I want to argue that ideology, propaganda, and ignorance are inevitable features of socially complex systems. Socially complex systems involve constellations of many subjects and, thus, of indefinitely many modes of being wrong. There is no central agency (the state, science, reason, or anything else) that would allow us to replace negotiations of complex subjective interests by a mere reference to objective knowledge. This is, of course, not a justification or endorsement of ideology, propaganda, and ignorance in the pernicious sense. My goal is rather to point out that the critique of ideology, propaganda, and ignorance at some point or other involves value judgments and, thus, subjective positions that in turn always have to be subjected to the type of critical evaluation used in detecting discursive shortcomings in one's political opponent. When it comes to conditions of social complexity, there is no way of transcending this position. For this reason, we need an account of negative epistemological and practical phenomena that does not ignore the positive contribution of the source of these phenomena to modern, socially complex arrangements.

Mutatis mutandis for ignorance, which not only designates an irresponsible lack of knowledge that can be produced and reproduced by nefarious sociopolitical actors (using tools of ideology, propaganda, fake news, manipulation, disinformation, etc.) but also refers to insight into our constitutive fallibility. The fact that we do not know which parts of our scientific and non-scientific knowledge claims are successful and which will turn out to be failures can be deemed both a neutral diagnosis of our fallibility and even a positive contribution to the value of epistemic humility.[9]

The fact that there are these uses associated with different (ethical and sociopolitical) evaluations of these modes of being wrong is evidence for the presence of subjectivity: Insofar as subjects make knowledge claims that cannot constitutively get reality right, we ought to value the social practices of generating dissent. For, we can only evaluate the quality of a given knowledge claim through a variety of competing knowledge claims that make subjects aware of their socially orchestrated corrigibility. By contrast, the exclusively pejorative usages of "ideology," "propaganda," and "ignorance" are typically part of critical diagnoses of modern society and its digital modes of mass communication. These critical diagnoses serve the function of getting distortions of social space into view. While this is a laudable endeavor, its shortcoming has been pointed out time and again: The critique of ideology, propa-

CONCLUSION

ganda, and ignorance is incapable of designing a concrete, realistic, and desirable alternative to the allegedly deluded status quo without resorting to its own brand of ideology, propaganda, and systemic ignorance concerning the socioeconomic conditions of the type of academic and political knowledge claims within which it unfolds. Any staunchly critical description of modern societies relies on a special position within modern society—a position that ideally serves the goal of improving social conditions by achieving a certain immanent distance from within the status quo.[10]

Ideology

In general, I propose to think of ideology in terms of false consciousness. Here (unlike in the Marxist and neo-Marxist tradition), "false consciousness" does not necessarily refer to the idea of a misguided and harmful (false) representation of the socioeconomic, material relations and overall conditions of the production of goods relevant to human survival and flourishing. Rather, "false consciousness" is to be taken as a failure in self-consciousness. Specifically, my use of "ideology" intends to pick out the notion that we have a subjective and, thus, constitutively partially erroneous conception of ourselves as conscious. We represent our status as specifically minded animals in terms of mentalistic and noetic vocabulary that serves the function of articulating a self-conception of humans in opposition to other types of denizens of natural reality. We thereby come to grasp ourselves as distinct from non-human animals, plants, inorganic nature, viruses, etc. and locate our position within the largest possible frame of existence accessible from our position. In short, we produce images of the human together with large-scale worldviews in order to come to terms with our status as conscious.

In this regard, I have argued throughout the book that worldviews and conceptions of consciousness are prone to global and local confusion and, thus, produce nonsense. This nonsense becomes harmful as soon as we treat it as an extension of the realm of sense into a comprehensive scientific conception of "the human place in the cosmos," to borrow a famous phrase of Max Scheler.[11] Contemporary paradigmatic examples of ideology in that sense abound in the popular science literature on how to interpret

213

physics in light of our existential need of finding meaning in the universe, of deciphering life, consciousness, intelligence, and so forth based on speculative extensions of actual scientific knowledge.[12]

To be sure, one might suspect that ideology in the literal sense of "false consciousness" (or rather "false self-consciousness") could be read as a symptom of ideology in the traditional sense such that the idea of science as a guide to the meaning of life, consciousness, and the human place in the cosmos would turn out to serve the function of screening agents off from their socioeconomic, material conditions. By distorting the nature of consciousness in virtue of thinking of it in terms of a piece of nature open to scientific investigation, one easily gets distracted from the socioeconomic realities. This might even be one route to extremist ethical ideologies such as *longtermism,* which is willing to sacrifice the actual well-being of masses of living and near-future human generations for the sake of a fictional long-term goal of the ultimate flourishing of specifically human intelligent achievements.[13]

Having said that, the notion of ideology as false self-consciousness is more general than the strictly Marxist application of it to a diagnosis of the systemic mechanisms of distortion operative in a given society. In particular, it allows for a critique of the Marxist notion in that it points out that the actual Marxist conception of human species-being is itself an ideological self-representation of human mindedness and, therefore, subject to its own critical tools.

Ideology is a particular mode of being wrong. It involves falsity with respect to ourselves as subjects of knowledge claims. For this reason, it is epistemically blameworthy. At the same time, we cannot step outside of our skins to identify a purified self-consciousness that could replace ideological illusions. Qua conscious agents, we embody an objectively existing illusion without which we could not achieve self-consciousness.

Propaganda

Like ideology, propaganda has a complicated relationship to truth. Historically, propaganda originates in the sector of public relations, advertisement, and overall behavioral control under conditions of modern mass societies.[14] It predates the infamous use of propaganda tools by evil actors associated with modern totalitarianism and contemporary authoritarian rule. Following Bussemer's proposal for a "super-definition" of propaganda, we can introduce the notion of propaganda "as the usually media-based formation of behaviorally relevant opinions and attitudes of political or social big groups though symbolic communication," which leads to the "production of public awareness at the service of specific interests."[15] Bussemer adds that propaganda subordinates truth to efficiency and that it naturalizes its messages, meaning that it presents its normative recommendations as scientific insights.[16]

In sum, propaganda is a mode of distributing often wide-ranging beliefs concerning human and non-human reality with the goal of action coordination and behavioral attitude adjustment to a proposition or theory with societal relevance that the propagandist takes to be both true and, more importantly, efficient for achieving a desirable political or socioeconomic goal. In that sense, vaccine campaigns during a pandemic are propaganda that some interpret as positive (those who focus on the beneficial health effects and known efficacy of a given vaccine) and others as negative (those who either have deviating beliefs concerning the efficacy of a given vaccine or even vaccines in general as well as those who believe that vaccine campaigns have unwanted collateral damage effects such as provoking anti-vaccine communities and other potentially dangerous social dissenters).

Rightly insisting on certain facts concerning the efficacy of vaccines, the reality of human-made climate change, or the destructive side effects of modern industrial capitalism is not free from its own illusions. For instance, all vaccines have some negative side effects for some people, and human-made climate change, made possible by modern industrial capitalism, among other things, results from our modern achievements of alleviating many millions from poverty. These examples only serve to point out that ideology, propaganda, and ignorance in our digital age are enormous factors of social complexity that cannot be reduced to a single type of explanation designed by an in-principle omniscient being, the scientific subject who simply tries to translate scientific knowledge of the human place in the cosmos into concrete policy. For, as desirable as this idea of a truly scientific technocracy might sound to some academic ears, it is entirely illusory when we face global challenges to humanity as a whole. That should not make us epistemic pessimists or cultural critics of the unsurmountable obstacle of the dangers of a post-truth era. The very idea of a post-truth era in which facts matter less and less and politically manipulated emotions take over is itself an ideological fantasy. Against this trend, which is part and parcel of the illusion that we live in some unified era or other (be it the scientific, digital, modern, postmodern, post-truth, or any other age), we should mobilize the virtue of epistemic humility. Identifying something as "propaganda" or "propagandistic," therefore, need not amount to rejecting it wholesale as false, manipulative, or in some other way dangerous. While this certainly holds of propaganda for politically harmful causes (the paradigm being war propaganda by aggressors designed to steer public opinion in favor of an evil cause), it cannot generalize to propaganda as such, as the mainstream of propaganda studies has been pointing out. It all depends on the specific uses of propaganda as well as on the details of the ethics of politically orchestrated belief formation in modern mass societies that cannot be condemned wholesale, as it has had many positive effects—including the wide distribution of largely correct information and normative recommendations in light of defeasible scientific evidence.

Again, we encounter the phenomenon that we cannot generalize the pejorative notion of propaganda to such an extent that we begin to suspect modern democratic mass societies as being reducible to a "spectacle," "simulacrum," "context of delusion," or even a kind of systemic, plutocratic conspiracy controlled by capitalism's stakeholders. Such a generalization ignores the presence of subjectivity and, thus, of fallibility in the very constitution of the public sphere(s).

The digital age is no exception to this rule. On the contrary, it exacerbates the conditions of subjectivity by allowing everybody to amplify their idiosyncrasy in terms of the algorithmic digital infrastructure of social media in particular, and of smartphones and the internet in general. In that sense, we can think of the digital revolution of the twenty-first century (which gradually started, of course, with new electronic mass media in the twentieth century) not as a pathological distortion of the consensus-, truth-, and reality-oriented public sphere under the control of informed gatekeepers, but rather as a manifestation of the constitutive function of dissent, subjectivity, illusion, and the manifold modes of being wrong for the achievement of action coordination.[17]

CONCLUSION

In short, we need to overcome the illusion of a possible illusion-free public sphere. The digital age does not aggravate an already problematic condition, but rather adds to social complexity and, thereby, contributes both to negative social disruption and to a dissemination of dissent. Hence, it is not a coincidence that moral progress and disinformation, emancipation and domination, both flourish under conditions of the digital age that can be seen as one factor of the novel phenomenon of polarization with its potentially harmful consequences for our capacities of mitigating the negative effects of dissent as socially disruptive.[18]

The right kind of social epistemology accepts both that knowers are subjects (and, thus, essentially wrong about some thing or other even in contexts of successful knowledge claims) and that they are inextricably bound up with the production and maintenance of social facts. Social epistemology must not dissolve the subject in its structural relations to other subjects—a reductionist paradigm often proven to be unfeasible.[19]

Ignorance

From the standpoint of the standard analysis of propositional knowledge, it seems straightforward to think of ignorance as a shortcoming concerning either truth, justification, or belief. In this context, ignorance could arise (1) from either not knowing the truth but believing something that is false, (2) from merely believing a true proposition while having a wrong justification, or (3) from not even believing a true proposition to which one ought to have a relevant doxastic attitude.[20]

As in the case of positive epistemology (i.e., epistemology dealing with the good case), negative epistemology of ignorance thereby tends to ignore the role of the subject in the formula "S knows that p" or "S is ignorant concerning p." By contrast, the New Realist theory of subjectivity as fallibility proposed in this book thinks of knowledge claims (whether successful or not) and, thus, of ignorance as phenomena within the full-blown reality of the unfolding of a subject's mental life. Ignorance is not a more or less accidental shortcoming such that we could devise methods of epistemic grooming to contain or even eliminate it.

SENSE, NONSENSE, AND SUBJECTIVITY

Subjectivity is essentially involved in nonsense. Due to the omnipresence of field confusion in the mental life of subjects, subjects capable of making knowledge claims can never guarantee the success of their claims in terms of a propositional analysis of their beliefs that are relevant for knowledge. As I argued throughout the book, this explains our fallibility without misleading us into a skeptical denial of the very possibility (and existence) of the full-blown case of reflexively available knowledge (including knowledge that one knows something or other). It also explains the positive value of ignorance. Grasping ourselves as subjects and, thus, as people who essentially get some things wrong (without being in a position to conclusively determine which of our beliefs are true and which false) makes us humble. Epistemic humility precisely differs from skepticism in that it neither denies the possibility nor the reality of knowledge. It merely accepts that knowledge cannot be achieved if we expect absolute guarantees for its success.

Ignorance is constitutive for successful knowledge claims in that subjects are bound to remain ignorant concerning some feature of their knowledge claim or other. We cannot guarantee that all conditions for a successful knowledge claim are met simply in virtue of knowing that we know certain things. As soon as we dig our heels deeper into the conceptual and nonconceptual ramifications of the social and mental reality of knowledge, we will encounter blind spots—a fact that comes out easily if we recognize how we typically fall short of having a full, clear, and distinct grasp of all concepts involved in the articulation and defense of a knowledge claim.

This is not a defense of the bliss of ignorance, let alone a justification of a blatant failure to recognize a truth or the stubborn rejection of facts by various forms of blameworthy denialism that indeed haunt the public sphere. However, the theory of subjectivity advanced here points out that there is no position from which to critique ideology, propaganda, and ignorance that would be entirely free from the shortcomings that are easier to identify in those who disagree with us on fundamental issues than in ourselves.

In this book I have been arguing that epistemic humility is grounded in a recognition of reality's hypercomplexity. Reality exceeds everything we will ever be able to grasp in terms of our practices of propositional sensemaking. Reality is objectively confusing, and it is confused at least insofar as we come to see our subjectivity as an integral part of reality. Nonsense cannot and, hence, need not be eradicated. Negative epistemological and practical phenomena are part of the peculiar "fate of human reason," as Kant pointed out at the beginning of his *Critique of Pure Reason*.[21]

That subjects constitutively fail in one respect or other, in both the theoretical and the practical realm, is no reason for pessimism. It is just a constitutive fact of subjectivity with which we will have to live as long as subjects are around who are capable of the highest achievements of the true, the good, and the beautiful. To be someone, a subject, thus, cannot generally count as a failure, as skepticism urges. It cannot count as an achievement either, as the vision of epistemological and ethical perfectionism suggests, according to which subjectivity is something we somehow have to achieve. Subjectivity is an ambivalent given; it manifests itself in the free exercise of capacities that never exist in a pure unactualized state. The human mind is always already part of reality and, thereby, involved in its heterogeneous, chaotic, uncertain, and ultimately unpredictable unfolding.

NOTES

Introduction

1. Aristotle, "Metaphysics," in *The Complete Works of Aristotle: Revised Oxford Edition,* vol. 2, ed. Jonathan Barnes, trans. William David Ross (Princeton, NJ: Princeton University Press, 1991), I1, 980a21.

2. For an account of knowledge as "non-accidentally true belief," see Andrea Kern, *Sources of Knowledge: On the Concept of a Rational Capacity for Knowledge,* trans. Daniel Smyth (Cambridge, MA: Harvard University Press, 2017), 1.

3. See Naomi Oreskes and Erik M. Conway, *Merchants of Doubt: How a Handful of Scientists Obscured the Truth on Issues from Tobacco Smoke to Global Warming* (New York: Bloomsbury, 2010); Naomi Oreskes, *Why Trust Science?* (Princeton, NJ: Princeton University Press, 2019); Quassim Cassam, Ian J. Kidd, and Heather Battaly, eds., *Vice Epistemology* (London: Routledge, 2021); Quassim Cassam, *Conspiracy Theories* (London: Polity, 2019); Quassim Cassam, *Vices of the Mind: From the Intellectual to the Political* (Oxford: Oxford University Press, 2019); Jason Stanley, *How Propaganda Works* (Princeton, NJ: Princeton University Press, 2015); Wayne Le Cheminant and John M. Parrish, eds., *Manipulating Democracy: Democratic Theory, Political Psychology, and Mass Media* (New York: Routledge, 2011); Jonathan Auerbach and Russ Castronovo, eds., *The Oxford Handbook of Propaganda Studies* (Oxford: Oxford University Press, 2013); Philip N. Howard, *Lie Machines: How to Save Democracy from Troll Armies, Deceitful Robots, Junk News Operations, and Political Operatives* (New Haven, CT: Yale University Press, 2020); Maurizio Ferraris, *Postverità e altri enigmi: Quanta verità c'è nella postverità* (Bologna: il Mulino, 2017); Lee McIntire, *Post-Truth* (Cambridge, MA: MIT Press, 2018).

4. In epistemology, there is a growing literature on fallibilism beyond the narrower realm of natural science where Popper's falsificationism is still prominent. See, for instance, Jessica Brown, *Fallibilism: Evidence and Knowledge* (Oxford: Oxford University Press, 2018); Geert Keil, *Wenn ich*

NOTES TO PAGES 4–8

micht nicht irre: Ein Versuch über die menschliche Fehlbarkeit (Stuttgart: Reclam Verlag, 2019). This recent work begins to point out that the bearer of fallibility is the subject of knowledge claims and not their knowledge that, qua good case, cannot go wrong. Subjects can get it right or wrong, while the propositions they endorse through their knowledge claims can be true or false. Knowledge is not in the category of things that can be wrong that does not make the person who makes a knowledge claim infallible. For a defense of the constitutive non-iterability of knowledge (i.e., the fact that "*S* knows that *p*" only in special cases, if at all, entails "*S* knows that *S* knows that *p*") as a constitutive conceptual contribution to our status as fallible, see Markus Gabriel, *The Limits of Epistemology,* trans. Alex Englander (Cambridge: Polity, 2020), 95–101.

5. Thanks to Jocelyn Benoist and Harald Atmanspacher for pointing out to me that getting it right is tied to the reality of knowledge claims and should, therefore, be distinguished from the mental state of actual knowledge.

6. Notice that the widespread way of reducing falsity to non-truth by stipulating that if *p* is true, then ~*p* is false, does not clarify falsity, but only stipulates that under conditions of bivalence the negation of a true proposition produces a false proposition. Yet, negation by itself cannot account for falsity, as negated propositions can, of course, be just as true as propositions without a negation symbol attached to them.

7. Markus Gabriel, *Fields of Sense: A New Realist Ontology* (Edinburgh: Edinburgh University Press, 2015).

8. Gottlob Frege, "On Sense and Reference," in *Translations from the Philosophical Writings of Gottlob Frege,* ed. and trans. Peter Thomas Geach and Max Black (Oxford: Blackwell, 1980), 56–78.

9. For an overview, see Markus Gabriel, ed., *Der Neue Realismus* (Berlin: Suhrkamp, 2014); Dominik Finkelde and Paul Livingston, *Idealism, Relativism, and Realism: New Essays on Objectivity beyond the Analytic-Continental Divide* (Berlin: De Gruyter, 2020); issue on "The New Realism," ed. Mario de Caro and Maurizio Ferraris, *The Monist* 98, no. 2 (2015).

10. This corresponds to what Anton Friedrich Koch has called "hermeneutic realism," a form of realism that puts fallible subjectivity at the core of philosophical methodology and recognizes its ineliminable presence in any respectable account of what there is. See Anton Friedrich Koch, *Hermeneutischer Realismus* (Tübingen: Mohr Siebeck, 2016), and his magnum opus *Versuch über Wahrheit und Zeit* (Paderborn: Mentis, 2006). *Mutatis mutandis* the theory of truth has to be embedded in a theory of getting it right and, thus, of objectivity that, since it has been at the center stage of the mainstream of epistemology, will not be the focus of this book.

11. Plato, *Theaetetus,* trans. John McDowell, with an introduction and notes by Lesley Brown (Oxford: Oxford University Press, 2014), 199b 1–9.

12. For a reconstruction of the landscapes of skepticism (ancient and modern), see Markus Gabriel, *The Limits of Epistemology,* trans. Alex En-

glander (Cambridge: Polity, 2019), and Markus Gabriel, *Skeptizismus und Idealismus in der Antike* (Berlin: Suhrkamp, 2009).

13. In Markus Gabriel, *Der Mensch als Tier: Warum wir trotzdem nicht in die Natur passen* (Berlin: Ullstein, 2022), I develop the idea that humans are the paradigmatic animals, that our self-conception as animals constitutes the meaning of "animal," whereas the so-called non-human animals are lifeforms that cannot be thought of as embodying a unified concept of animality. The concept of an animal suffers from the weakness that it has been designed (at least since Aristotle) to think of humans as animals of a particular kind, such as rational or political animals. If other, non-human animals count as animals, there would have to be a notion of an animal that is common to both humans and non-human animals. But that notion would be the notion of a human animal without human specificity, hence, a deficient human being. Thus, the concept of an animal inherits the constitutive unclarity of the notion of a human that thinks of itself as part of a broader animal kingdom. The relationship between animality and subjectivity is a thorny issue beyond the bounds of this book. It will suffice to point out that human thinkers, knowers, and agents are animals endowed with subjectivity. Thanks to Carla Franciska Spielmann for pointing out to me that it ultimately matters for the theory of subjectivity that our own animality is, to say the least, complicated, such that the theory of subjectivity and of human animality are conceptually interwoven. For the purposes of this book, it is sufficient to think of subjectivity as a feature of specifically minded animals without providing a full account of the relationship between animality and subjectivity.

14. For a critique of the idea of metaphysics as investigating the "world without spectators" (as well as the world as such), see Markus Gabriel, *Why the World Does Not Exist,* trans. Gregory S. Moss (Cambridge: Polity, 2015), 15. The metaphor of a "cosmic exile" is due to Willard Van Orman Quine, *Word and Object* (Cambridge, MA: MIT Press, 1960), 275.

15. For an elaboration of a novel type of dual-aspect monism that draws on the ontology of fields of sense, see Harald Atmanspacher and Dean Rickles, *Dual-Aspect Monism and the Deep Structure of Meaning* (New York: Routledge, 2022).

I. Sense

1. Zed Adams has rightly been pointing out to me that there are unclear constraints on a controlled use of the metaphor of a perspective beyond the literal realm of optical analysis. On this see James Elkins, *The Poetics of Perspective* (Ithaca, NY: Cornell University Press, 1994). There are other influential visual metaphors used in epistemology and the philosophy of mind to draw boundaries to knowledge, such as point of view, standpoint, visual field, or horizon. Thanks to Elisabeth Camp, Noël Carroll, Hans Ulrich

NOTES TO PAGES 10-15

Gumbrecht, Paul Kottman, Stephen Neale, and Joel Snyder for discussion of the vague boundary between metaphor and literal use of visual terminology in accounts of perceptual and social knowledge during the 3rd meeting of the Institute of Philosophy and the New Humanities at The New School for Social Research in September 2022.

2. Immanuel Kant, *Critique of Pure Reason,* ed. and trans. Paul Guyer and Allen W. Wood (Cambridge: Cambridge University Press, 1998), A363, A364, A659 / B687.

3. On the radiation theory of perceptual modes of presentation, see Markus Gabriel, *The Power of Art* (Cambridge: Polity, 2020).

4. See Markus Gabriel, *Fields of Sense: A New Realist Ontology* (Edinburgh: Edinburgh University Press, 2015), chap. 13.

5. While we know that there are many unknowns, we are in touch with the unknowns by way of the *de dicto* characterization of the unknowns as unknowable in one way or another. The unknowables really are unknowable; their unknowability is one of their ways to be, i.e., a (actually the only) sense through which they appear to us.

6. Markus Gabriel, *The Meaning of Thought,* trans. Alex Englander (Cambridge: Polity, 2020), chap. 1.

7. For an account of primitive accuracy or veridicality conditions that sets in at the lowest possible layers, see the monumental Tyler Burge, *Origins of Objectivity* (Oxford: Oxford University Press, 2010).

8. Carla Franciska Spielmann has made me aware of the fact that the concept of reality I am using here is potentially deceptive in that it serves a function analogous to the notion of the world or even the external world as a sum total of mind-independent items and events in the non-subjective environment of subjects. As the vocabulary of FOS is unfolded throughout the book, it should become clearer that instead of a unified "reality" we should think of fos populated by objects when we characterize the various object domains of objective thought. For more, see the section "Reality: Why It Is Roughly What It Seems."

9. Hubert Dreyfus and Charles Taylor, *Retrieving Realism* (Cambridge, MA: Harvard University Press, 2015).

10. Thanks to Umrao Sethi and John Campbell for convincing me during a visiting professorship at UC Berkeley in 2013 that the relational theory of perceptual appearing can be added to FOS as an element in its theory of perceptual senses.

11. On this, see Umrao Sethi, "Diaphaneity and the Way Things Appear," in *Gabriel's New Realism,* ed. Jan Voosholz (Cham, Switzerland: Springer, forthcoming).

12. See Hilary Putnam, "Sense, Nonsense, and the Senses: An Inquiry into the Powers of the Human Mind," *Journal of Philosophy* 91, no. 9 (1994): 445–517, here 487. Putnam's influential critique of an interface model of per-

NOTES TO PAGE 16

ception presupposes that interfaces between the subjective and the objective are on the subjective side.

13. The *factual* perceptual correlation does not undermine the straightforwardly *factive* structure of propositional perceptual knowledge. If S knows that p by perceiving her environment, it follows that p is the case. If she perceives elements in a situation that does not include her perception of the situation, the content of p is not affected by the factual correlation. For this (and other reasons), there is no mystery of how we can come to know something about the external world even though our perception of it constitutively involves us.

14. I owe this formulation to Zachary Hall. Thanks for his written comments on an earlier draft of the chapters.

15. An important source of inspiration for the type of realism at stake here has been my encounter with drafts of Mark Johnston's *The Manifest* that circulated at New York University in 2005–2006. See Mark Johnston, *Saving God: Religion after Idolatry* (Princeton, NJ: Princeton University Press, 2011), which argues for the idea of reality's constitutive manifestness. It would lead too far afield here to compare this to Hegel's notion that "Geist," i.e., human mindedness, essentially is a mode of manifestation on the basis of which we come to know that reality cannot as such be separated from its knowability. See Markus Gabriel, "What Kind of an Idealist (If Any) Is Hegel?," *Hegel Bulletin* 37, no. 2 (2016): 181–208; and "Hegel's Account of Perceptual Experience in His Philosophy of Subjective Spirit," in *Hegel's Philosophy of Spirit: A Critical Guide,* ed. Marina F. Bykova (Cambridge: Cambridge University Press, 2019), 104–124.

16. Thanks to Zachary Hall for proposing the positive realist complement formulation of reality as "that to which thought is answerable" that complements the idea of a domain of entities (the real) that accounts for the failures of thinking and acting. In sum, in what follows, let "reality" cover not only the answerability of thought to the domains of entities (fields of sense) at which it is directed in a given situation but also the idea of evidence-transcendent facts, i.e., of facts whose structure is not available to *de re* thought. Answerability and corrigibility thus are both aspects of the epistemic modal category of "reality" as a concept that does not reduce the real to its relationship to thought and language. For a robust account of answerability to a world composed of both true and false facts in terms of "the realist's doctrine of answerability" (7), see Richard Gaskin, *Language, Truth, and Literature: A Defence of Literary Humanism* (Oxford: Oxford University Press, 2013), 7–11. Gaskin's approach at this level does not provide an account of the knowing and, thus, also fallible subject that is not covered by the notion of a propositionally structured "world." Remarkably, he recently moved away from the realist version of answerability to a resolute form of linguistic idealism in his *Language and the World: A Defence of Linguistic Idealism* (London: Routledge, 2022).

225

NOTES TO PAGES 17–19

17. A concept introduced by Quentin Meillassoux, *After Finitude: An Essay on the Necessity of Contingency,* trans. Ray Brassier (London: Continuum, 2008), 5. For an attempt to clarify the notion, see Gabriel, *Fields of Sense,* 284–288.

18. On the particular worry concerning a focus on the human standpoint as reflexive starting point of a thoroughly realist treatment of object-object relations, see Graham Harman, *Object-Oriented Ontology: A New Theory of Everything* (London: Pelican Books, 2018).

19. Recently, Jocelyn Benoist has objected against FOS that reality is a category that essentially differs from anything we can hope to find in the realm of sense. Reality, for him, is, as it were, the thickness of being. The realm of sense, according to Benoist, consists of norms that can be applied to a given reality. Senses are normative and can be used to deal with reality in a certain way. In this way, they categorically differ from reality, as he conceives of it. While he is right to draw a distinction between a reality that is not of our own making and to which we apply norms in order to measure it in fallible and generally defeasible ways, he is wrong in concluding that this makes senses somehow unreal. Senses are part of the historical reality that we happen to encounter as we are introduced into the realm of linguistic sense. Linguistic senses (meanings) too are objects of scientific (linguistic) investigation, such that they are what they are, namely, legitimate parts of reality. Thus, being normative and being part of reality cannot contrast on a metaphysical level. To be sure, some sense is made in that its meaning depends on social, historical practices of language use. But reference to that fact alone does not demonstrate that there is something wrong with the idea of objective, pre-linguistic senses. The fact that linguistic practices and thereby linguistic meaning is real evidently does not entail that sense is essentially linguistic. And it certainly does nothing to motivate the idea that reality used to be utterly senseless until practices of sensemaking emerged. See Jocelyn Benoist, *Toward a Contextual Realism* (Cambridge, MA: Harvard University Press, 2021), and Jocelyn Benoist, *Von der Phänomenologie zum Realismus: Die Grenzen des Sinns* (Tübingen: Mohr Siebeck, 2022).

20. For the details of an ontology based on this tenet, see Gabriel, *Fields of Sense,* chaps. 2–6.

21. For recent accounts of objective thought, see Sebastian Rödl, *Self-Consciousness and Objectivity: An Introduction to Absolute Idealism* (Cambridge, MA: Harvard University Press, 2018), and James F. Conant, "Subjective Thought," in *Parisian Notebooks, No. 3* (Paris: University of Chicago Center, 2007), 234–258.

22. For the contrast of objectivity, see Markus Gabriel, *The Limits of Epistemology,* trans. Alex Englander (Cambridge: Polity, 2019), chap. 2.

23. Markus Gabriel, "How Mind Fits into Nature—Mental Realism after Nagel," in *Parallax: The Dependence of Reality on Its Subjective Constitu-*

NOTES TO PAGES 19–23

tion, ed. Dominik Finkelde and Christoph Menke (London: Bloomsbury, forthcoming).

24. As Crispin Wright pithily puts it in a somewhat polemical remark about verificationism as "a thesis about the bounds of reality—the thought that, as it were, the totality of facts if conveniently (but mysteriously) trimmed to ensure that there is nothing there that outreaches human inquisitiveness" (*Truth and Objectivity* (Cambridge, MA: Harvard University Press, 1994), 159).

25. Markus Gabriel, ed., *Der Neue Realismus* (Berlin: Suhrkamp, 2014), 10. This is a premise that I share with Jocelyn Benoist, who also does not identify the category of reality (or reality) with a particular kind of entity (such as physical objects).

26. Huw Price, *Naturalism without Mirrors* (New York: Oxford University Press, 2011), 230.

27. See Markus Gabriel, *Why the World Does Not Exist,* trans. Gregory S. Moss (Cambridge: Polity, 2015), chap. 3, and Gabriel, *Fields of Sense,* chap. 7.

28. Here, an absolute whole is a whole such that everything without exception (thus, including the whole itself) is a (proper) part of said whole. One way of stating the no-world-view is that there is no such whole. For detailed discussions of this dimension of the no-world-view, see Markus Gabriel and Graham Priest, *Everything and Nothing* (Cambridge: Polity, 2022).

29. To be sure, there are philosophical and non-philosophical usages of the term "the world" that are not committed to the types of totality rejected by my no-world-view. For instance, we can think of a world (as in "possible world") in terms of maximally consistent sets of propositions. Or, in the phenomenological tradition, we could understand "the world" as a realm of meaningful encounters with objects, as a subject's "life-world." Thanks to one of the anonymous reviewers for pointing out that possible worlds talk can be reconstrued without assuming that worlds are totalities in the sense rejected by FOS. It would lead too far afield to see to which extend we can actually restrict the use of "world" in possible worlds semantics to a metaphysically neutral language that does not assume that the actual world together with all possible worlds makes up precisely the kind of totality repudiated by FOS. In any event, FOS does not reject the idea of wholes or bounded totalities, such as the idea of a maximally consistent set of propositions concerning a given fos, say. As the reviewer points out, on this level FOS could even be seen as advancing a form of "world pluralism" according to which worlds in this sense of maximally consistent sets of propositions are "sense-relative."

30. Martin Heidegger, "Letter on 'Humanism," in *Pathmarks,* ed. William McNeill, trans. Frank A. Capuzzi (Cambridge: Cambridge University Press, 1998), 239: "Language is the house of being."

31. See prominently John McDowell, *Perception as a Capacity for Knowledge* (Milwaukee, WI: Marquette University Press, 2011), and the further

NOTES TO PAGES 23–25

development of the idea in Irad Kimhi, *Thinking and Being* (Cambridge, MA: Harvard University Press, 2018) and Rödl, *Self-Consciousness and Objectivity.*

32. John McDowell, *Mind and World* (Cambridge, MA: Harvard University Press, 1996), 33.

33. A "boundary between cognition and the Absolute that completely separates them" (Georg Wilhelm Friedrich Hegel, *Phenomenology of Spirit,* trans. Arnold V. Miller (Oxford: Oxford University Press, 1977), 46).

34. Markus Gabriel, *Der Mensch im Mythos: Untersuchungen über Ontotheologie, Anthropologie und Selbstbewußtseinsgeschichte in Schellings "Philosophie der Mythologie"* (Berlin: Walter de Gruyter, 2006), §§4–10, and Markus Gabriel, *Skeptizismus und Idealismus in der Antike* (Frankfurt am Main: Suhrkamp, 2009), §3.

35. Kimhi, *Thinking and Being,* 99–101.

36. As I will argue in due course, this account has to be corrected too: where there are knowledge claims, the idea of a deontological difference between the claim and its success is operative. This is why Aristotle characterizes truth-apt thought (thought capable of getting it right or wrong) not as a fusion but as a "synthesis" of thoughts, *as if* they are one. See Aristotle, *On the Soul/De anima* 430a 26–28: "The thinking of indivisibles is found in those cases where falsehood is impossible: where the alternative of true or false applies, there we always find a sort of combining of objects of thought in a quasiunity" (Ἡ μὲν οὖν τῶν ἀδιαιρέτων νόησις ἐν τούτοις περὶ ἃ οὐκ ἔστι τὸ ψεῦδος, ἐν οἷς δὲ καὶ τὸ ψεῦδος καὶ τὸ ἀληθὲς, σύνθεσις τις ἤδη νοημάτων ὥσπερ ἓν ὄντων). *The Complete Works of Aristotle: Revised Oxford Edition,* vol. 1, ed. Jonathan Barnes, trans. J. A. Smith (Princeton, NJ: Princeton University Press, 1985).

37. Mark Johnston, "Objective Mind and the Objectivity of Our Minds," *Philosophy and Phenomenological Research* 75, no. 2 (2007): 233–268.

38. Johnston, *Saving God,* 132.

39. Johnston, *Saving God,* 132.

40. Including Deleuze who repeatedly points out in his *Logic of Sense* that sense is made, for instance, when he praises Freud as "the prodigious discoverer of the machinery of the unconscious by means of which sense is produced always as a function of nonsense." Gilles Deleuze, *Logic of Sense,* trans. Mark Lester with Charles Stivale, ed. Constantin V. Boundas (New York: Columbia University Press, 1990), 72.

41. Against this, see Johnston, *Saving God,* 134–136.

42. It is not a coincidence that reconstructions of Frege's theory of judgment typically ascribe some dualism or other to him. See, for instance, Maria van der Schaar, "Frege on Judgement and the Judging Agent," *Mind* 127, no. 505 (2018): 225–250. Van der Schaar argues that Frege on judgment can be understood in terms of "the distinction between an empirical and a logical notion of judgement" (226). Here, a logical notion is one that does not refer to an event in the world that can be grasped from the standpoint of the third

person. First-person, logical judgment is commitment to the truth of a proposition and, hence, as such incorrigible, which does not mean that it is infallible in that a thinker can revise her commitment after being corrected by a third person. However, that does not solve the problem as to how an empirical thinker, some actual person, can grasp concepts or full propositions for that matter. Ultimately, then, Kimhi, *Thinking and Being,* 32n11 is right in his diagnosis of a particular form of dualism in Frege: "Frege is psychologistic with respect to phenomenal episodes including sensations and images, but not with respect to thinking [here I disagree]. But this division of the mind into logical and subjective parts is itself characteristic of psycho-logical dualism." For a robust rejection of Frege's hidden psychologism, see Gabriel, *Fields of Sense,* chap. 13.

43. For more on the notion (and my rejection) of flat ontology, see Gabriel, *Fields of Sense,* chap. 9.

44. Johnston, *Saving God,* 148. He is a professed naturalist elsewhere, though, which comes as a surprise; Mark Johnston, *Surviving Death* (Princeton, NJ: Princeton University Press, 2010).

45. Thanks to Jan Voosholz for repeatedly pointing out to me that I ought to reject fusion even in the context of an account of the good case. This is also one way of aligning realism about sense with Benoist's insistence that senses are normative. If they are essentially normative, then no sense can be such that it is a one-way road to epistemic or referential success.

46. Compare the extension of the concept of a "point of view" in Adrian W. Moore, *Points of View* (Oxford: Oxford University Press, 1996), 6:

> By a point of view I shall mean a location in the broadest possible sense. Hence points of view include points in space, points in time, frames of reference, historical and cultural contexts, different roles in personal relationships, points of involvement of other kinds, and the sensory apparatuses of different species. My question, in these terms, is whether there can be thought about the world that is not from any point of view.

While this work can serve as an example for the conceptual extension of the notion of a point of view or standpoint beyond the "literal" optical case, the set of questions generated by Moore's assumption of the existence of the world as a metaphysical anchor for "talk about the unity of reality" (22) is misguided. Points of view in the extended sense are not representations of a singular, all-encompassing world from different perspectives, and the problem of objectivity of location-dependent knowledge claims is not one of the relationship between an allegedly unified reality and our different modes of representation of it.

47. Dreyfus and Taylor, *Retrieving Realism.*

48. Dreyfus and Taylor, *Retrieving Realism,* 2.

49. Markus Gabriel, "Neutral Realism," *The Monist* 98, no. 2 (2015): 181–196. Only recently did I realize that Kit Fine holds a view somewhat similar to what I dub "neutral realism" in the context of his fragmentalism in the philosophy of time. See Kit Fine, *Modality and Tense: Philosophical Papers* (Oxford: Clarendon, 2005), 279–280, 286. He too speaks of the "neutral realist" who holds the view that "reality is *irreducibly* relative" to a subjective standpoint. His arguments "in favour of some sort of neutral realism" that takes "the case of first-personal realism more seriously as a model" (286) are drawn from the philosophy of tense. It would lead too far afield here to explore the idea in detail that FOS might be motivated from within the philosophy of time.

50. Dreyfus and Taylor, *Retrieving Realism*, 93.

51. Dreyfus and Taylor, *Retrieving Realism*, 93.

52. Dreyfus and Taylor, *Retrieving Realism*, 131.

53. Dreyfus and Taylor, *Retrieving Realism*, 154.

54. Dreyfus and Taylor, *Retrieving Realism*, 154.

55. Dreyfus and Taylor, *Retrieving Realism*, 160.

56. Gabriel, *The Limits of Epistemology*, chap. 2, and Gabriel, "Neutral Realism." Despite his otherwise deflationary take on the issue of realism, Jocelyn Benoist puts this in an ontological key when he writes: "Thus we get, it seems, the basic idea of a full-blooded—as opposed to *illusory*—realism, that is, the ontological grounding of truth. What is true or not depends fundamentally on *how things are*. Let us call it *reality*. Without this point there is no realism" (Benoist, *Toward a Contextual Realism*, 172).

57. For a recent sophisticated strategy of establishing a global expressivist semantics that can be read as a defense of global anti-realism, see Price, *Naturalism without Mirrors*, chap. 12.

58. Wright, *Truth and Objectivity*, 1.

59. On this, see Markus Gabriel and Malte D. Krüger, *Was ist Wirklichkeit? Neuer Realismus und hermeneutische Theologie* (Tübingen: Mohr Siebeck, 2018), 63–77, and Gabriel, *The Meaning of Thought*, chap. 5.

60. That does precisely not rule out that there are more or less mundane unknowns as well as known unknowns (known insofar as we have identified them as problems within a given scientific enterprise) and unknown unknowns. The fact that we can grasp the thought that no one knows absolutely everything is a crucial route to the thought of reality's independence. For details on this, see Gabriel, *The Limits of Epistemology*, chap. 4.

61. For instance, it is not hard to grasp the surprisingly much-debated concept of ancestrality proposed by Quentin Meillassoux as a hallmark of realism. Ancestral facts are facts obtaining before the existence of thinkers. Thinking that some ancestral fact obtains is thinking about a reality that does not include the thinker. While the reality of the thought directed at an ancestral fact evidently includes the thinker, what she thereby thinks about is constituted by her absence. Thus, thinking one's absence in that sense requires

NOTES TO PAGES 33–36

an act of abstraction that provides the thinker with easy access to how things are regardless of her taking things to be a certain way. The act of abstraction that puts us in touch with objective senses as such does not thereby distort their content. Otherwise put, it does not secretly convert them into subjective senses. Meillassoux, *After Finitude,* 28. For a recent discussion, see G. Anthony Bruno, "Jacobi's Dare: McDowell, Meillassoux, and Consistent Idealism," in *Idealism, Relativism, and Realism: New Essays on Objectivity Beyond the Analytic-Continental Divide,* ed. Dominik Finkelde and Paul M. Livingston, (Berlin: De Gruyter, 2020), 35–56.

62. As early as in his *Philosophy of Arithmetic* (1891), Husserl tries to reconcile the objectivity of mathematical and logical concepts with psychologically realistic methods of mathematical abstraction. In this context, he rightly criticizes Frege's earlier identification of a concept with its extension; see *Philosophy of Arithmetic: Psychological and Logical Investigations with Supplementary Texts from 1887–1901,* trans. Dallas Willard (Dordrecht: Springer, 2003), 123–129, and Frege's reply in "Review of Dr. E. Husserl's *Philosophy of Arithmetic,*" trans. Eike-Henner W. Kluge, *Mind* 81, no. 323 (1972): 321–337.

63. Kimhi, *Thinking and Being,* 30–52.

64. Kimhi, *Thinking and Being,* 32n11.

65. Kimhi, *Thinking and Being,* 52.

66. Kimhi, *Thinking and Being,* 56.

67. Such a conception of the synthetic activity of a thinker who is introduced in our logical theory in order to account for the unity of logical space is reminiscent of Husserl, who is surprisingly absent from Kimhi's theory.

68. Ludwig Wittgenstein, *Remarks on the Foundations of Mathematics,* trans. Gertrude E. M. Anscombe, ed. Georg H. von Wright, Gertrude E. M. Anscombe, and Rush Rhees (Oxford: Blackwell, 1998), 84.

69. Compare the notion of a "furnishing function" in David Chalmers, "Ontological Anti-Realism," in *Metametaphysics: New Essays on the Foundations of Ontology,* ed. David Chalmers, David Manley, and Ryan Wasserman (New York: Oxford University Press, 2009), 77–129, here 104–110. As transpires from the title of his paper, Chalmers's use of the concept is part of a very different theoretical orientation. For details, see Markus Gabriel, "Grenzen des Realismus? Neuere sprachphilosophische Einwände gegen den semantischen Realismus," in *Wirklichkeit oder Konstruktion? Sprachtheoretische und interdisziplinäre Aspekte einer brisanten Alternative,* ed. Ekkehard Felder and Andreas Gardt (Berlin: De Gruyter, 2018), 45–64.

70. Which is not to say: way beyond the reach of mathematics. Mathematics might well have the conceptual resources to encode FOS, as Eduardo Luft already pointed out to me around 2011–2012. Yet, this option should not be combined with the problematic idea of foundations of mathematics, which he sees in category theory (rather than in the analytic metaphysician's preferred realm of set theory). It is entirely unsettled whether it makes sense to

NOTES TO PAGES 36–39

look for foundations of mathematics, as the realm of mathematical objects and structures during the twentieth century turned out to extend way beyond the scope of *Principia Mathematica* and related foundationalist projects (such as Frege's).

71. Technically, subjective sense can be represented as indices on fos that correspond to the semantic maneuver of inscribing the subjective into thought with recourse to indexicality.

72. Gabriel, *The Meaning of Thought.*

73. Markus Gabriel, *I am not a Brain: Philosophy of Mind for the Twenty-First Century,* trans. Christopher Turner (Cambridge: Polity, 2017).

74. Gabriel, *The Meaning of Thought.*

75. Mark Johnston, *Saving God: Religion after Idolatry* (Princeton, NJ: Princeton University Press, 2011), 132.

76. On this, see Markus Gabriel, *Fictions,* trans. Wieland Hoban (Cambridge: Polity, 2023), §§6–11.

77. Markus Gabriel, *Neo-Existentialism: How to Conceive of the Human Mind after Naturalism's Failure* (Cambridge: Polity, 2018).

78. Graham Priest, *Beyond the Limits of Thought* (Oxford: Oxford University Press, 2002), 61–78.

79. See Robert B. Brandom, *Tales of the Mighty Dead: Historical Essays in the Metaphysics of Intentionality* (Cambridge, MA: Harvard University Press, 2002), 50: "Concept P is *sense dependent* on concept Q just in case one cannot count as having grasped P unless one counts as having grasped Q. Concept P is *reference dependent* on concept Q just in case P cannot apply to something unless Q applies to something." See my discussion of this distinction in Gabriel, *The Limits of Epistemology,* chap. 15.

80. The starting point of recent debates surrounding so-called Speculative Realism (see paradigmatically Meillassoux, *After Finitude,* and Levi Bryant, Graham Harman, and Nick Srnicek, eds., *The Speculative Turn* (Melbourne: re:press, 2011), and its subsequent variants (including various forms of materialism) paradoxically makes the same mistake as the correlationism it officially opposes. While there is a correlational circle whenever a knowledge claim actually takes place in the mental life of a knowledgeable animal, this does not mean that the thinker is debarred from grasping a reality that would have been the way she discovers it to be had no one ever sprung into existence in order to put forth knowledge claims. The correlational circle here consists merely in the idea that the knower and the known are part of a fos that encompasses both of them. In some prominent strands of new materialism this has led to a rapprochement of ontology and quantum theoretical basic concepts; see, for instance, Karen Barad, *Meeting the Universe Halfway: Quantum Physics and the Entanglement of Matter and Meaning* (Durham, NC: Duke University Press, 2007), and Jane Bennett, *Vibrant Matter: A Political Ecology of Things* (Durham, NC: Duke University Press, 2010).

NOTES TO PAGES 40-45

81. Gabriel, "Neutral Realism," 181–196.

82. See Markus Gabriel, "Truths and Posits—The Realm of Sense According to Fichte's Wissenschaftslehre 1794," in *Palgrave Handbook of German Idealism and Analytic Philosophy,* ed. James F. Conant and Jonas Held (Basingstoke, UK: Palgrave Macmillan, forthcoming).

83. Compare Markus Gabriel and George Ellis, "Physical, Logical, and Mental Top-Down Effects," in *Top-Down Causation and Emergence,* ed. Markus Gabriel and Jan Voosholz (Cham, Switzerland: Springer, 2021), 3–39.

84. Gabriel, *Fictions,* Chapter 3 of this volume, and John McDowell, *Having the World in View: Essays on Kant, Hegel, and Sellars* (Cambridge, MA: Harvard University Press, 2009).

85. For a form of idealism about linguistic meaning and, thereby, of the articulation of subjective sense see Thomas Hofweber, *Idealism and the Harmony of Thought and Reality* (Oxford: Oxford University Press, 2023).

86. Benoist, *Toward a Contextual Realism,* 171.

87. Gottlob Frege, "Sense and Reference," *The Philosophical Review* 57, no. 3 (1948): 209–230, here 216–217.

88. Harald Atmanspacher and Dean Rickles, *Dual-Aspect Monism and the Deep Structure of Meaning* (New York: Routledge, 2022). To be sure, New Realism has no truck with the postmodern critique of reference; it is not in the business of denying the existence of a reference relationship (say between a name and what it designates). Rather, FOS insists that neither meaning nor sense ought to be modeled in terms of the assumption that the reference relationship is paradigmatic for our understanding of intensionality and intentionality. Being in touch with how things are on the level of conscious perception should not be thought of as a variety of linguistic reference. Hence, New Realism's overall rejection of one of the main motives of the linguistic turn, which identifies thought with its linguistic expression.

89. Thanks to Zachary Hall for pointing out to me that there is nothing wrong with assuming that a meaning-as-use theorist could think of meanings that are in the business of tracking senses in the good case relate us to sense in a way that allows us to say that our concepts fully express senses and thereby allow us to construe those linguistic meanings as "limited insight into the realm of sense," as he put it.

90. The term "linguistic turn" has different though related meanings. After its introduction by Gustav Bergmann it became a name for a method in the context of Richard Rorty's influential collection of material under the title "the linguistic turn." Richard Rorty, ed., *The Linguistic Turn: Essays in Philosophical Method; With Two Retrospective Essays* (Chicago: University of Chicago Press, 1992). Rorty refers to "the view that philosophical problems which may be solved (or dissolved) either by reforming language, or by understanding more about the language we presently use" (Rorty, *The Linguistic Turn,* 2).

233

NOTES TO PAGES 45–50

A related, but different sense of the term refers to ideas according to which language and thought are inextricably linked, maybe to the point of being identical. For a recent reconstruction of some of the connections between the linguistic turn as a method and the linguistic turn as a series of (contentious) claims concerning human mindedness as linguistically structured, see Charles Taylor, *The Language Animal: The Full Shape of the Human Linguistic Capacity* (Cambridge, MA: Belknap Press of Harvard University Press, 2016), and Michael N. Forster, *Herder's Philosophy* (Oxford: Oxford University Press, 2018).

91. Benoist, *Toward a Contextual Realism,* 181.

92. Benoist, *Toward a Contextual Realism,* 187.

93. Benoist, *Toward a Contextual Realism,* 177.

94. Benoist, *Toward a Contextual Realism,* 172, 181, 180.

95. For a recent discussion of the relationship between perception and language that is both philosophically and scientifically sophisticated, see Ned Block, *The Border Between Seeing and Thinking* (Oxford: Oxford University Press, 2023).

96. Again, see Burge, *Origins of Objectivity.*

97. On the associated worry of an arbitrariness of grammar that arises for the linguistic case but cannot be translated into an account of logical thought (which cannot be arbitrary in the way in which language use is), see the excellent discussion in Michael N. Forster, *Wittgenstein on the Arbitrariness of Grammar* (Princeton, NJ: Princeton University Press, 2004).

98. On pre-linguistic human minds and how they achieve sense-based objectivity, see Alison Gopnik, *The Philosophical Baby: What Children's Minds Tell Us about Truth, Love, and the Meaning of Life* (New York: Picador, 2009), and Susan Carey, *The Origin of Concepts* (Oxford: Oxford University Press, 2011).

99. Atmanspacher and Rickles, *Dual-Aspect Monism,* xii.

100. Atmanspacher and Rickles, *Dual-Aspect Monism,* xii–xiii.

101. Atmanspacher and Rickles, *Dual-Aspect Monism,* 36.

102. For a convincing argument for the irreducibility of reference to causal contact (the "noneffectiveness of reference and semantics," as he puts it), see Brian Cantwell Smith, *The Promise of Artificial Intelligence: Reckoning and Judgment* (Cambridge, MA: MIT Press, 2019), 12–21.

103. Atmanspacher and Rickles, *Dual-Aspect Monism,* xi.

104. Robert B. Brandom, *Tales of the Mighty Dead: Historical Essays in the Metaphysics of Intentionality* (Cambridge, MA: Harvard University Press, 2002), 50.

105. Atmanspacher and Rickles, *Dual-Aspect Monism,* 37.

106. Hilary Putnam, "The Meaning of Meaning," in *Language, Mind and Knowledge,* ed. Keith Gunderson (Minneapolis: University of Minnesota Press, 1975), 131–193, here 144.

NOTES TO PAGES 51–54

107. As Cavell pithily put it in Stanley Cavell, *Must We Mean What We Say?* (Cambridge: Cambridge University Press, 2015), 91: "We know of the efforts of such philosophers as Frege and Husserl to undo the 'psychologizing' of logic (like Kant's undoing Hume's psychologizing of knowledge): now, the shortest way I might describe such a book as the *Philosophical Investigations* is to say that it attempts to undo the psychologizing of psychology, to show the necessity controlling our application of psychological and behavioral categories; even, one could say, show the necessities in human action and passion themselves."

108. See the excellent philosophical reconstruction of the stakes of the context principle in Frege in Charles Travis, *Frege: The Pure Business of Being True* (Oxford: Oxford University Press, 2021). On the historical context of the problem of the unity of the proposition in early analytic philosophy, see Richard Gaskin, *The Unity of the Proposition* (Oxford: Oxford University Press, 2008).

109. Frege stops at the unity (the whole) of thoughts and decomposes thoughts into parts without considering the integration of thoughts into larger wholes that in turn provide rules for their decomposition into thoughts. Concerning Frege's holism, see, for instance, Gottlob Frege, "Aufzeichnungen für Ludwig Darmstädter," in *Nachgelassene Schriften und wissenschaftlicher Briefwechsel,* ed. Hans Hermes, Friedrich Kambartel, and Friedrich Kaulbach, vol. 1 (Hamburg: Meiner, 1983), 273–277, in Charles Travis's translation in "Where Words Fail," in *The Logical Alien: Conant and His Critics,* ed. Sofia Miguens (Cambridge, MA: Harvard University Press, 2020), 222–280, here 224–225:

> What is distinctive in my view of logic is made recognizable, first of all, by the fact that I put the content of the word "true" at the forefront, and then by the fact that I let thoughts follow immediately as that by which truth can come into question at all. Thus I do not begin with concepts and build thoughts, or judgements, out of them, but I arrive at thought-elements by the decomposition of thoughts.

According to Travis's reading: "*Sinn* is a species with two genera: *whole* thoughts (ways for truth to come into question) and thought-elements" (Travis, "Where Words Fail," 225).

110. Frege, "Sense and Reference," 213.

111. McDowell, of course, argues that "thinking does not stop short of the facts" (*Mind and World* [Cambridge, MA: Harvard University Press, 1996], 33), and that this insight is central in understanding perception's grip on reality.

112. See my introduction to Gabriel, *Der Neue Realismus,* 8–16.

113. For a recent conception of consciousness as not putting us in touch with anything, but rather obscuring metaphysical reality, see Donald D.

Hoffman, *The Case against Reality: Why Evolution Hid the Truth from Our Eyes* (New York: W. W. Norton, 2019).

114. Hoffman, *The Case against Reality,* xiii.

115. Hoffman, *The Case against Reality,* xvii.

116. Hoffman, *The Case against Reality,* xviii.

117. Hoffman, *The Case against Reality,* 184.

118. Hoffman, *The Case against Reality,* 191.

119. Hoffman, *The Case against Reality,* 191.

120. John Campbell and Quassim Cassam, *Berkeley's Puzzle: What Does Experience Teach Us?* (Oxford: Oxford University Press: 2014), 2.

121. Hoffman, in *The Case against Reality,* 195–196, believes that "many key ideas of conscious realism and the interface theory of perception have appeared in prior sources, from ancient Greek philosophers such as Parmenides, Pythagoras, and Plato through more recent German philosophers such as Leibniz, Kant, and Hegel, and from eastern religions such as Buddhism and Hinduism to mystical strands of Islam, Judaism, and Christianity. The British philosopher and bishop George Berkeley clearly summarized some of the key ideas." While this is true to a certain extent, it is mysterious how conscious realism could possibly be "precise and testable" and allow "the ideas to be refined under the watchful eye of the scientific method" (196). In this context, *subjective idealism* is a heterodox form of realism about sense. It is the view that results from being realistic about subjective sense while denying the existence of objective sense.

122. Kant, *Critique of Pure Reason,* B133–155.

123. On the issue of the plural decomposability of a Fregean thought see Travis, *Frege,* 19–36.

124. Gottlob Frege, *Function and Concept,* trans. Peter Thomas Geach (Oxford: Basil Blackwell, 1960), 32, quoted in Travis, *Frege,* 59:

> The question now arises what is here being called an object. A textbook definition I take to be impossible because we have to do here with something which, on account of its simplicity, does not admit of logical analysis. It is only possible to gesture at what is meant. Here one can only say in brief: an object is anything which is not a function, thus whose expression carries with it no empty place.

125. For a clear exposition of the problem, see Graham Priest, *Beyond the Limits of Thought,* 179–184.

126. Theodore Sider, "Ontological Realism," in Chalmers, Manley, and Wasserman, *Metametaphysics,* 384–423, here 400.

127. This addresses a point raised by one of the reviewers of this book who asked for a clarification of the modal status of a subject's fallibility. While it is indeed "not implausible that all actual subjects are wrong," as the reviewer

NOTES TO PAGE 61

notes, it strikes them as more contentious to maintain that it is constitutive of a subject to be wrong about something (while being right about many things). One way to get a grip on how to evaluate the modal range here is in terms of the conception of an omniscient being on the one hand and a being "which is brought briefly into being and then out of it" (as the reviewer puts it). On the other hand, concerning the omniscient being, my reply is that that being would not be a subject in that it would precisely not be fallible and, therefore, would not formulate knowledge claims or even have to exercise epistemic capacities in a way that is subject to normative assessment. Given that the omniscient being cannot fail in their thoughts, the Platonic-Aristotelian-Neoplatonic tradition (which is paradigmatic in that area of metaphysical investigation) precisely held that God is pure actuality and his thoughts are in relevant ways precisely not subjective. Concerning the other case, that of a subject that briefly comes into existence and thinks exactly one true thought (or a series of true thoughts for that matter), I would reply that there could not be such a subject, unless we allow for possible worlds in which there are thinkers with epistemic capacities that are in no way embodied and, thus, in no way tied to conditions of sensory registrations that are in principle subject to error. As soon as a subject comes into existence whose epistemic registrations are subject to error in principle, their representations will contain a distorting element (such as their sensory consciousness of objects from their perspective) that makes their thought subjective, i.e., their thought rather than an anonymous event. Having said that, it would be too far afield here to rehearse my account of the modalities that argues that the very idea of a possible world cannot be articulated sufficiently clearly in order to use thought experiments about disembodied omniscient thinkers in other possible worlds as evidence for modal claims concerning actual thinkers. For my account of the modalities that does not rely on possible worlds talk, see Gabriel, *Fields of Sense,* chaps. 10–11.

128. On the associated phenomenological accounts of non-truth see Rudolf Bernet, "Phänomenologische Begriffe der Unwahrheit bei Husserl und Heidegger," in *Heidegger und Husserl,* Heidegger-Jahrbuch 6, ed. Rudolf Bernet, Alfred Denker, and Holger Zaborowski (Freiburg: Verlag Karl Alber, 2012), 108–130. Thanks to Tobias Keiling for this reference and for discussion of negative epistemological phenomena in classical phenomenology.

129. Compare Frege's statement of this point in terms of his sense-reference distinction in "Sense and Reference," 210–211:

> The sense of a proper name is grasped by everybody who is sufficiently familiar with the language or totality of designations to which it belongs; but this serves to illuminate only a single aspect of the referent, supposing it to exist. Comprehensive knowledge of the referent would require us to be able to say immediately whether every given sense belongs to it. To such knowledge we never attain.

NOTES TO PAGES 63–66

See also the analysis in Travis, *Frege,* 66–68.

130. See the famous and influential rhetorical question in Plato, *The Sophist,* 248e7–249a2, in *Loeb Classical Library, Plato II,* ed. and trans. Harold North Fowler (Cambridge, MA: Harvard University Press, 1952), 382–383:

> But for heaven's sake, shall we let ourselves easily be persuaded that motion and life and soul and mind are really not present to absolute being, that it neither lives nor thinks, but awful and holy, devoid of mind, is fixed and immovable? [ὡς ἀληθῶς κίνησιν καὶ ζωὴν καὶ ψυχὴν καὶ φρόνησιν ἦ ῥαδίως πεισθησόμεθα τῷ παντελῶς ὄντι μὴ παρεῖναι, μηδὲ ζῆν αὐτὸ μηδὲ φρονεῖν, ἀλλὰ σεμνὸν καὶ ἅγιον, νοῦν οὐκ ἔχον, ἀκίνητον ἑστὸς εἶναι].

131. The recent knowledge-first tradition disagrees in that it rejects the very idea of an analyzability of knowledge into components such as truth, belief, and justification. The most influential statement to date is Timothy Williamson, *Knowledge and Its Limits* (Oxford: Oxford University Press, 2002). However, even if knowledge were a general factive mental state *sui generis,* subjects would still have to claim knowledge in order to manifest their states to themselves and to others, which brings in the dimension of justification so that the problem of justification remains unsolved by merely putting knowledge first in that sense.

132. See, of course, Plato, *Theaetetus,* 201c8–d1: ἔφη δὲ τὴν μὲν μετὰ λόγου ἀληθῆ δόξαν ἐπιστήμην εἶναι. English translation by John McDowell in *Clarendon Plato Series,* ed. M. J. Woods (Oxford: Oxford University Press, 1991), 94: "He said that true judgement with an account is knowledge, and the kind without an account falls outside the sphere of knowledge."

133. Graham Priest, *An Introduction to Non-Classical Logic: From If to Is* (Cambridge: Cambridge University Press, 2008).

134. For my part, I surmise that some form of *logical pluralism* comes out true to the extent to which we can answer the question whether there is a single all-encompassing "background" logic against which we formulate different lower-level logical systems (such as classical, free, paraconsistent, quantum etc. logic). For a recent overview, see Nathan Kellen, Nikolaj J. L. L. Pedersen, and Jeremy Wyatt, eds., *Pluralisms in Truth and Logic* (Basingstoke, UK: Palgrave Macmillan, 2019).

135. On the crucial difference between prima facie and *ideal* conceivability, see David Chalmers, "Does Conceivability Entail Possibility?," in *Conceivability and Possibility,* ed. Tamar Gendler and John Hawthorne (Oxford: Oxford University Press, 2002), 145–200.

136. For a discussion of some other contemporary forms of ontological pluralism in terms of modes of being and categories, see Gabriel, "Neutral Realism."

NOTES TO PAGES 68-71

137. Plato was probably the first to distinguish between a name (ὄνομα) and a predicate (ῥῆμα), which paved the way for Aristotelian logics. On this history, see Francesco Ademollo, "Names, Verbs, and Sentences in Ancient Greek Philosophy," in *Linguistic Content: New Essays on the History of Philosophy of Language,* ed. Margaret Cameron and Robert J. Stainton (Oxford: Oxford University Press, 2015), 33–54.

138. Herein lies a heavy, unresolved problem for Frege. In his "Sense and Reference," he introduces the true and the false as referents of well-formed thoughts thus:

> We are therefore driven into accepting the truth value of a sentence as constituting its reference. By the truth value of a sentence I understand the circumstance that it is true or false. There are no further truth values. For brevity I call the one the True, the other the False. Every declarative sentence concerned with the reference of its words is therefore to be regarded as a proper name, and its reference, if it has one, is either the True or the False. These two objects are recognized, if only implicitly, by everybody who judges something to be true—and so even by a sceptic. (216)

An assertion is a proper name for one of two objects: it either names the true or the false. But that means that we can think of a book such as *PM* as a conjunctive proposition that we can symbolize as the assertion *p*. Now, let us imagine that *PM* were entirely true. Then how do we distinguish different propositions contained in the presentation of its overall assertion? Here, Frege's realm of sense enters the picture. Senses account for the cognitive difference associated with the various expressions of assertions found throughout *PM*. However, how do senses connect with what they present if they are not themselves part of what there is? And if they are part of what there is, they can be designated and thought of in the same way in which we can access their referents, i.e., through senses. And what about the false? What does it even mean to say that the false is an object on the level of the true, i.e., on the level of the pure referents of thoughts? Does this mean that alethic reality is split into two parts, the true and the false? And if this is the case, how does sense manage to split the true and the false, respectively, into a manifold of thoughts half of which mean the true and the other half the false?

139. Plato uses the term "δεσμός" (see, for instance, *Parmenides,* 162a4) to signify the binding together of subject and predicate, which is the origin of the history of the copula. For more details, see Charles H. Kahn, "On the Terminology for *Copula* and *Existence,*" in Kahn, *Essays on Being* (Oxford: Oxford University Press, 2009), 41–61.

140. On this, see Gabriel, *Fields of Sense,* 230–242.

NOTES TO PAGES 72–74

141. Gabriel and Priest, *Everything and Nothing.*

142. I believe that it is appropriate because Leibniz himself thought of monads as non-well-founded totalities, which he constructed on the basis of identifying the paradigmatic form of judgment with the fundamental form of reality. This leads to the notion that every object is its own universe, entirely sealed off from all other objects. However, this makes it hard to understand the view of monadology itself, as monadology itself (i.e., the view held by Leibniz) has to be sealed off from all other monads in just the way it predicts for those monads of which it can take no actual cognizance.

143. See Gabriel, *Fields of Sense,* 253–254.

144. The following draws on Markus Gabriel, *Sinn und Existenz: Eine realistische Ontologie* (Berlin: Suhrkamp, 2016), 224. In the original English version of *Fields of Sense,* I did not attempt to summarize the arguments against the world by providing a unified argument for the no-world-view. I added this to the German translation of *Fields of Sense* in order to respond to some objections that had been raised in the meantime.

145. To be distinguished from me-ontological thought, i.e., thought directed at non-existence (μὴ ὄν). We will get to that in Chapter 2.

146. The formulation of the no-world-view in this paragraph owes much to the discussion with Graham Priest, who has made me aware of a lacuna in earlier formulations of the argument. The lacuna consists in an absence of the demonstration that, if anything, we are in a well-founded reality where fos are wholes with parts without a looping structure that allows the absolute whole to be a proper part of itself. To be sure, I have excluded this option since *Why the World does not Exist* on the ground that I postulated a form of mereological pluralism according to which FOS does not rest on the notion of a singular concept of the part–whole relationship. Having said that, I recognize that FOS to a certain extent can be modeled in terms of mereology that requires a change in the formulation of the argument. For details, see Gabriel and Priest, *Everything and Nothing.*

147. Following Jocelyn Benoist, in this context I repudiate the "myth of white objects [le mythe des 'objets blancs']." *Éléments de philosophie réaliste* (Paris: Vrin, 2011), 59.

148. Which need not be associated with the view that objects necessarily have their properties or the weaker claim that objects have some of their properties (the substantial ones) necessarily.

149. Gabriel, *Fields of Sense,* chap. 2.

150. There are different meta-logical accounts of the nature of the descriptive character of concepts like identity. But most of them share the idea that identity is constituted in virtue of something that allows it to function in a rule-governed fashion that, for instance, could be stated in the form of Leibniz's laws of identity or symbolically in terms of substitution rules for terms or other kinds of expression within a well-defined formal system.

NOTES TO PAGES 74-77

151. Notice that it became standard after Aristotle precisely not to think of being as the highest genus. Porphyry himself was an ontological pluralist and, like Aristotle, rejected the idea of metaphysics as ontology. See, for instance, the introduction into Aristotle's category theory by the major Neoplatonist Porphyry who rightly reads Aristotle as maintaining that there are ten categories that are all on the same level without being grounded in being as ultimate genus. He explicitly distinguishes between the idea of Zeus as the highest God and the absence of a single top of the hierarchy in the order of genera and species. See his statement of an ontological pluralism in category theory in Porphyre, *Isagoge,* Texte grec et latin, traduction par Alain de Libera et Alain-Philippe Segons, introduction et notes par Alain de Libera (Paris: Vrin, 1998), 6 [my translation]:

> But if one ascends in genealogies up to one, such as to Zeus, so as to reach the highest principle, this will not be the case for the genera and species. Being is not a single common genus to everything and it is not the case either that everything is homogeneous with respect to one as the highest genus, as Aristotle said. Instead, let's posit, just as in the *Categories,* that the ten first genera behave like ten first principles. And if someone wanted to call all of everything beings, he would speak homonymously but not synonymously [my translation of the Greek: Ἀλλ'ἐπὶ μὲν τῶν γενεαλογιῶν εἰς ἕνα ἀνάγουσι, φέρε εἰπεῖν τὸν Δία, τὴν ἀρχὴν ὡς ἐπὶ τὸ πλεῖστον, ἐπὶ δὲ τῶν γενῶν καὶ τῶν εἰδῶν οὕτως ἔχει. Οὐ γάρ ἐστι κοινὸν ἓν γένος πάντων τὸ ὂν οὐδὲ πάντα ὁμογενῆ καθ'ἓν τὸ ἀνωτάτω γένος, ὥς φησιν ὁ Ἀριστοτέλης. Ἀλλὰ κείσθω, ὥσπερ ἐν ταῖς Κατηγορίαις, τὰ πρῶτα δέκα γένη οἷον ἀρχαὶ δέκα πρῶται. κἂν δὴ τις ὄντα καλῇ, ὁμωνύμως, φησί, καλέσει, ἀλλ'οὐ συνωνύμως].

152. Richard Rorty, "The World Well Lost," *Journal of Philosophy* 69, no. 19 (1972): 649-665.

153. See prominently Kit Fine, "The Question of Realism," *Philosopher's Imprint* 1 (2001): 1-30; "What Is Metaphysics?," in *Contemporary Aristotelian Metaphysics,* ed. Tuomas E. Tahko (Cambridge: Cambridge University Press, 2011), 8-25; David Chalmers, *Reality+: Virtual Worlds and the Problems of Philosophy* (New York: Norton, 2022).

154. Jocelyn Benoist, *Le bruit du sensible* (Paris: CERF, 2013).

155. Gabriel, "Neutral Realism," and the debate in Thomas Buchheim, ed., *Markus Gabriel—Neutraler Realismus: Jahrbuch-Kontroversen 2* (Freiburg: Alber, 2016).

156. Maurizio Ferraris, *The External World,* trans. Sarah de Sanctis (Edinburgh: Edinburgh University Press, 2021).

157. Chalmers, *Reality+,* 108-114, distinguishes five ways of thinking about reality: (1) reality as existence, (2) reality as causal power, (3) reality as

NOTES TO PAGES 77–79

mind-independence, (4) reality as non-illusoriness, and (5) reality as genuineness. He neither provides a full account of reality nor commits to one way of thinking about it. FOS spells out the notion of reality as existence, which leads to a view roughly similar to Chalmers's inchoate notion of "Reality+: a multiverse of both physical and virtual realities" (108). He goes on to claim: "All of these realities (worlds) are part of reality (the cosmos)" (108). I reject the idea that the realities (fields of sense) are part of a single reality. Chalmers surprisingly remains silent about the crucial question of what it means for his realities to be part of a singular reality.

158. Willard Van Orman Quine, *Word and Object* (Cambridge, MA: MIT Press, 1960), 275–276.

159. Gabriel, *The Limits of Epistemology,* 251.

160. Markus Gabriel, *Transcendental Ontology: Essays in German Idealism* (London: Bloomsbury, 2013).

161. A phrase introduced by him in his seminar at Bonn's International Center for Philosophy in May–June 2018.

162. See Carlo Rovelli, *Reality Is Not What It Seems: The Journey to Quantum Gravity* (London: Penguin, 2017), and similarly Carlo Rovelli, *Helgoland: The Strange and Beautiful Story of Quantum Physics* (London: Penguin, 2022); Brian Greene, *Until the End of Time* (London: Penguin, 2021); Sean Carroll, *The Big Picture: On the Origins of Life, Meaning and the Universe Itself* (New York: Dutton, 2016).

163. Gertrude Elisabeth M. Anscombe, *An Introduction to Wittgenstein's Tractatus* (London: St. Augustine's Press, 1959), 151.

164. See famously Erwin Schrödinger, *Mind and Matter* (Cambridge: Cambridge University Press, 1958). In contemporary philosophy of quantum physics, an interpretation of quantum mechanics in Schrödinger's wake is prominently defended by Michel Bitbol, *Schrödinger's Philosophy of Quantum Mechanics* (Dordrecht: Kluwer, 1996), and more recently *La pratique des possible: une lecture pragmatiste et modale de la mécanique quantique* (Paris: Hermann, 2015).

165. See Markus Gabriel, "Being Human in the Digital Age: Comments on Floridi's Sketch for a New Political Ontology," in *The Green and the Blue: Digital Politics in Philosophical Discussion,* ed. Luciano Floridi and Jörg Noller (Baden-Baden: Verlag Karl Alber, 2022), 71–84; see also, in the same volume, Luciano Floridi, "Reply to Broy, Gabriel, Grunwald, Hagengruber, Kriebitz, Lütge, Max, Misselhorn, and Rehbein," 171–192, and my meta-reply, 197–199.

166. See the brilliant exposition of this point about appearances in Jocelyn Benoist, *Logique du phénomène* (Paris: Hermann, 2016).

167. Kimhi, *Thinking and Being,* 16. Quine pithily characterizes syncategorematic expressions as "meaningful in context but *naming* nothing." Willard Van Orman Quine, "Designation and existence," *Journal of Philosophy* 36, no. 26 (1939): 701–709, here 704.

NOTES TO PAGES 79–82

168. See, of course, the locus classicus Gottlob Frege, "On Concept and Object," in *Translations from the Philosophical Writings of Gottlob Frege,* ed. and trans. Peter Thomas Geach and Max Black (Oxford: Blackwell, 1980), 42–55.

169. Hegel, *The Science of Logic,* trans. George Di Giovanni (Cambridge: Cambridge University Press, 2010), 562: "The positive judgment has in fact no truth through its form as positive judgment; whoever calls *truth* the *correctness* of an *intuition* or a *perception,* the agreement of *representation* with the subject matter, has for a minimum no expression left for that which is the subject matter and the aim of philosophy." And Martin Heidegger, *Vom Wesen der Wahrheit: Zu Platons Höhlengleichnis und Theätet* (Frankfurt am Main: Klostermann, 1997).

170. See the collection of essays in Joachim Bromand and Guido Kreis, eds., *Was sich nicht sagen lässt: Das Nicht-Begriffliche in Wissenschaft, Kunst und Religion* (Berlin: De Gruyter, 2010).

171. For a radical, global account of vagueness (according to which vagueness abounds in all regions of thought), see Kit Fine, *Vagueness: A Global Approach* (Oxford: Oxford University Press, 2020).

172. Gregory S. Moss and Robert H. Scott, eds., *The Significance of Indeterminacy: Perspectives from Asian and Continental Philosophy* (New York: Routledge, 2019).

173. By the term "world," Husserl explicitly refers to a "universal horizon [*Universalhorizont*]." Edmund Husserl, *The Crisis of European Sciences and Transcendental Phenomenology: An Introduction to Phenomenology,* trans. David Carr (Evanston, IL: Northwestern University Press, 1970), 108. He explicitly equates this with a unity of "manners of givenness" [*Gegebenheitsweisen*] rather than with an object on the level of reference, which he calls "*onta*":

> Let us direct our attention to the fact that in general the world or, rather, objects are not merely pregiven to us all in such a way that we simply have them as the substrates of their properties but that we become conscious of them (and of everything ontically meant) through subjective manners of appearance, or manners of givenness, without noticing it in particular; in fact we are for the most part not even aware of it at all. Let us now shape this into a new universal direction of interest; let us establish a consistent universal interest in the "how" of the manners of givenness and in the *onta* themselves, not straightforwardly but rather as objects in respect to their "how"—that is, with our interest exclusively and constantly directed toward *how,* throughout the alteration of relative validities, subjective appearances, and opinions, the coherent, universal validity *world—the* world—comes into being for us; how, that is, there arises in us the constant consciousness of the universal existence,

243

NOTES TO PAGES 83–85

of the universal horizon, of real, actually existing objects, each of which we are conscious of only through the alterations of our relative conceptions [*Aufassungen*] of it, of its manners of appearing, its modes of validity, even when we are conscious of it in particularity as something simply being there. (144–145)

Husserl unequivocally distinguishes between the world as "horizon" and objects that appear within the world and for this reason does not think of the world as an object, but as belonging to a categorically different (ultimately subjective) sphere:

The world, on the other hand, does not exist as an entity, as an object, but exists with such uniqueness that the plural makes no sense when applied to it. Every plural, and every singular drawn from it, presupposes the world-horizon. This difference between the manner of being of an object in the world and that of the world itself obviously prescribes fundamentally different correlative types of consciousness for them. (143)

Thanks to Tobias Keiling for directing me to those references and for discussion of this point.

174. Gregory S. Moss, *Hegel's Foundation Free Metaphysics: The Logic of Singularity* (London: Routledge, 2022), 239; Gabriel and Priest, *Everything and Nothing*.

175. See the field theory of consciousness in Richard M. Zaner and Lester Embree, eds., *The Collected Works of Aron Gurwitsch (1901–1973)*, vol. 3, *The Field of Consciousness: Phenomenology of Theme, Thematic Field, and Marginal Consciousness* (Dordrecht: Springer, 2010).

176. Alison Gopnik, *The Philosophical Baby: What Children's Minds Tell Us about Truth, Love, and the Meaning of Life* (New York: Picador, 2009), 163.

2. Nonsense

1. For the shortcomings of the case against category mistakes, see Ofra Magidor, *Category Mistakes* (Oxford: Oxford University Press, 2013). See also Jan Westerhoff, *Ontological Categories: Their Nature and Significance* (Oxford: Oxford University Press, 2005).

2. See the wide-ranging critique of the methodological foundations of analytic metaphysics (he goes as far as claiming that all of analytic philosophy is subject to the same problem, an idea I do not share) in Peter Unger, *Empty Ideas: A Critique of Analytic Philosophy* (New York: Oxford University Press, 2014), and the recent (metaphysical!) critique of analytic philosophy (whose "bankruptcy" [xxii] he declares) in Michael Della Rocca, *The Parmenidean Ascent* (Oxford: Oxford University Press, 2020), in particular chap. 11. For a dis-

cussion of how ontology got resuscitated in the wake of the later Carnap (and the debate between him and Quine), see the papers in Stephan Blatti and Sandra Lapointe, eds., *Ontology after Carnap* (Oxford: Oxford University Press, 2016). A paradigmatic introduction and defense of the very idea of an analytic metaphysics despite analytic philosophy's antimetaphysical founding gesture still is Peter van Inwagen, *Metaphysics,* 4th ed. (New York: Routledge, 2018). All three parts of that book are dedicated to the world (they respectively deal with the way it is, why it is, and what its inhabitants are). For his most recent defense of a substantial approach to analytic metaphysics against Huw Price's and Amie Thomasson's neo-Carnapian deflations of the ambitions of metaphysics, see Peter van Inwagen, "The Neo-Carnapians," *Synthese* 197 (2020): 7–32.

3. Wilfrid S. Sellars, *Science, Perception, and Reality* (London: Routledge & Kegan Paul, 1963), 1.

4. This should mislead one into extremist neo-Eleatic positions such as Emmanuele Severino's theory of error according to which error's paradigm is the allegedly false belief that there is change and temporality in the first place Severino. See Emanuele Severino, "Ritornare a Parmenide," *Rivista di Filosofia Neo-Scolastica* 56, no. 2 (1964): 137–75; *Essenza del nichilismo,* 2nd ed. (Milan: Adelphi, 1982); and *La potenza dell'errare: Sulla storia dell'Occidente* (Milan: Rizzoli, 2014). For a similar form of resolute monism based on Parmenidean considerations, see della Rocca, *The Parmenidean Ascent.*

5. While the issue of ontological nonsense is not identical to the approach to nonsense as meaninglessness, there is an overlap in theoretical results from FOS and from early analytic philosophers' desire to overcome metaphysics from within language. In a sense, FOS argues that there is an ontological depth structure to the articulation of linguistic meaning in that an important part of language is in the business of formulating propositional thought with identifiable parts of objective and subjective sense. Those parts of language which are not in that business are indeed involved in nonsense, as I argue in the chapter. However, the identification of ontological nonsense in thought and thought expression is not an accusation, as it were, because I will reject the idea that propositional, regimented, scientific discourse is an isolated module of our minds. In the reality of our minds, it is integrated into nonsense. Moreover, ontological nonsense is part of the glue that connects fos. It opens the possibility of change and of objectively existing forms of confusion, paradigmatically represented by consciousness (both as a reality and as a topic). Thanks to two reviewers for pointing out to me that ontological nonsense, thus articulated, after all, indirectly contributes to the nonsense-as-meaninglessness tradition without sharing its specific ambition of a language reform designed in light of problematic overgeneralizations of the articulation of propositional thought.

NOTES TO PAGES 86–87

6. Which is not to say that there is a finite list of categories in the sense of the logically closest conceptual divisions right below being. Against such a conception of categories, see Otávio Bueno, Jacob Busch, and Scott A. Shalkowski, "The No-Category Ontology," *The Monist* 98, no. 3 (2015): 233–245, and Markus Gabriel, "Hegels Kategorienkritik," in *Kategoriendeduktion in der klassischen deutschen Philosophie,* ed. Rainer Schäfer, Nicolas Bickmann, and Lars Heckenroth (Berlin: Duncker & Humblot, 2020), 100–111.

7. Jürgen Habermas expressed exactly this worry during our Starnberg meeting on May 20, 2022. In this context, he portrayed realism about sense as a form of post-metaphysical Platonism, as he put it, a position that according to him requires a fallibilist or, rather, pragmatist addendum to make sense of the dimension of justification essential for any socially meaningful account of the activity of claiming knowledge. I agree with the thrust of the argument, as can be seen from my earlier account of justification in Markus Gabriel, *The Limits of Epistemology,* trans. Alex Englander (Cambridge: Polity, 2019), and from the third part of Markus Gabriel, *Fictions,* trans. Wieland Hoban (Cambridge: Polity, 2023). However, Habermas went a significant step further where we begin to diverge. For he wanted me to provide an account of the "innerworldly happening" (*innerweltliches Geschehen*) of the evolution of social spheres embedded in larger-scale forms of evolution of nature to ground the type of theory of subjectivity on offer within FOS. However, this threatens to revert to metaphysics as a monistic overall theory of reality, as it brings the concept of "world" back into the picture. For a discussion of Habermas's notion of the world as presupposition of discourse, see Markus Gabriel, *Why the World Does Not Exist,* trans. Gregory S. Moss (Cambridge: Polity, 2015), 46–49. Having said that, the entire book you are reading can be seen as a response to the worry that FOS might be overly Eleatic in its fundamental outlook and, therefore, hostile to history, evolution, temporality, and subjectivity, which I think is a mistake that ignores the epistemological and social-ontological dimensions of FOS, as they have already been presented in Markus Gabriel, *Fields of Sense: A New Realist Ontology* (Edinburgh: Edinburgh University Press, 2015), chaps. 11–12. In any event, I thank Habermas for pushing me to clarify this dimension of FOS further in order to fend off a "Platonistic" or, rather, Eleatic reading of FOS.

8. Sigmund Freud, *Civilization and Its Discontents* (New York: Norton, 1961), 11–13. On this, see William Parsons, *The Enigma of the Oceanic Feeling* (New York: Oxford University Press, 1999).

9. For a by now classical philosophical presentation, see Jaegwon Kim, *Mind in a Physical World* (Cambridge: Cambridge University Press, 1998), and *Physicalism, or Something Near Enough* (Princeton, NJ: Princeton University Press, 2005). A contemporary overall account of metaphysical naturalism can be found in Alexander Rosenberg, *The Atheist's Guide to Reality: Enjoying Life Without Illusions* (New York: W. W. Norton, 2011). Rosenberg has attempted

246

to demonstrate that the humanities (in particular, history) and the social sciences can be replaced by suitable forms of natural-scientific investigation so as to ultimately fulfill the naturalistic promise to show that there is nothing that withstands the modes of explanation characteristic of the natural sciences. See Alexander Rosenberg, *Sociobiology and the Preemption of Social Sciences* (Oxford: Basil Blackwell, 1981), and *What History Gets Wrong: The Neuroscience of Our Addiction to Stories* (Cambridge, MA: MIT Press, 2019). Elsewhere, I have argued that these assumptions lead to a nonsensical account of action explanation. See Markus Gabriel, *Neo-Existentialism: How to Conceive of the Human Mind after Naturalism's Failure,* ed. Jocelyn Maclure, with contributions by Jocelyn Benoist, Andrea Kern, and Charles Taylor (Cambridge: Polity, 2018).

10. John MacFarlane made me aware of a similarity between my view about field confusion and Joseph L. Camp Jr., *Confusion: A Study in the Theory of Knowledge* (Cambridge, MA: Harvard University Press, 2002).

11. See for example, the paradigmatic discussions in Sofia Miguens, ed., *The Logical Alien: Conant and His Critics* (Cambridge, MA: Harvard University Press, 2020).

12. Wittgenstein, *Tractatus Logico-Philosophicus,* trans. Frank P. Ramsey and Charles Kay Ogden (London: Kegan Paul, 1922), 6.54. On the idea of category mistakes as inference traps, see Jody Azzouni, "A White Horse Is Not a Horse: Markus Gabriel's New Realism," in *Gabriel's New Realism,* ed. Jan Voosholz (Cham, Switzerland: Springer, forthcoming).

13. Crispin Wright, *Truth and Objectivity* (Cambridge, MA: Harvard University Press, 1994), 159.

14. On this, see the classic Susan Wolf, "Moral Saints," *Journal of Philosophy* 79, no. 8 (1982): 419–439, and my notion of an ethical "principle of leniency [Prinzip der Nachsicht]" in Markus Gabriel, *Moral Progress in Dark Times: Universal Values for the Twenty-First Century,* trans. Wieland Hoban (Cambridge: Polity, 2022), 97.

15. See the transition from skepticism to a non-skeptical epistemology in Gabriel, *The Limits of Epistemology,* a project carried further in Gabriel, *Fields of Sense,* chaps. 12–13.

16. See Sebastian Rödl, *Self-Consciousness and Objectivity: An Introduction to Absolute Idealism* (Cambridge, MA: Harvard University Press, 2018); Andrea Kern, *Sources of Knowledge: On the Concept of a Rational Capacity for Knowledge,* trans. Daniel Smyth (Cambridge, MA: Harvard University Press, 2017).

17. Markus Gabriel, *Sinn und Existenz: Eine realistische Ontologie* (Berlin: Suhrkamp, 2016), §7. For some clarification on this issue, see the exchange in Peter Gaitsch, Sandra Lehmann, and Philipp Schmidt, eds., *Eine Diskussion mit Markus Gabriel: Phänomenologische Positionen zum Neuen Realismus* (Vienna: Turia + Kant, 2017), 171–190, 251–255.

18. Wittgenstein, *Tractatus Logico-Philosophicus,* 5.473.

NOTES TO PAGES 90–97

19. In this context, throughout the chapter I elaborate my position vis-à-vis various prominent accounts of nonsense stemming from discussions about Wittgenstein's and Heidegger's respective critiques of metaphysics. This is a follow up on an ongoing debate with Taylor Carman. See Taylor Carman, "Gabriel's Metaphysics of Sense," *Harvard Review of Philosophy* 23 (2016): 53–59, and my reply in Gaitsch, Lehmann, and Schmidt, *Eine Diskussion mit Markus Gabriel,* 221–224.

20. David Lewis, *On the Plurality of Worlds* (Oxford: Blackwell, 1986).

21. For a nuanced contemporary discussion of this charge, see Yitzhak Y. Melamed and Eckart Förster, eds., *Spinoza and German Idealism* (Cambridge: Cambridge University Press, 2012); Yitzhak Y. Melamed, *Spinoza's Metaphysics: Substance and Thought* (Oxford: Oxford University Press, 2013); Yitzhak Y. Melamed, ed., *Spinoza's Ethics: A Critical Guide* (Cambridge: Cambridge University Press, 2017); Yitzhak Y. Melamed, ed., *A Companion to Spinoza* (Oxford: Blackwell, 2021).

22. See Markus Gabriel, "What Kind of an Idealist (If Any) Is Hegel?," *Hegel Bulletin* 37, no. 2 (2016): 181–208.

23. See Markus Gabriel, *Transcendental Ontology: Essays in German Idealism* (London: Bloomsbury, 2013); Gregory S. Moss, *Hegel's Foundation Free Metaphysics: The Logic of Singularity* (London: Routledge, 2022), 22–23.

24. At this point, it is sufficient to commit to what has been called a "deflationary" or "easy" approach in meta-physics. See Amie L. Thomasson, *Ontology Made Easy* (New York: Oxford University Press, 2015). One need not (though I think one should) be more robust about the relevant kind of ontological realism required to state one's case for the existence of mathematical objects in physics.

25. See David Deutsch, *The Fabric of Reality: The Science of Parallel Universes—and Its Implications* (London: Penguin, 1997).

26. Max Tegmark, *Our Mathematical Universe: My Quest for the Ultimate Nature of Reality* (New York: Alfred A. Knopf, 2014).

27. Berkeley holds this, not simply *"esse* is *percipi."* George Berkeley, "Principles of Human Knowledge," in *Principles of Human Knowledge and Three Dialogues,* ed. Howard Robinson (Oxford: Oxford University Press, 1999), 1–95, here 25; but, as the full version of his famous dictum goes, "Existence is *percipi* or *percipere."* George Berkeley, "Philosophical Commentaries," in *The Works of George Berkeley Bishop of Cloyne,* vol. 1, ed. A. A. Luce and T. E. Jessop (London: Thomas Nelson and Sons, 1948), 1–139, here 55, Notebook A, no. 429.

28. Douglas Hofstadter, *I Am a Strange Loop* (New York: Basic Books, 2007).

29. Markus Gabriel, *Skeptizismus und Idealismus in der Antike* (Berlin: Suhrkamp, 2009).

NOTES TO PAGES 98–101

30. For this reason of the gist of the transcendental dialectic, see Markus Gabriel, *Der Mensch im Mythos: Untersuchungen über Ontotheologie, Anthropologie und Selbstbewußtseinsgeschichte in Schellings "Philosophie der Mythologie"* (Berlin: Walter de Gruyter, 2006), §5.

31. Anil Seth, *Being You: A New Science of Consciousness* (London: Faber & Faber, 2021), 53.

32. Seth, *Being You,* 53.

33. Seth, *Being You,* 53.

34. Robert B. Brandom, *Tales of the Mighty Dead: Historical Essays in the Metaphysics of Intentionality* (Cambridge, MA: Harvard University Press, 2002), 49.

35. This is one of the rationales for the idea that information (in the sense of content associated with negative determination) is first and foremost monadic or "intrinsic," as the proponents of the integrate information theory of consciousness put it. See Masafumi Oizumi, Larissa Albantakis, and Giulio Tononi, "From the Phenomenology to the Mechanisms of Consciousness: Integrated Information Theory 3.0," *PLoS Computational Biology* 10, no. 5 (May 2014): e1003588.

36. Immanuel Kant, *Critique of Pure Reason,* ed. and trans. Paul Guyer and Allen W. Wood (Cambridge: Cambridge University Press, 1998), B207–218. See also Wolfram Hogrebe, *Ligaturen* (Frankfurt am Main: Vittorio Klostermann, 2022), 55–66.

37. Raimundus Lullus, *Die neue Logik,* ed. Charles Lohr, introduction by Vittorio Hösle (Hamburg: Meiner, 1985), 174.

38. Kant, *Critique of Pure Reason,* B41: "Now how can an outer intuition inhabit the mind that precedes the objects themselves, and in which the concept of the latter can be determined *a priori?* Obviously not otherwise than insofar as it has its seat merely in the subject, as its formal constitution for being affected by objects and thereby acquiring *immediate representation,* i.e., *intuition,* of them, thus only as the form of outer *sense* in general."

39. Seth, *Being You,* chap. 4.

40. Lullus, *Die neue Logik,* 180, no. 87.

41. Insofar as consciousness is temporal, it is an objectively existing confusion, i.e., a blurry blending of different conscious states whose identity- and difference-conditions can never be determinately stated, as I will argue in Chapter 3.

42. Gabriel, *Fields of Sense,* 187.

43. See, for instance, Christian Wolff, *Philosophia prima sive ontologia,* ed. Jean Ecole (Hildesheim: Georg Olms, 1962), §226, 188: *"Ens singular,* sive *Individuum* esse illud, quod omnimode determinatum est." On this notion of individuation, see Jorge J. E. Garcia, "Christian Wolff on Individuation," *History of Philosophy Quarterly* 10, no. 2 (1993): 147–164.

249

NOTES TO PAGES 102–106

44. Which is not to deny that so-called non-human animals are also conceptually competent sensers, perceivers, and thinkers. However, the concept of an "animal" is problematic in this context, not so much the idea that lions, dolphins, or bees, sense, perceive, and think. See Markus Gabriel, *Der Mensch als Tier: Warum wir trotzdem nicht in die Natur passen* (Berlin: Ullstein, 2022).

45. Steven Pinker, *Rationality: What It Is, Why It Seems Scarce, Why It Matters* (New York: Viking, 2021).

46. See Gabriel, *Fields of Sense,* 254.

47. That sense is real means, among other things, that objects really are organized in the way in which we represent them as being in knowledge. Knowledge as a *sui generis* factive mental state puts us in touch with how things really are without thereby fusing with its objects. For it to be factive cannot consist in the wrongheaded notion that some parts of our minds are infallible (as they constitute knowledge). This is not to say that knowledge is fallible, either. If "knowledge" designates the success case of having grasped how things are, it cannot be wrong. But that remark does nothing to show that we are ever in a position to distinguish an actual piece of knowledge from being wrong by somehow inspecting the success case further. The success case does not necessarily look or feel successful, knowledge is not necessarily accompanied by certainty or a feeling of clarity. For knowledge to be an epistemological and not a psychological concept is for it to be subject to a worry that might mislead into skepticism but does not have to. The worry is simply that there is an epistemological difference between a knowledge claim and knowledge. Even if I know that *p,* my claim that I know that *p,* categorially differs from a claim to the effect that I know that I know that *p.* Knowledge does not iterate ad libitum, and where it does iterate, we have local reasons to support our reasons for a knowledge claim in a particular manner. For more details on this epistemological dimension of realism, see Gabriel, *The Limits of Epistemology,* 95–101.

48. See Stanislas Dehaene, Hakwan Lau, and Sid Kouider, "What Is Consciousness, and Could Machines Have It?," in *Robotics, AI, and Humanity: Science, Ethics, and Policy,* ed. Joachim von Braun, Margaret S. Archer, Gregory M. Reichberg, and Marcelo Sánchez Sorondo (Cham, Switzerland: Springer, 2021), 43–56.

49. On the "concept" of "pure consciousness," see Thomas Metzinger, "Minimal Phenomenal Experience: Meditation, Tonic Alertness, and the Phenomenology of 'Pure' Consciousness," *Philosophy and the Mind Sciences* 1, no. 1, art. 7 (2020): 1–44.

50. Markus Gabriel, "The Paradox of Self-Consciousness: A Conversation with Markus Gabriel," Edge.org, November 2019, https://www.edge.org /conversation/markus_gabriel-the-paradox-of-self-consciousness.

51. Seth, *Being You,* chap. 3.

250

NOTES TO PAGES 107–109

52. Friedrich Nietzsche, *Beyond Good and Evil: Prelude to a Philosophy of the Future,* ed. Judith Norman and Rolf-Peter Horstmann, trans. Judith Norman (Cambridge: Cambridge University Press, 2001), §15:

> To study physiology with a good conscience, we must insist that the sense organs are not appearances in the way idealist philosophy uses that term: as such, they certainly could not be causes! Sensualism, therefore, at least as a regulative principle, if not as a heuristic principle.—What? and other people even say that the external world is the product of our organs? But then our body, as a piece of this external world, would really be the product of our organs! But then our organs themselves would really be—the product of our organs! This looks to me like a thorough reductio ad absurdum: given that the concept of a causa sui is something thoroughly absurd. So does it follow that the external world is not the product of our organs—?

Thanks to Alex Englander for directing me to this passage in Nietzsche.

53. Donald D. Hoffman, *The Case against Reality: Why Evolution Hid the Truth from Our Eyes* (New York: W. W. Norton, 2019), 106.

54. Hoffman, *The Case Against Reality,* 106–107.

55. Schopenhauer unequivocally identifies the transcendental subject, or "intellect" as he says, with the brain and claims that the brain "fabricates" material reality through its forms, "time, space, and causality." Arthur Schopenhauer, *The World as Will and Representation,* vol. 1, trans. Judith Norman, Alistair Welchman, and Christopher Janaway (Cambridge: Cambridge University Press, 2010), 50. He maintains that "transcendental philosophy" entails "that what we recognize as the objective world does not belong to the essence of things in themselves, but rather only to its appearance, and is conditioned by those very forms that lie a priori in the human intellect (i.e. the brain), and thus that the world can contain nothing but appearances." (Schopenhauer, *The World as Will and Representation,* 1:448). See also Arthur Schopenhauer, *The World as Will and Representation,* vol. 2, trans. Judith Norman, Alistair Welchman, and Christopher Janaway (Cambridge: Cambridge University Press, 2018), 24: "For while the nerves of the sense organs invest the appearing objects with colour, sound, taste, smell, temperature, etc.; the brain imparts to them extension, form, impenetrability, mobility, etc., in short, all that can be represented only by means of time, space, and causality."

56. Hoffman, *The Case against Reality,* 37.

57. I owe the last two sentences to comments by Alex Englander. For an interesting argument for a similar conclusion based on a demonstration that the notion of a causal closure of the universe is unscientific in the context of any account of consciousness as correlated with the physical, see Johannes

Kleiner and Stephan Hartmann, "The Closure of the Physical is Unscientific" (forthcoming).

58. Thomas Nagel, "The Psychophysical Nexus," in *New Essays on the A Priori,* ed. Paul A. Boghossian and Christopher Peacocke (Oxford: Oxford University Press, 2000), 433–471.

59. See Keith Frankish, ed., *Illusionism as a Theory of Consciousness* (Exeter, UK: Imprint Academic, 2017), and the critical discussion in *The Monist* issue on mental fictionalism: *The Monist* 96, no. 4 (2013).

60. Harald Atmanspacher and Dean Rickles, *Dual-Aspect Monism and the Deep Structure of Meaning* (New York: Routledge, 2022), 156. The family of positions in the vicinity of neutral monism (associated with a sophisticated account of a plurality of aspects grounded in a unity) is already on its way out of nonsense, so I will not deal with it here.

61. Thanks to one of the anonymous reviewers for asking me to clarify the relationship between my critique of infallibilism and skepticism. The thought is that the good case of knowledge is such that the success can, of course, not be a failure at the same time. This is what motivates infallibilism. Skepticism draws on the opposite tendency inherent in the concept of a knowledge claim, namely that it can go wrong, and tries to show that we can never guarantee that we are in the good case. While I believe that we can guarantee sometimes that we are in the good case (in virtue of being in it), this does not show that successful knowledge *claims,* let alone the subject of knowledge is therefore infallible. The knowledge claim that underpins the successful mental state of knowledge can go wrong in all sorts of ways in that it is embedded in a subject's life. The guarantee involved in the good case is evidently not always a priori. Hence, there has to be room for invoking fallibility of knowledge claims even in the case where a subject actually gets it right. The strong guarantee that justifies a knowledge claim is not necessarily higher-order: A subject can be wrong concerning whether she gets it right or wrong even in a case of actual knowledge. There might be exceptions (such as cogito cases or some forms of a priori knowledge), but that neither demonstrates that infallibilism can be extended to successful knowledge claims as such nor that skepticism is off the table in virtue of the fact that there is some strongly guaranteed form of knowledge. For my own overall strategy of taming skepticism by re-interpreting its argumentative thrust in terms of a focus on the shifting contexts of knowledge claims without ever amounting to a successful demonstration of the impossibility of knowledge, see again Gabriel, *The Limits of Epistemology.*

62. Charles Travis argues that there is a similar gap (a normative, i.e., deontological difference) between a thought's sense and its being true (or false) in "Where Words Fail," in *The Logical Alien: Conant and His Critics,* ed. Sofia Miguens (Cambridge, MA: Harvard University Press, 2020), 228–229:

NOTES TO PAGES 111–115

Having the truth-value it does *cannot* be part of what identifies a thought (or its question of truth) as the one it is. Truth cannot belong to what brings itself into question. Otherwise it would not be fixed what thought was at issue until it was fixed whether what was in question was a *true* thought or a false one. In a thought, something is represented *as* being something: the way things are as being some way there *is* for things to be (e.g., such that Sid smokes). Truth now enters the picture with the question of whether things *are* as thus represented. A thought is identified by what is thus variable: the second factor. Where truth belonged to bringing itself into question, *how* a thought represented things as being would not be fixed until it was fixed whether such was representing truly. But *such* reduces the behavior of a thought, and of representing-as, to the behavior of something else entirely: *factive* meaning, or (where falsity plays the identifying role) factive counter-meaning. Factive meaning leaves no room for the question of whether things are as represented: if not, then they simply were not so represented. Representing-as, so truth, would thus be abolished.

63. Christof Koch, *The Feeling of Life Itself: Why Consciousness Is Widespread but Can't Be Computed* (Cambridge, MA: MIT Press, 2020).

64. See famously Friedrich Hölderlin, "Judgement and Being," *Graduate Faculty Philosophy Journal* 11, no. 1 (1986): 17–18, and Friedrich Wilhelm Joseph Schelling, "Of the I as Principle of Philosophy, or on the Unconditional in Human Knowledge," in *The Unconditional in Human Knowledge: Four Early Essays (1794–1796)*, ed. and trans. Fritz Marti (London: Associated University Press, 1980), 63–128.

65. Georg Wilhelm Friedrich Hegel, *Aesthetics: Lectures on Fine Art*, trans. Thomas M. Knox (Oxford: Clarendon Press, 1975), 128–129.

66. For a recent reconstruction of these accounts in the context of contemporary philosophy of language see Magidor, *Category Mistakes*.

67. Wittgenstein, *Tractatus Logico-Philosophicus*, 6.54. On the idea of category mistakes as inference traps, see Azzouni, "A White Horse is Not a Horse."

68. This holds across levels. The kinds of objects, events, facts, and processes that are consciously available to us in virtue of our mesoscopic position (which is defined relative to the highly relevant scale at which our survival is at stake) hang together with objects, events, facts, and processes in other fos whose otherness can be thought of in terms of a difference in scaling. Nano- and microscopic levels intersect with meso- and macroscopic ones in ways not even entirely transparent to the intellectually most impressive theoretical accounts of correlation across levels of the universe, i.e., those derivable from physics.

253

NOTES TO PAGES 115–124

69. Benedictus Spinoza, *The Collected Writings of Spinoza,* vol. 1: *Ethics,* trans. Edwin Curley (Princeton, NJ: Princeton University Press, 1985): "Una substantia quae iam sub hoc iam sub illo attributo comprehenditur" (Eth. II, prop. VII, schol.).

70. Gabriel, *Fields of Sense,* 230–231.

71. Graham Harman, "Objects and Fields of Sense: Reflections on Markus Gabriel's Ontology," in Voosholz, *Gabriel's New Realism.*

72. Gabriel, *Fields of Sense,* 13.

73. Harman, "Objects and Fields of Sense."

74. See Graham Harman, *The Quadruple Object* (Winchester, UK: Zero Books, 2011), and Maurizio Ferraris, *Emergenza* (Turin: Einaudi, 2016).

75. See the introduction to Sir Arthur Eddington, *The Nature of the Physical World* (Ann Arbor: University of Michigan Press, 1958), xi–xix.

76. Thanks to Joseph Pomp, who asked me to clarify the notion of ontological nonsense even in the absence of subjective confusion.

77. This wrongheaded metaphysical picture assumes that there are pure objects that are then sorted into different categories in one way or another, an idea Benoist has rejected under the critical label of "the myth of pure objects (le mythe des objets blancs)." Jocelyn Benoist, *Éléments de philosophie réaliste* (Paris: Vrin, 2011), 59.

78. Introduced in his seminar at Bonn's *International Center for Philosophy* in May–June 2018.

79. Ludwig Wittgenstein, *Remarks on the Foundations of Mathematics,* trans. Gertrude E. M. Anscombe, ed. Georg H. von Wright, Gertrude E. M. Anscombe, and Rush Rhees (Oxford: Blackwell, 1998), 84.

80. Wittgenstein, *Tractatus Logico-Philosophicus,* 6.54.

81. Taylor Carman, "Gabriel's Metaphysics of Sense," *Harvard Review of Philosophy* 23 (2016): 53–59, and subsequently Taylor Carman, "Existentialism as Anti-Rationalism," in Voosholz, *Gabriel's New Realism.* I use the epithet "neo-" quite deliberately to flag the difference between Heidegger (at least as I read him) and Carman. I think that Carman's Heidegger only loosely resembles the actual Heidegger, though in interesting enough ways to count as some kind of continuation of certain lines of thought present in Heidegger.

82. Carman, "Gabriel's Metaphysics of Sense," 54–55.

83. Carman, "Gabriel's Metaphysics of Sense," 55.

84. Carman, "Gabriel's Metaphysics of Sense," 59.

85. Martin Heidegger, *The Question Concerning Technology and Other Essays,* trans. and with an introduction by William Lovitt (New York: Garland, 1977), 17.

86. See also Tobias Keiling, *Seinsgeschichte und phänomenologischer Realismus: Eine Interpretation und Kritik der Spätphilosophie Heideggers* (Tübingen: Mohr Siebeck, 2015), and Jaroslaw Bledowski, *Zugang und Fraktur:*

254

NOTES TO PAGES 125–128

Heideggers Subjektivitätstheorie in "Sein und Zeit" (Tübingen: Mohr Siebeck, 2021).

87. Amir Eshel, *Poetic Thinking Today: An Essay* (Stanford, CA: Stanford University Press, 2019).

88. Carman, "Gabriel's Metaphysics of Sense," 54.

89. Carman, "Gabriel's Metaphysics of Sense," 53.

90. Georg Wilhelm Friedrich Hegel, *The Phenomenology of Spirit,* ed. and trans. Terry Pinkard (Cambridge: Cambridge University Press, 2018), 22.

91. Carman, "Gabriel's Metaphysics of Sense," 54.

92. Carman, "Gabriel's Metaphysics of Sense," 59.

93. Carman, "Gabriel's Metaphysics of Sense," 59.

94. Carman, "Existentialism as Anti-Rationalism."

95. Carman, "Existentialism as Anti-Rationalism."

96. Thanks to Harald Atmanspacher for clarifying some of the fundamental notions of physics referred to here in his written comments on this chapter.

97. To be sure, Heidegger runs into difficulties with correlationism, but these difficulties are much more theoretically refined than Carman's dogma that to appear is to appear to someone suggests. See Markus Gabriel, "Ancestrality and (In-)Dependence: On Heidegger on Being-In-Itself," *British Journal for the History of Philosophy* 30, no. 3 (2022): 535–546, and Gabriel, *Fields of Sense,* 197–200. Carman does not bother to mention the detailed readings of Heidegger and his critique of metaphysics throughout *Fields of Sense,* a revealing lacuna.

98. See the classical statement of a tenable form of descriptivism in John R. Searle, "Proper Names," *Mind* 67, no. 266 (1958): 166–173. Notice that Searle neither argues that the meaning of a proper name is identical with its descriptive content nor that a speaker has to be in a position to specify the descriptive content of a given proper name. His view is only "that the descriptive force" of a statement such as "this is Aristotle" "is to assert that a sufficient number of these statements are true of this object. Therefore, referring uses of "Aristotle" presuppose the existence of an object of whom a sufficient but so far unspecified number of these statements are true" (171). Given that we cannot and, thus, need not specify all "characteristics" that "constituted the identity of Aristotle," there is a constitutive use of proper names in which they are not reducible to descriptions, though any proper name is associated with an unspecified range of descriptions without which we could not use the name in the context of the intention to refer to some existing object or other. Searle explicitly argues that proper names, therefore, are not "logically equivalent" to any "set of descriptions." For "if this were the case we would be in the position of only being able to refer to an object by describing it. Whereas in fact this is just what the institution of proper names enables us to avoid and what distinguishes proper names from descriptions" (171). Qua proper names,

255

NOTES TO PAGES 128–129

then, terms such as "Aristotle" "function not as descriptions, but as pegs on which to hang descriptions" (171). Yet, this entails that there is an essential relationship between descriptions and objects referred to by proper names.

99. Again, while he somewhat correctly describes one way of getting to the no-world-view at the beginning of his article, within just a few paragraphs he moves to a maximally uncharitable reading by claiming that my "conclusion that 'objects are individuated by descriptions' *evidently* amounts to no more than the thesis that facts are metaphysically fundamental. That is not a trivial thesis, but it is a metaphysical thesis." Carman, "Gabriel's Metaphysics of Sense," 54; emphasis added.

100. In Markus Gabriel, "Sinn, Existenz und das Transfinite," in *Welt und Unendlichkeit: Ein deutsch-ungarischer Dialog in memoriam László Tengelyi,* ed. Markus Gabriel, Csaba Olay, and Sebastian Ostritsch (Freiburg: Verlag Karl Alber, 2017), 187–204, I discuss Fernando Pessoa's poem "The King of Gaps" (in *A Little Larger than the Entire Universe: Selected Poems* [London: Penguin, 2006], 420):

> There lived, I know not when, never perhaps—
> But the fact is he lives—an unknown king,
> Whose kingdom was the strange Kingdom of Gaps.
> He was lord of what is twixt thing and thing,
> Of interbeings, of that part of us
> That lies between our waking and our sleep,
> Between our silence and our speech, between
> Us and the consciousness of us; and thus
> A strange mute kingdom did that weird king keep
> Sequestered from our thought of time and scene.
> Those supreme purposes that never reach
> The deed—between them and the deed undone—
> He rules, uncrowned. He is the mystery which
> Is between eyes and sight, nor blind, nor seeing,
> Himself is never ended nur begun,
> Above his own void presence empty shelf.
> All He is but a chasm of his own being,
> The lidless box holding not-being's no-pelf.
> All think that he is God, except himself.

101. Marisa Galvez, "Unthought Medievalism," *Neophilologus* 105 (2021): 365–389, here 371.

102. Galvez, "Unthought Medievalism," 371.

103. See the famous reflections on meaning and how it is grounded in stimulus meaning in Willard van Orman Quine, *Word and Object* (Cambridge,

256

MA: MIT Press, 1960), 32–36, encapsulated in the statement from page 32: "For meaning, supposedly, is what a sentence shares with its translation; and translation at the present stage turns solely on correlations with non-verbal stimulation."

104. William Shakespeare, *Macbeth*, 5.5:25–27: "A tale / told by an idiot, full of sound and fury / signifying nothing." In *The New Oxford Shakespeare: The Complete Works; Modern Critical Edition*, ed. Gary Taylor, John Jowett, Terri Bourus, and Gabriel Egan (Oxford: Oxford University Press, 2016), 2505–2563, here 2561.

105. Quoted from Marisa Galvez, "The Production of Medieval Life Forms in the Work of Gumbrecht," Arcade: Literature, Humanities, and the World, accessed October 4, 2022, https://arcade.stanford.edu/content/pro duction-medieval-life-forms-work-gumbrecht.

106. Ludwig Wittgenstein, *Culture and Value*, ed. Georg H. von Wright, trans. Peter Winch (Oxford: Blackwell, 1980), 56.

107. Carman, "Existentialism as Anti-Rationalism."

108. See Gabriel, *Why the World Does Not Exist*, 221: "We find ourselves together on a great expedition—we have arrived here from nowhere, and together we set out into the infinite."

109. Huw Price famously made a case for "the view from nowhen" according to which entropy is a red herring and does not establish the existence of an arrow of time within physics. See Huw Price, *Time's Arrow and Archimedes' Point: New Directions for the Physics of Time* (Oxford: Oxford University Press, 1998).

110. Some read FOS as a rather Eleatic view, an ontological version of a four-dimensional block universe. See David Espinet, "Stillgestellte Existenz? Gegenstand und Ereignis," in Gaitsch, Lehmann and Schmidt, *Eine Diskussion mit Markus Gabriel*, 128–145, and my reply in the same volume, 244–247.

111. See the ontology of the modalities in Gabriel, *Fields of Sense*, chaps. 10–11.

112. James Hill, "Markus Gabriel against the World," *Sophia* 56, no. 2 (2017): 471–481.

113. Gabriel, *Fields of Sense*, 200–201.

114. James Hill, "Does the World Exist? Markus Gabriel and Absolute Generality," *Philosophy Today* 66, no. 3 (2022): 491–506.

115. Hill, "Does the World Exist?," 497.

116. Hill, "Does the World Exist?," 493.

117. Hill, "Does the World Exist?," 497.

118. Theodore Sider, *Writing the Book of the World* (Oxford: Oxford University Press, 2011), 18.

119. Richard Rorty, "The World Well Lost," *Journal of Philosophy* 69, no. 19 (1972): 649–665.

NOTES TO PAGES 133–142

120. Remarkably, Schopenhauer does not bother to tell his readers what he means by "the world" at all. This is even more surprising given that his opus magnum is dedicated to his "discovery" that there is a "world as representation" and a "world as will," which seems to presuppose that there is something (namely the world) that manifests itself to the thinker under two broad kinds of conception. How this works, and how Schopenhauer knows this, remains a mystery.

121. Friedrich Nietzsche, *The Birth of Tragedy and Other Writings,* ed. Raymond Geuss and Ronald Speirs, trans. Ronald Speirs (Cambridge: Cambridge University Press, 1999), 33.

122. Nietzsche, *The Birth of Tragedy,* 33.

123. Wittgenstein, *Philosophical Investigations,* trans. G. E. M. Anscombe, P. M. S. Hacker, and Joachim Schulte, rev. 4th ed. by P. M. S. Hacker and Joachim Schulte (Oxford: Wiley-Blackwell, 2009) 11ᵉ. See also Carman, "Gabriel's Metaphysics of Sense," 53.

124. As Azzouni claims in his response to FOS in Azzouni, "A White Horse Is Not a Horse."

125. Raoul Moati, *Derrida / Searle: Deconstruction and Ordinary Language,* trans. Timothy Attanucci and Maureen Chun (New York: Columbia University Press, 2014), and Philip Freytag, *Die Rahmung des Hintergrunds: Eine Untersuchung über die Voraussetzungen von Sprachtheorien am Leitfaden der Debatten Derrida-Searle und Searle-Habermas* (Frankfurt am Main: Klostermann, 2019).

126. Jacques Derrida, *Limited Inc.* (Evanston, IL: Northwestern University Press, 1988), 16–17.

127. Wittgenstein, *Tractatus Logico-Philosophicus,* slightly altered translation of 6.54.

128. Wittgenstein, *Tractatus Logico-Philosophicus,* 5.631.

129. Wittgenstein, *Tractatus Logico-Philosophicus,* 5.632.

130. Ernest Sosa, *Knowing Full Well* (Princeton, NJ: Princeton University Press, 2011).

131. As I argued extensively in Gabriel, *The Limits of Epistemology.*

132. Markus Gabriel and Slavoj Žižek, *Mythology, Madness, and Laughter: Subjectivity in German Idealism* (London: Continuum, 2009).

3. Subjectivity

1. For a popular appraisal of this feature of subjectivity, see Kathryn Schulz, *Being Wrong: Adventures in the Margin of Error* (New York: Harper-Collins, 2010). For a recent philosophical and ethical analysis, see Costica Bradatan, *In Praise of Failure: Four Lessons in Humility* (Cambridge, MA: Harvard University Press, 2023).

NOTES TO PAGES 142–147

2. Christoph Horn's question in an online workshop with Daniel Kahneman on *Noise* (see note 3 below) on March 1, 2022, organized by The New Institute in Hamburg, Germany.

3. Daniel Kahneman, Olivier Sibony, and Cass R. Sunstein, *Noise: A Flaw in Human Judgment* (London: William Collins, 2021).

4. Kahneman, Sibony, and Sunstein, *Noise,* 78.

5. As Kahneman pointed out in the same conversation, psychological evidence clearly indicates that large-scale individual behavioral change as a consequence of an insight into one's noisy tendencies is, if anything, an exception to the rule of our ultimately unruly minds. Moral progress—to the extent to which it exists—is thus not a cumulative affair, but disturbed by psychosocial patterns that could in principle become the object of social-scientific investigations led by normative insight into how we ought to act.

6. Quassim Cassam, *Vices of the Mind: From the Intellectual to the Political* (Oxford: Oxford University Press, 2019), 109–110.

7. The term "rational reconstruction" is borrowed from Carnap who, in his *The Logical Structure of the World,* engages in the activity of "rational reconstruction of an entity which has already been constructed in a partly intuitive, partly rational way in daily life or in the sciences." Rudolf Carnap, *The Logical Structure of the World and Pseudoproblems in Philosophy,* trans. Rolf A. George (Chicago: Open Court, 2003), 156, §98. To be sure, he thought that rational reconstruction should take a particular logical form rather than engage in overall conceptual analysis guided by controlled moves in a game of giving and asking for reasons. This technical part of his enterprise is obsolete.

8. See Markus Gabriel, *The Limits of Epistemology,* trans. Alex Englander (Cambridge: Polity, 2020), 251.

9. Georg Wilhelm Friedrich Hegel, *The Phenomenology of Spirit,* ed. and trans. Terry Pinkard (Cambridge: Cambridge University Press, 2018), 22.

10. See again Sebastian Rödl, *Self-Consciousness and Objectivity: An Introduction to Absolute Idealism* (Cambridge, MA: Harvard University Press, 2018). For a fuller picture, see Klaus Düsing, *Das Problem der Subjektivität in Hegels Logik: Systematische und entwicklungsgeschichtliche Untersuchungen zum Prinzip des Idealismus und zur Dialektik* (Hamburg: Meiner, 1995).

11. See John McDowell, *Mind and World* (Cambridge, MA: Harvard University Press, 1996), 27, where McDowell draws on Ludwig Wittgenstein, *Philosophical Investigations* (Oxford: Basil Blackwell, 1963), I, §95.

12. See the collection of essays Andrea Kern and Christian Kietzmann, eds., *Selbstbewusstes Leben* (Berlin: Suhrkamp, 2017).

13. See paradigmatically Michael Thompson, *Life and Action: Elementary Structures of Practice and Practical Thought* (Cambridge, MA: Harvard University Press, 2012).

NOTES TO PAGES 147–154

14. Which of course does not mean that we never reach them or that we are somehow screened off from them as a matter of principle, as the skeptic maintains. See again Gabriel, *The Limits of Epistemology.*

15. See Markus Gabriel, *Moral Progress in Dark Times: Universal Values for the Twenty-First Century,* trans. Wieland Hoban (Cambridge: Polity, 2022).

16. Aristotle, *Metaphysics,* I 1, 980a 21.

17. For this account of the humanities and their specific objectivity, see Markus Gabriel, *Fictions,* trans. Wieland Hoban (Cambridge: Polity, 2023), and the discussion paper Markus Gabriel et al., *Towards a New Enlightenment: The Case for Future-Oriented Humanities* (Bielefeld: Transcript Verlag, 2022).

18. Skepticism can be used as a tool for generating self-knowledge in virtue of putting our knowledge claims into context. As I have argued in *Transcendental Ontology* and *The Limits of Epistemology,* too many contemporary epistemologists recklessly neglect a decisive insight from the Kantian and Post-Kantian tradition: There is no way to begin to understand knowledge without accounting for actual self-knowledge. Without actual self-knowledge, we could not get knowledge as an object of further investigation into view.

19. See McDowell, *Mind and World;* John McDowell, "Criteria, Defeasibility and Knowledge," *Proceedings of the British Academy* 68 (1982): 455–479; John McDowell, "The Disjunctive Conception of Experience as Material for the Transcendental Argument," in *Disjunctivism: Perception, Action, Knowledge,* ed. Adrian Haddock and Fiona Macpherson (New York: Oxford University Press, 2008), 376–389; Timothy Williamson, *Knowledge and Its Limits* (Oxford: Oxford University Press, 2000).

20. To be distinguished from the view that the fallibilism / infallibilism distinction concerns the status of evidence for the truth of the proposition known. On this, see Jessica Brown, *Fallibilism: Evidence and Knowledge* (Oxford: Oxford University Press, 2018). She believes that the issue of fallibilism turns on a decision between the fallibilist view about evidence ("one can know that p even though one's evidence does not guarantee the truth of p") and its infallibilist counterpart ("one can know that p only if one's evidence guarantees the truth of p") (2).

21. See Richard Gaskin, *The Unity of the Proposition* (Oxford: Oxford University Press, 2008).

22. Bertrand Russell, *Philosophical Essays* (London: Routledge, 1966), 174–175; Richard Cartwright, *Philosophical Essays* (Cambridge, MA: MIT Press, 1987), 79–84; Gaskin, *The Unity of the Proposition,* 48–53, 109–111.

23. See Graham Priest, *In Contradiction: A Study of the Transconsistent,* 2nd ed. (Oxford: Clarendon Press, 2006); Graham Priest, *Doubt Truth to Be a Liar* (Oxford: Oxford University Press, 2006); and Graham Priest, *An Introduction to Non-Classical Logic: From If to Is,* 2nd ed. (Cambridge: Cambridge University Press, 2008).

NOTES TO PAGES 155–164

24. See Irad Kimhi, *Thinking and Being* (Cambridge, MA: Harvard University Press, 2018).

25. See Geert Keil, *Wenn ich micht nicht irre: Ein Versuch über die menschliche Fehlbarkeit* (Stuttgart: Reclam Verlag, 2019), and my earlier work in Markus Gabriel, *Propos réalistes* (Paris: Librairie philosophique J. Vrin, 2020).

26. This is Fichte's actual insight. See Markus Gabriel, "Truths and Posits—The Realm of Sense according to Fichte's Wissenschaftslehre 1794," in *The Palgrave Handbook of German Idealism and Analytic Philosophy,* ed. James Conant and Jonas Held (London: Palgrave Macmillian, forthcoming).

27. See Stanley Cavell, *The Claim of Reason: Wittgenstein, Skepticism, Morality, and Tragedy* (Cambridge, MA: Harvard University Press, 1979), 178: "We begin to feel, or ought to, terrified that maybe language (and understanding, and knowledge) rests upon very shaky foundations—a thin net over an abyss."

28. Or, as Hilary Putnam famously put it in *Reason, Truth, and History* (Cambridge: Cambridge University Press, 2012), xi, "Mind and world jointly make up mind and world."

29. See Tyler Burge, "Perceptual Entitlement," *Philosophy and Phenomenological Research* 67, no. 3 (2003): 503–548, and more recently Tyler Burge, "Psychological Content and Ego-Centric Indexes," in *Blockheads! Essays on Ned Block's Philosophy of Mind and Consciousness,* ed. Adam Pautz and Daniel Stoljar (Cambridge, MA: MIT Press, 2019), 41–69.

30. See José Luis Bermudez, *The Paradox of Self-Consciousness* (Cambridge, MA: MIT Press, 1998).

31. Kenneth Williford, "The Self-Representational Structure of Consciousness," in *Self-Representational Approaches to Consciousness,* ed. Uriah Kriegel and Kenneth Williford (Cambridge, MA: MIT Press, 2006), 111–142, here 113: "According to the oldest objection, ubiquity is involved in at least one of two infinite regresses. Put as a dilemma, it is that ubiquity entails either that there are infinitely many distinct conscious mental states or that a single conscious mental state must represent infinitely many objects individually."

32. Hugo von Hofmannsthal, *The Lord Chandos Letter: And Other Writings,* trans. Joel Rotenberg (New York: NYRB Classics, 2012).

33. See Markus Gabriel, "The Paradox of Self-Consciousness: A Conversation with Markus Gabriel," Edge.org, November 2019, https://www.edge.org/conversation/markus_gabriel-the-paradox-of-self-consciousness.

34. Thanks to one of the anonymous reviewers for asking me to clarify this particular point.

35. The drawing appears for the first time in Ernst Mach, *Beiträge zur Analyse der Empfindungen* (Jena: Fischer, 1886), 15.

36. See Henri Bergson, *Time and Free Will: An Essay on the Immediate Data of Consciousness,* trans. F. L. Pogson (1889; repr., Whitefish, MT:

NOTES TO PAGES 164–172

Kessinger, 1910), 219, 229 and William James, *The Principles of Psychology* (1890; repr., Cambridge, MA: Harvard Press, 1981), 236.

37. Relatedly, famous work by the neurophysiologist Eric Kandel (like Kahneman, a recipient of the Nobel Prize) is widely regarded as having shown that there are non-conscious, nay, unconscious mental and / or physiological processes that make up an iceberg the tip of which might be consciousness. Eric R. Kandel, *In Search of Memory: The Emergence of a New Science of Mind* (New York: Norton, 2006).

38. On this gap and how it is the source of the famous "explanatory gap" introduced by Joseph Levine, see Markus Gabriel, *Neo-Existentialism: How to Conceive of the Human Mind after Naturalism's Failure* (Cambridge: Polity, 2018), 17–18. On the explanatory gap, see Joseph Levine, *Purple Haze: The Puzzle of Consciousness* (Oxford: Oxford University Press, 2004).

39. Andrea Kern, *Sources of Knowledge: On the Concept of a Rational Capacity for Knowledge,* trans. Daniel Smyth (Cambridge, MA: Harvard University Press, 2017).

40. Plato, *Theaetetus,* 201c9–d1.

41. Georg Wilhelm Friedrich Hegel, "On the Relationship of Skepticism to Philosophy, Exposition of Its Different Modifications and Comparison of the Latest Form with the Ancient One," in *Between Kant and Hegel: Texts in the Development of Post-Kantian Idealism,* ed. George Di Giovanni and H. S. Harris, trans. H. S. Harris (Indianapolis: Hackett, 2000), 311–362, here 354.

42. See Markus Gabriel, *Skeptizismus und Idealismus in der Antike* (Frankfurt am Main: Suhrkamp, 2009).

43. See Immanuel Kant, *Critique of Pure Reason,* ed. and trans. Paul Guyer and Allen W. Wood (Cambridge: Cambridge University Press, 1998), §16 (B132–136).

44. As I put it in Gabriel, *The Limits of Epistemology,* 134, 175.

45. Freud identifies the unconscious as the "mark of the mental" in the sense of the "psychical." See Sigmund Freud, *The Interpretation of Dreams,* ed. and trans. James Strachey (New York: Basic Books, 2010), 607: "The unconscious is the larger sphere, which includes within it the smaller sphere of the conscious. Everything conscious has an unconscious preliminary stage; whereas what is unconscious may remain at that stage and nevertheless claim to be regarded as having the full value of a psychical process. The unconscious is the true psychical reality; in its innermost nature it is as much unknown to us as the reality of the external world, and it is as incompletely presented by the data of consciousness as is the external world by the communications of our sense organs."

46. Franz Müller-Lyer, "Optische Urteilstäuschungen," *Archiv für Anatomie und Physiologie, Physiologische Abteilung* 2, suppl. (1889): 263–270.

47. See Stephen Biggs, Mohan Matthen, and Dustin Stokes, eds., *Perception and Its Modalities* (Oxford: Oxford University Press, 2014).

NOTES TO PAGES 172–181

48. With reference to seminar work by Michael Anderson, "Neural Reuse: A Fundamental Organizational Principle of the Brain," *Behavioral and Brain Sciences* 33, no. 4 (2010): 245–266.

49. Harald Atmanspacher and Dean Rickles, *Dual-Aspect Monism and the Deep Structure of Meaning* (New York: Routledge, 2022), §3.2.

50. Anderson, "Neural Reuse."

51. I owe this version of the paragraph to Harald Atmanspacher, who provided me with written comments on the chapter.

52. Markus Gabriel, *Der Mensch als Tier: Warum wir trotzdem nicht in die Natur passen* (Berlin: Ullstein, 2022).

53. Heraclitus, DK B123: φύσις κρύπτεσθαι φιλεῖ. Eng. trans. by Charles H. Kahn in *The Art and Thought of Heraclitus* (Cambridge: Cambridge University Press, 1979), 32, 33: "Nature loves to hide."

54. Quantum mechanics and its commitment to some form of indeterminacy poses no obstacle to physicalism thus understood, as it merely amounts to an insight into novel mathematical features in the description of physical properties (i.e., their non-commutativity) that leads to restrictions on their simultaneous determinacy and, as a consequence, measurability. This indeterminacy is reflected in the mathematical apparatus of quantum mechanics and does not as such speak in favor of any relevant limitation of physicalism. Physicalism in the sense of a commitment to a full coincidence of mathematical accessibility and being is not disproved by the existence of phenomena that require new modes of mathematical thinking.

55. Gabriel, *Der Mensch als Tier.*

56. Markus Gabriel, *Fiktionen* (Berlin: Suhrkamp, 2020), 80, grounded in Fredrick Kroon, Stuart Brock, and Jonathan McKeown-Green, eds., *A Critical Introduction to Fictionalism* (London: Bloomsbury, 2019); Mark Eli Kalderon, ed., *Fictionalism in Metaphysics* (Oxford: Clarendon Press, 2005); Richard Mark Sainsbury, *Fiction and Fictionalism* (London: Routledge, 2010); and Kwame Anthony Appiah, *As If: Idealization and Ideals* (Cambridge, MA: Harvard University Press, 2017).

57. Hans Vaihinger, *The Philosophy of "As If": A System of the Theoretical, Practical and Religious Fictions of Mankind,* trans. C. K. Ogden (Mansfield Center, CT: Martino, 2009).

58. George F. R. Ellis, Krzysztof A. Meissner, and Hermann Nicolai, "The Physics of Infinity," *Nature Physics* 14, no. 8 (2018): 770–772.

59. Arthur Fine, "Fictionalism," *Midwest Studies in Philosophy* 18, no. 1 (1993): 1–18.

60. See Markus Gabriel, *The Meaning of Thought,* trans. Alex Englander (Cambridge: Polity, 2020), 170, where I define "basic reality" (*Basiswirklichkeit*) as the domain of "anything that is itself neither a simulation nor something that came into being via a human intention to produce an artefact."

NOTES TO PAGES 181–189

61. Notice that I am not revising my earlier claim that mind-independence is not the hallmark of reality, let alone of realism, as minds exist in any relevant sense of the term, and are thereby objects of realist thought and discourse. The earlier claim never amounted to the much stronger (and false) view that there is no mind-independent reality. Yet, I certainly hold that there is no mind-independent world, but not because the world is mind-dependent, but rather because it does not exist. See Gabriel, "Neutral Realism."

62. On this puzzle, see Eugene Wigner, "The Unreasonable Effectiveness of Mathematics in the Natural Sciences," *Communications in Pure and Applied Mathematics* 13 (1960): 1–14; Atmanspracher and Rickles, *Dual-Aspect Monism and the Deep Structure of Meaning,* §§7.2 (173–176) and 7.5 (185–188).

63. Markus Gabriel, "Neutral Realism," *The Monist* 98, no. 2 (2015): 185–187, and *The Meaning of Thought,* chap. 5.

64. Again, thanks to Harald Atmanspacher for correcting some of the physics-related formulations in an earlier version of this paragraph.

65. This speaks in favor of an interventionist theory of causation, at least in the field of natural scientific explanation. See James Woodward, *Making Things Happen: A Theory of Causal Explanation* (Oxford: Oxford University Press, 2003).

66. Emil Heinrich Du Bois-Reymond, "The Limits of Our Knowledge of Nature," *Popular Science Monthly* 5 (1884): 17–32.

67. Du Bois-Reymond, "The Limits of Our Knowledge of Nature," 29.

68. Du Bois-Reymond, "The Limits of Our Knowledge of Nature," 24.

69. Du Bois-Reymond, "The Limits of Our Knowledge of Nature," 29.

70. On this point, see Harald Atmanspacher, "Why Physics Does Not Inform the Human Condition, But Its Boundaries Do," forthcoming in *Foundations of Science.*

71. Du Bois-Reymond, "The Limits of Our Knowledge of Nature," 29.

72. Thanks to George Ellis for repeatedly pointing this out during our ongoing conversation on the relationship between physics and the parts of mathematics that should not be treated as referring to events and structures in the universe.

73. On the importance of a distinction between a "philosophical dualism and a philosophical distinction," see Hilary Putnam, *The Collapse of the Fact/Value Dichotomy and Other Essays Including the Rosenthal Lectures* (Cambridge, MA: Harvard University Press, 2002), 9–12.

74. Atmanspacher and Rickles, *Dual-Aspect Monism and the Deep Structure of Meaning* propose such a field theory of sense in §7.4.

75. I owe this paragraph and some of the formulations to written comments by Alexander Englander. Thanks to Harald Atmanspacher, Stephan Hartmann, George Ellis, and Delícia Kamins for discussion of exactly this point during our workshop on mind and the universe at The New Institute in Hamburg on May 24–25, 2022.

NOTES TO PAGES 190–199

76. The first statement of this particular worry is from Jens Rometsch, "Ontologie ohne Metaphysik?," in *Das neue Bedürfnis nach Metaphysik / The New Desire for Metaphysics,* ed. Markus Gabriel, Wolfram Hogrebe, and Andreas Speer (Berlin: De Gruyter, 2015), 201–206.

77. Let alone a Meillassouxian hyperchaos in the sense of Quentin Meillassoux, *After Finitude: An Essay on the Necessity of Contingency,* trans. Ray Brassier (London: Continuum, 2008), 64.

78. As imagined by Lisa Randall, *Warped Passages. Unraveling the Mysteries of the Universe's Hidden Dimensions* (New York: Ecco, 2005).

79. See Immanuel Kant, *Groundwork of the Metaphysics of the Moral,* vol. 4, trans. Mary Gregor and Jens Timmermann (Cambridge: Cambridge University Press, 2012), 414, 439. A Kantian holy will is incapable of forming maxims (roughly: intentions) that do not automatically coincide with the moral law. A holy will would, therefore, not count as subjective in the sense laid out in the main text. On the issue of moral saints and why they are not required for understanding the demands of actual morality, see again Susan Wolf, "Moral Saints," *Journal of Philosophy* 79, no. 8 (1982).

80. For details, see the social ontology presented in Gabriel, *Fictions,* §§12–17.

81. See Takahiro Nakajima, "Human Co-becoming: Redefining What It Means to Be Human for the Super Smart Society," *Hitachi Review* 68, no. 5 (November 2019): 572–573, https://www.hitachi.com/rev/column/ei/pdf /P004-005_R5_experts_insight01.pdf.

82. All quotes are from a not-yet-published book manuscript on ordinary self-consciousness. Thanks to Lucy O'Brien for sharing the material in the context of the seminar on her work sponsored by the Humboldt Research Award, which she received in 2021, and for her permission to quote from the manuscript here. For an outline of her theory, see also her "Ordinary Self-Consciousness," in *Consciousness and the Self: New Essays,* ed. JeeLoo Liu and John Perry (Cambridge: Cambridge University Press, 2011), 101–122.

83. Markus Gabriel, "What Kind of an Idealist (If Any) Is Hegel?," *Hegel Bulletin* 37, no. 2 (2016): 181–208.

84. The relationship should not be reduced to con-specifics; it also holds inter-species. As she rightly emphasizes later, "there is no reason to think that basic forms of evaluation are not spread widely across the animal kingdom."

85. See Markus Gabriel, *I am Not a Brain: Philosophy of Mind for the Twenty-First Century,* trans. Christopher Turner (Cambridge: Polity, 2017); Gabriel, *Neo-Existentialism;* and Gabriel, *Fictions.*

86. Gabriel, *I am Not a Brain,* chap. 5.

87. Gabriel, *Der Mensch als Tier,* 34–38.

88. In light of such a consideration, Derek Parfit goes as far as claiming: "The body below the neck is not an essential part of us." Derek Parfit, "We Are Not Human Beings," in *Animalism: New Essays on Persons, Animals, and*

NOTES TO PAGES 201–206

Identity, ed. Stephan Blatti and Paul F. Snowdon (Oxford: Oxford University Press, 2016), 31–49, here 40.

89. For some more details, see Gabriel, *Moral Progress in Dark Times.*

90. Bernard Gert and Joshua Gert, "The Definition of Morality," in *The Stanford Encyclopedia of Philosophy* (Fall 2020 edition), ed. Edward N. Zalta, https://plato.stanford.edu/archives/fall2020/entries/morality-definition.

91. See Nakajima, "Human Co-becoming."

92. As Gert Scobel and I put it in our conversations on the foundations of ethics in Markus Gabriel and Gert Scobel, *Zwischen Gut und Böse: Philosophie der radikalen Mitte* (Hamburg: Edition Körber, 2021).

93. See Gabriel, *Moral Progress in Dark Times.*

94. Evidently, this is a reference to Thomas M. Scanlon's seminal *What We Owe to Each Other* (Cambridge, MA: Belknap Press of Harvard University Press, 1998). In particular, I follow him in his restriction of ethics to a smaller domain than that of "morality" in the broadest sense of the term which, as he surmises, might not be "a single subject that has a similar unity" (7) to that of the domain of our mutual obligations. As is well known, his account of the structure of morally relevant mutual obligations is based on the view "that thinking about right and wrong is, at the most basic level, thinking about what could be justified to others on grounds that they, if appropriately motivated, could not reasonably reject." (5) In general, moral motivation draws on the idea that people are "moved to find principles for the general regulation of behavior that others, similarly motivated, could not reasonably reject." (4) In this context, I introduce the concept of human mindedness (*Geist*) in order to account for the source of our capacity to act both in light of a self-conception (self-determination) and to be corrigible by others with whom we share the common feature of humanity, i.e., the capacity for self-determination that is always actualized in diverse modes of actually being human. This corresponds to a certain extent to Scanlon's idea of the value of human (that is, for him, rational) life; see 103–107.

95. See Frans de Waal, *Good Natured: The Origins of Right and Wrong in Humans and Other Animals* (Cambridge, MA: Harvard University Press, 1996), and Frans de Waal, *Primates and Philosophers: How Morality Evolved,* ed. Stephen Macedo and Josiah Ober (Princeton, NJ: Princeton University Press, 2016).

96. Kant, *Groundwork of the Metaphysics of the Moral,* 4:439.

97. On radical evil as propensity to deviate from the universal moral law, see Immanuel Kant, "Religion within the Boundaries of Mere Reason, Part One: Concerning the Indwelling of the Evil Principle alongside the Good, or, of Radical Evil in Human Nature," in *Religion within the Boundaries of Mere Reason and Other Writings,* ed. and trans. Allen Wood and George Di Giovanni (Cambridge: Cambridge University Press, 2018), 45–73.

NOTES TO PAGES 208-212

Conclusion

1. Markus Gabriel, *Fictions,* trans. Wieland Hoban (Cambridge: Polity, 2023), §§12–17.

2. See Michael Tomasello, *A Natural History of Human Morality* (Cambridge, MA: Harvard University Press, 2016).

3. See Gabriel, *Fictions,* §13.

4. See again Philip N. Howard, *Lie Machines: How to Save Democracy from Troll Armies, Deceitful Robots, Junk News Operations, and Political Operatives* (New Haven, CT: Yale University Press, 2020). On a reading of ChatGPT's so-called hallucination of content (i.e., its making up alleged facts concerning, for instance, political theories or fictional characters, based on its statistical mode of calculating the probability that, say, someone is both a democrat and a defender of the division of powers) in terms of Harry Frankfurt's notion of bullshit as a form of discourse that is not even in the business of pretending to speak the truth, see Jocelyn Maclure's recent opinion piece "ChatGPT, baratineur," *La Presse,* January 18, 2023, https://www.lapresse.ca/debats/opinions/2023-01-18/chatgpt-baratineur.php.

5. For a map of the various critical-negative uses of "ideology," see the essays in Slavoj Žižek, ed., *Mapping Ideology* (London: Verso, 1994). For a nuanced account of ideology in the context of a social theory of mass communication, see John B. Thompson, *Ideology and Modern Culture: Critical Social Theory in the Era of Communication* (Cambridge: Polity, 1990). For an overview of the history of ideology and ideology critique, see Jan Rehmann, *Einführung in die Ideologietheorie* (Hamburg: Argument Verlag, 2008).

6. For a philosophical and linguistic analysis of the negative use and function of propaganda in the contemporary public sphere, see Jason Stanley, *How Propaganda Works* (Princeton, NJ: Princeton University Press, 2015).

7. See Harry Frankfurt, *On Bullshit* (Princeton, NJ: Princeton University Press, 2005).

8. See Jonathan Auerbach and Russ Castronovo, eds., *The Oxford Handbook of Propaganda Studies* (Oxford: Oxford University Press, 2013), in particular the introduction, 1–16, and the comprehensive study in Thymian Bussemer, *Propaganda: Konzepte und Theorien,* mit einem einführenden Vorwort von Peter Glotz, 2, überarbeitete Auflage (Wiesbaden: VS Verlag für Sozialwissenschaften, 2008).

9. For such a positive use in the context of an "ethics of not-knowing," see Markus Gabriel, *Der Mensch als Tier: Warum wir trotzdem nicht in die Natur passen* (Berlin: Ullstein, 2022), 217–292. See also Stuart Firestein, *Ignorance: How It Drives Science* (New York: Oxford University Press, 2012). For a comprehensive overview of the field, see Matthias Gross and Linsey McGoey,

eds., *Routledge International Handbook of Ignorance Studies,* 2nd ed. (London: Routledge, 2022).

10. On social critique as immanent, see Rahel Jaeggi, *Critique of Forms of Life,* trans. Ciaran Cronin (Cambridge, MA: Belknap Press of Harvard University Press, 2018).

11. Max Scheler, *The Human Place in the Cosmos,* trans. Manfred S. Frings, with an introduction by Eugene Kelly (Evanston, IL: Northwestern University Press, 2008).

12. Recent examples for this ideological genre are Sean Carroll, *The Big Picture: On the Origins of Life, Meaning, and the Universe Itself* (New York: Dutton, 2016), and Max Tegmark, *Life 3.0: Being Human in the Age of Artificial Intelligence* (London: Allen Lange, 2017).

13. See prominently Toby Ord, *The Precipice: Existential Risk and the Future of Humanity* (New York: Hachette, 2020), and William MacAskill, *What We Owe the Future* (New York: Basic Books, 2022).

14. For a classic (itself propagandistic) defense of propaganda, see Edward Bernays, *Propaganda,* with an introduction by Mark Crispin Miller (1928; repr., New York: Ig Publishing, 2005). For a classic, general critical account of it, see the equally influential Jacques Ellul, *Propaganda: The Formation of Men's Attitudes,* trans. Konrad Kellen and Jean Lerner, with an introduction by Konrad Kellen (New York: Vintage Books, 1973).

15. My translation of Bussemer, *Propaganda,* 33: "*als die in der Regel medienvermittelte Formierung handlungsrelevanter Meinungen und Einstellungen politischer oder sozialer Großgruppen durch symbolische Kommunikation und als Herstellung von Öffentlichkeit zugunsten bestimmter Interessen.*"

16. See Bussemer, *Propaganda,* 33.

17. See Gabriel, *Fictions,* §17, with reference to Habermas's account of electronic mass media in the preface to the 1990 edition of *The Structural Transformation of the Public Sphere: An Inquiry into a Category of Burgeois Society,* trans. Thomas Burger with the assistance of Frederick Lawrence (Cambridge, MA: MIT Press, 1991), and Habermas's own most recent *Ein neuer Strukturwandel der Öffentlichkeit und die deliberative Politik* (Berlin: Suhrkamp, 2022).

18. I owe the insight that polarization in democratic societies, like ideology and propaganda, can be classified as positive and negative to discussions with members of the "depolarizing public debates" program at the New Institute in Hamburg, led by Michael Brüggemann. For how to translate some of the tools of Habermas's theory of the communicative action and the associated account of the public sphere to contemporary media theory, see Hartmut Wessler, *Habermas and the Media* (Cambridge: Polity, 2018).

19. For my own specific reasons for rejecting a fully socialist account of subjectivity in terms of structural, intersubjective relations, see again Gabriel, *Fictions,* §§12–17, and Markus Gabriel, "A Very Heterodox Reading of the Lord-

Servant-Allegory in Hegel's *Phenomenology of Spirit,"* in *German Idealism Today,* ed. Markus Gabriel and Anders Moe Rasmussen (Berlin: De Gruyter, 2017), 95–120.

20. For an overview over those strategies, including a proposal for how to unify these propositional epistemological analyses of ignorance with the idea of ignorance as a social mistake, see Nadja El Kassar, "What Ignorance Really Is: Examining the Foundations of Epistemology of Ignorance," *Social Epistemology,* 32, no. 5 (2018): 300–310.

21. Immanuel Kant, *Critique of Pure Reason,* ed. and trans. Paul Guyer and Allen W. Wood (Cambridge: Cambridge University Press, 1998), A5.

ACKNOWLEDGMENTS

During the conception and the writing of this book, various institutions and colleagues to whom I am grateful supported my work. First and foremost, I thank my research teams at the chair in epistemology, modern and contemporary philosophy, the International Center for Philosophy, and the Center for Science and Thought at the University of Bonn for their thoughtful philosophical and editorial comments on earlier stages of the manuscript. Particular thanks to Philipp Bohlen, Charlotte Gauvry, Alex Englander, Delicia Kamins, Jérôme Schickschneit, Carla Franciska Spielmann, Jens Rometsch, Jan Voosholz, Victor Bruhn-Pedersen Weisbrod, and David Zapero. In this context, I am also grateful for written comments on the first complete draft of some of the chapters by Zed Adams, Zachary Hall, James T. Hill, and Anton Friedrich Koch.

The first draft of the manuscript was completed during a fellowship at The New Institute in Hamburg (2021–2022), which allowed me to write the bulk of the chapters. I am grateful to the institute for their generous support of my research.

Due to the COVID-19 pandemic, a fellowship at the Stanford Humanities Center had to be postponed until March 2022, which turned out to be the right moment, as I was writing the chapter on nonsense. Stanford's inspiring context in the humanities allowed me to appreciate the difference between nonsense and meaninglessness and to better understand what it takes to get non-propositional thinking into view without sacrificing methodological precision. I learned a lot from a workshop dedicated to future-oriented humanities (sponsored by The New Institute) in Stanford. Thanks to Andrea Capra, Amir Eshel, Roland Greene (also in his capacity as the director of the Stanford Humanities Center), Hans Ulrich

ACKNOWLEDGMENTS

Gumbrecht, Courtney Blair Hodrick, Robert Pogue Harrison, Paul Kottman, Teathloach Wal Nguot, and Laura Wittman.

The material on self-consciousness and subjectivity was first presented during my seminars and public lectures as Tang Chun-I Visiting Professor at the Chinese University of Hong Kong in spring 2021. Particular thanks are owed to Gregory Moss and Chong-Fuk Lau for discussion of various crucial points.

The final stage of revision after working through the helpful and productive peer reviews owes a lot to the careful work of Joseph Pomp, my editor at Harvard University Press, who offered very helpful advice in structuring the material.

As always, this book owes most to the support of my loved ones, Stefanie, Marisa, and Leona.

INDEX

aboutness, 18, 54, 82, 86, 138; literal meaning and, 129; semantic, 45

accountability, 2, 202, 205

Adams, Zed, 223n1

agnotology (theory of ignorance), 3, 4

analytic philosophy, 245n2, 245n5; of language, 44, 53; return of metaphysics in, 85

ancestrality, 230n61

Anderson, Michael, 173

animals, human, 8, 12, 27, 42, 223n13; complex agency of, 194; ethics and, 203; separation from non-human animals, 198–199; as social, self-determining agents, 200

animals, non-human, 38, 195, 213, 250n44, 265n84; kingdom of ends and, 205; as paradigmatic thinkers, 42; prosocial behavior in, 203; relation to content, 43; as thinkers without language, 48; thinking and, 37

Anscombe, Elizabeth, 78

answerability, 65, 77, 80, 225n16

anthropology, ethics and, 201–207

Aristotle, 2, 158, 167, 223n13; category theory, 74, 241n151; *Metaphysics,* 2, 91, 148; physics of, 79; on truth-apt thought, 228n36

artificial intelligence, 4, 159, 162

Atmanspacher, Harald, 48–49, 50, 51, 172

Austin, John L., 135

Baumgarten, Alexander Gottlieb, 99

being, 44, 112, 241n151; Heidegger's "Seyn" and, 124; knowability and, 39

Benoist, Jocelyn, 112, 226n19, 227n25, 229n45; on analytic philosophy of language, 44, 53; conception of realism, 45–46; on ontological nonsense, 122; on realism, 76, 230n56

Bergmann, Gustav, 233n90

Bergson, Henri, 99

Berkeley, George, 236n121

biology, 13, 122

brain, 108, 173, 187, 251n55

Brandom, Robert B., 39, 50

Brown, Jessica, 260n20

Buddha, the, 158

bullshit, 210, 211, 267n4

bundle theory of objects, 71

Burge, Tyler, 13, 40, 158

Bussemer, Thymian, 215

Campbell, John, 57

capitalism, 215–216

Carman, Taylor, 123–136, 254n81, 255n97

Carnap, Rudolf, 8, 84, 86, 113; language and, 128; on rational reconstruction, 259n7; sharp line drawn between sense and nonsense, 129

Cassam, Quassim, 57

category theory, 231n70

Cavell, Stanley, 235n107

273

INDEX

Chalmers, David, 108, 231n69, 241–242n157

ChatGPT, 210, 267n4

confusion. *See* field confusion

consciousness, 8, 19, 20, 40, 75, 131; amphibious, 54; analytic and synthetic unity of, 58; as both objective and subjective, 41; epistemic field confusion and, 94; false, 211, 212; historically varied meanings of, 106; "I" embodied as finite thinker, 34; as illusion, 110, 155, 171–175; integrated information theory of, 249n35; limits of physics and, 186–187; Lord Chandos problem, 38, 161–163, 165, 171, 193; nature and, 148; neural tissue and, 49; nonsense and, 98–112; objects as correlates of, 82; ontological depth and, 54; as psychological concept in narrow sense, 38; pure, 104, 105, 108; reality associated with, 85; reality imbued with, 13–14; sense and, 53–57; subjective idealism and, 96; subjectivity tied to, 42; as temporal unfolding of objects and processes, 99, 100, 249n41; as ultimate representational layer, 54. *See also* self-consciousness

contact picture, 29, 30

correlationism, 17, 127–128, 232n80, 255n97

Crick, Francis, 107

Daniel, Arnaut, 128–129

delusions, 1, 3, 90, 142, 153, 211; context of delusion, 216; of grandeur, 17; moral judgment and, 204; as obstacle to knowledge, 144; theoretical subjectivity and, 194

Derrida, Jacques, 135–136

Descartes, René, 144

descriptivism, ontological, 73–74, 117, 125, 128, 130

determinacy, 118, 263n54

dialectics, 38, 75, 98

dialetheism, 75, 83

difference, deontological, 77, 145

Dirac distributions, 46

Dreyfus, Hubert, 14, 29, 30

dualism: Cartesian, 188; fos-dualism, 188; metaphysical, 9, 22–29; mind and world, 124; MNCC and, 105; "psycho-logical," 33, 37; of subject and object, 86, 124

Du Bois-Reymond, Emil Heinrich, 186–187

economics, behavioral, 3, 142, 206

Edelman, Gerlad Maurice, 98

epistemic capacities approach, 167

epistemology, 2, 4, 24, 39, 63; basic rule of, 41; blind spot of, 3; Cartesian strand in, 172; detached from ontology, 76; disjunctivism, 151–152; epistemic authority, 60; fallibility and, 150; interface with ontology, 8, 38; negative epistemological phenomena, 153; Platonic, 6; social epistemology, 217

Eshel, Amir, 125

ethics, 84, 196, 201–207, 266n94

existence, 20, 65, 72, 119; defined by FOS, 67, 131; etymology of, 5; non-propositional dimension of, 126; of objective reality, 56; of sense, 49; of subjects, 39; unintelligibility and, 125. *See also* ontology

facticity, 12, 124, 125, 152, 192; argument from, 30; mathematics and, 121–122

facts, 2, 4, 9, 25, 82, 87, 225n16, 253n68; ancestral, 230n61; contrast of objectivity and, 31; denialism of, 3, 218; distance / deviation from, 176, 184; ethics grounded in, 196; false facts, 153, 155, 225n16; FOS and, 72, 80; ignorance and, 157; illusions and, 215; limits of knowledge and, 186, 187; linguistic meaning and, 129; mathematical, 32–33; metaphysics and, 86, 90, 256n99; mind-independent, 50; moral, 200, 201, 202, 203, 210; non-linguistic, 68; objective, 32; objects embedded in, 69–70, 71, 81, 130, 131; physical, 92; post-truth idea and, 216; practical subjectivity and, 194; propositional judgment and, 136; social, 194, 195, 197, 198, 200, 217; temporality and, 8; totality of, 21, 88, 227n24; true descriptions and, 123; without objects, 80–83

fake news, 3, 211, 212

274

INDEX

fallibilism, 7, 155–156, 260n20

fallibility, 8, 28, 31, 149–157, 171; fallible self-determination, 196–200; modal status of, 236–237n127; objective senses and, 42–43; as property of knowers, 182; sociality and, 208; subjectivity and objectivity intertwined in, 157; theory of subjectivity and, 169. *See also* wrong, being

false beliefs, 7, 141, 150

false thought, 59–60, 70, 172, 175

falsity, 3, 6, 143, 154; "absolute falsity," 138; bullshit discourse and, 211; distinguished from being wrong, 4; as not-truth, 4, 222n6

Ferraris, Maurizio, 76, 119, 122

Fichte, Johann Gottlieb, 112

Fichte paradigm, 159–160

fictionalism, 178–183

field confusion, 8, 86, 117, 218; epistemic, 94; first-order metaphysics as, 86–97; global, 103; local, 98, 100, 102; ontic, 94; as phenomenon of the in-between, 93

fields, 19, 36, 81; furnishing function for, 36; objects and, 43, 53, 68, 74, 123, 127; vector fields, 17. *See also* fos; FOS

Fields of Sense (Gabriel), 89, 117, 131, 133, 240n144, 255n97

Fine, Kit, 76, 230n49

fos (fields of sense), 21, 36, 43, 71–72, 127; all-encompassing, 98; defined, 18; fictionalism and, 183; fos-confusion, 188, 189; fos-dualism, 188; hypercomplexity of, 206; metaphysics and, 190; mind-independent, 19; neutral, 189; nonsense and, 103; objects as elements of, 93; ontological reductionism and, 94–95; part–whole relationship and, 240n146; physics and, 121; relations among objects in, 61; singular (monad), 72; world as absolute whole, 65

FOS (fields of sense), ontology of, 5, 11, 61, 74, 80–83, 224n8, 226n19; anti-physicalism and, 95; Carman's objections to, 123, 125; Eleatic view of reality, 130, 257n110; existence and, 67, 131; "field theory of meaning" and, 48–49, 51; first-order metaphysics and, 132; as form

of ontological pluralism, 191; functionally universal concepts of, 190; fundamental concepts of, 67–72; meta-physics and, 90; motivations of, 21; nonsense and, 114, 118, 119, 122, 133; ontological descriptivism and, 73–74; reality described by, 77, 78; reference in, 113; senses as furnishing functions, 101; subjectivity and, 246n7; totalities rejected by, 227n29; univocal use of "sense" in, 36; world as object rejected by, 30

Frankfurt, Harry, 211, 267n4

Frege, Gottlob, 5–6, 11, 12, 13, 20; on comprehensive knowledge of referents, 237n129; concept of sense, 35, 50–51; on decomposition of thoughts, 235n109; on definition of object, 236n124; on distinction between sense and reference, 115; dualism and, 228–229n42; "field theory of meaning" and, 51–52; Husserl's criticism of, 231n62; idealism and, 113; linguistic meaning and, 45; logical and mathematical thought as starting point, 80; paradox of self-consciousness and, 159; psychologism and, 33–34; realism of sense, 101; on representations (*Vorstellungen*), 13, 53, 63; role of senses in mathematical thought and, 33; on senses (*Sinne*), 25; telescope allegory of, 52; on thought as true or false objects, 44; on true and false referents, 239n138

Freud, Sigmund, 164, 165, 171, 262n45

fusion theory (fusion of thinking and being), 24, 25, 26, 29; infallibilism and, 112; refined, 27–28; weaknesses of, 31–32

Galvez, Marisa, 128

Gaskin, Richard, 225n16

Gert, Bernard, 201–202

good case scenarios, 147

Gopnik, Alison, 83

Gumbrecht, Hans Ulrich, 128

Habermas, Jürgen, 246n7

Hall, Zachary, 225n16, 233n89

hallucinations, 3, 108, 211; of content, 267n4; controlled, 99, 106, 107

INDEX

hard problems, 49, 108

Harman, Graham, 117, 119

Hegel, G. W. F., 23, 125, 167, 225n15, 228n33, 236n121; on opposite meanings of sense, 112–113; on truth and correctness, 81, 243n169

Heidegger, Martin, 22, 81, 82, 119, 133; Carman's neo-Heideggerian perspective, 123–124, 254n81; correlationism and, 255n97; critique of metaphysics, 124; *Dasein* concept, 127; poetic thinking and, 129; "Seyn," 124

Helmholtz, Hermann von, 107

Heraclitus, 176

hermeneutical realism, 222n10

heuristics, 7, 108

Hill, James, 132

Hoffman, Donald, 55–57, 107, 108, 109, 236n121

Hofmannsthal, Hugo von, 161

Hölderlin, Friedrich, 112

holy will, Kantian, 194, 265n79

humanities, 13, 21, 84, 151, 247n9

Hume, David, 235n107

Husserl, Edmund, 20, 33, 231n62, 231n67, 235n107; on nature of consciousness, 99; phenomenological realism and, 127; on statements about the world, 82, 243–244n173

idealism, subjective, 57, 96, 97

identity, 12, 74, 240n150

identity theories, 104, 109

ideology, 3, 196, 210; critical diagnoses of modern society and, 212; as false consciousness, 212–213; as inevitable feature of complex systems, 212; as social formation of practical negativity, 211

ignorabimus thesis, 187

ignorance, 1, 3, 170, 194, 196, 210, 217–218; critical diagnoses of modern society and, 212; as inevitable feature of complex systems, 212; as social formation of practical negativity, 211; theory of false thought and, 4

illusion, 3, 32, 170, 217; consciousness as, 8, 55–56, 171–175; semantic, 9

incoherence, 1, 4, 88, 125, 190

indeterminacy, 82, 92, 263n54

indexicality, 50, 232n71

infallibilism, 87, 104, 110; fusion theory of, 112; skepticism and, 252n61

infallibility, claims to, 60

inference traps, 113

information technology, 210

integrated information theory (IIT), 104

intelligibility, 3, 104, 126, 127; of FOS, 132; of nature, 88; of reality, 24, 77, 89

intentionality, perceptual, 61

Johnston, Mark, 24–25, 38, 225n15; dualistic metaphysics and, 26–27; in tradition of Frege, 28

judgment, 34, 76, 103, 110, 154; categorical, 68, 71; false, 3, 16, 85, 153; flawed, 138, 142, 143; mistakes and, 115; propositional, 136; true, 154, 155, 170–171; variables and, 119

justification, 1, 63, 166, 169, 207, 210, 218; ignorance and, 217; justificatory gap, 165–171; knowledge claims and, 2, 7, 149, 246n7; knowledge-first tradition and, 238n131; non-accidental, 2, 167; practical subjectivity and, 194; skepticism and, 8

Kahneman, Daniel, 142, 143, 164–165, 259n5

Kandel, Eric R., 164–165, 262n37

Kant, Immanuel, 10, 58, 194, 202, 235n107, 236n121; *Critique of Pure Reason,* 98, 219; on intuition (*Anschauung*), 99, 249n38; on nonsense as transcendental illusions, 112; on pure practical reason (the will), 206; synthetic unity of consciousness, 105, 168; on things in themselves, 107; transcendental dialectics of, 98

Kimhi, Irad, 24, 33, 229n42; logical I as syncategorematic expression, 79, 242n167; on "psycho-logicism," 33–34

knowledge, 2, 23, 41; absolute, 97; boundaries to, 223n1; epistemological difference with knowledge claims, 250n47; fallibilism about, 155–156; first-order, 145, 158; knowledge production, 4, 80; limits of, 40, 139; mediational theory of,

276

INDEX

29; objective, 7, 149, 156, 158, 209, 210, 212; objectivity of, 5; propositional, 2, 152, 225n13; scientific, 157; subjectivity and, 17; true belief and, 63, 167. *See also* self-knowledge

knowledge acquisition, 7, 60, 87, 121, 146, 182; justification and, 166; scientific, 40; successful, 4

knowledge claims, 1, 2, 9, 39, 66; answerability to reality, 72; conditions for success of, 64; epistemic capacities approach and, 167–168; evaluation of, 212; failed, 170; fallible, 3, 7, 16, 222n4; false thought and, 60; infallibilism and, 110, 147, 252n61; justification for, 7, 63, 238n131; in Plato's pigeon simile, 6; right and wrong, 3–4; subjectivity and, 4, 141, 194; successful, 7, 24, 217, 218

known unknowns, 230n60

Koch, Anton Friedrich, 222n10

Koch, Christof, 111

Lacan, Jacques, 117

language, 18, 19, 113, 182, 226n19, 261n27; analytic philosophy of, 44, 53; compared to a city, 135; evolution of natural languages, 47; fictionalism and, 180, 181; grammatical principles, 47, 234n97; nonsense and, 123; philosophy of, 45; realism about sense and, 192

Laplace's demon, 186

Leibniz, Gottfried Wilhelm, 99, 108, 236n121, 240n142, 240n150

Lewis, David, 91

linguistics, 54, 68

linguistic turn, 21, 45, 233n88, 233–234n90

Llull, Ramon, 99–100

logical space, 6, 34, 64

logics, 5, 68, 84, 89, 123; Aristotelian, 239n137; coherent forms of, 154; logical pluralism, 65, 238n134; nonsense and, 84; no-world-view and, 191

logos, 3, 82

Lord Chandos problem, 38, 161–163, 165, 171, 193

Luft, Eduardo, 231n70

Mach, Ernst, 164

materialism, 102, 232n80

mathematics, 33, 36, 42, 118; coordinate systems and, 95; FOS and, 231n70; incompleteness and independence theorems, 64; mathematical sense, 12, 13; paradox of self-reference in, 158; physical science and, 103; pure thinking in, 65, 192

McDowell, John, 23, 53, 147, 235n111

meaning, 22, 44, 71, 127, 214; of consciousness, 106, 108, 162, 163; denial of existence of, 50; factive meaning, 253n62; field theory of, 48–49, 51; linguistic, 43–53, 113, 129, 226n19, 233n89, 245n5; nonsense and, 84, 136; two-tiered ontology of, 51

measurement problem, 92

mediational theories, 29–30

Meillassoux, Quentin, 17, 127, 230n61

mereology, 20, 65, 176, 189, 194, 240n146

Merleau-Ponty, Maurice, 127

meta-physics, 78, 90–91, 182, 248n24

metaphysics, 8, 21, 75, 81, 112; analytic, 85, 245n2; dualist, 9, 22–29, 57, 77; extensionalistic, 132; as field confusion, 86–97; first-order, 91, 92, 94, 96, 97, 103, 132; higher-order (critical), 91, 92; "knee-jerk realism" and, 133; meaninglessness of, 84; meanings of, 90–91; monist, 30; as nonsense, 90; Sartrean, 124; as theory of absolutely everything, 91

Metaphysics (Aristotle), 2, 91, 148

mind, 23; animality / corporeality of, 199; as an interface, 37–43; as objective component of reality, 24; ontology of, 174; as part of nature, 20, 182; pre-linguistic, 48

mind, philosophy of, 8, 23, 40, 162, 223n1; Cartesian strand in, 172; epistemology and, 151; fusion theory and, 24; Lord Chandos problem and, 161, 163; metaphysical source of confusion in, 148; mind–brain correlation, 173; neurocentrism and, 110; paradox of self-reference in, 158–159; theory of nonsense and, 112

mind-dependence, 15, 17, 39, 40, 77; fos and, 19; ontological realism and, 54; self-identity of mind and, 169

mind-independence, 15, 19, 54, 77, 181, 264n61

INDEX

mind sciences, 38, 161, 173

minimal neural correlate of consciousness (MNCC), 104–106, 108

modes of presentation. *See* presentation, modes of

monads and monadology, 72, 240n12

monism, 34, 96, 252n60

Moore, Adrian W., 229n46

morality, 201–202

Moss, Gregory, 80, 83

Müller-Lyer illusion, 171

Nāgārjuna, 168

Nakajima, Takahiro, 196, 202

naturalism, 25

nature, 31, 46; ecological crisis and, 195; as the in-itself, 176; mind as part of, 20; *natura naturata* and *natura naturans,* 184, 190, 192–193; as non-mental reality, 174; philosophy of, 148; realism about sense and, 192; subjectivity and, 87, 174–193; the universe distinguished from, 177, 183–184, 185; unknowable fos of, 103

Neo-Aristotelians, 170

neo-existentialism, 123

neural patterns, 63

neurocentrism, 104, 108

neuroconstructivism, 106–108, 112

neuroscience, 8, 107, 161

New Realism, 5, 19, 43, 75, 76, 174; contact theory and, 29; epistemological thesis of, 89; mind-independence repudiated by, 53, 66; reference relationships and, 233n88; skepticism rejected by, 88; theory of subjectivity, 123, 217

Nietzsche, Friedrich, 107, 134, 164, 165, 167, 251n52

Noigandres group, 128

noise, 3, 76, 143; as flawed judgment, 138; as source of error, 142

nonsense, 21, 81; as field confusion, 102; global and local, 86, 112; as meaninglessness, 84, 85; overlap with sense, 178; poetry and, 128–129, 130

nonsense, ontological, 8, 83, 86, 112–123, 124, 152, 245n5; consciousness as, 187; objects as regress stoppers and, 93, 100,

116, 118, 126; as ontological signature of subject, 136–140; pre-ontological experience and, 132

no-world-view, 21, 67, 96, 227nn28–29, 240n144, 240n146; fusion and confusion in, 134; local incompleteness and, 125; metaphysical reading of FOS and, 131; metaphysics and, 191; nonsense and, 133; sense and, 73–75

objective sense, 11, 12, 26, 40; accessed through subjective sense, 25, 43; consciousness and, 41; fallibility and, 42–43; grasping of, 32, 33, 42; linguistic meaning and, 43–53; mathematical object and, 16; mind-independence and, 15; reality as whole of, 28; refined fusion theory and, 27; self-referential, 28; subjects and, 14. *See also* subject–object relation, interface of

objective thought, 18–19

objectivity, 14, 76, 80, 115, 151; contrast of, 18, 31, 39–40, 65; linguistic meaning and, 47; of mathematical and logical thought, 33; mind-independence and, 15, 39; psychologism and, 33

objects, 20, 53, 74, 115, 116; bundle theory of, 71; as correlates of consciousness, 82; embedded in facts, 68, 69, 70, 71; facts without objects, 80–83; field as domain of, 36; intentional, 96; mind-independent, 17, 19, 96; non-linguistic, 68; object–object relations, 17, 117; object-slot of thinking, 117, 118; ontological nonsense and, 126; perception of, 15–16; properties of, 10, 14, 53, 74; relations to other objects, 61; representation of, 99; spatiotemporal, 56

O'Brien, Lucy, 196, 197

On the Plurality of Worlds (Lewis), 91

ontology, 4, 65, 71; detached from epistemology, 76; dualist metaphysics and, 22; flat, 26, 28; interface with epistemology, 8, 38; metaphysical, 74; ontological blurriness, 81, 82; ontological descriptivism, 73–74, 117, 125, 130; ontological pluralism, 5, 21, 119, 121, 191; ontological properties, 74; ontological relativity, 121–122, 131; Platonic, 6; plural realism and, 30;

278

INDEX

radical ontological pluralism, 66, 75; realist, 8; sense in ontological order, 17; theorem of the functional ontological difference, 103; transcendental, 77, 91
ontology of fields of sense. *See* FOS
Origins of Objectivity (Burge), 13

panpsychism, 13–14
Parfit, Derek, 265n88
Parmenides, 236n121
part–whole relationship, 240n146
perception, 10, 13, 14, 15, 32, 40, 106; complex physical systems and, 41; consciousness and, 162; dichotomy with cognition, 65; interface theory of, 56, 236n121; perceptual experience, 61
Pessoa, Fernando, 256n100
phenomenology, 30, 61, 81, 82, 227n29
philology, 90
philosophy, 1, 38, 94, 145
philosophy of mind. *See* mind, philosophy of
physicalism, 88, 93, 95, 96, 177, 185, 263n54
physics, 17, 36, 78–79, 103; arrow of time in, 257n109; complex numbers and, 179–180; concept of field in, 127; mathematical, 92, 95, 177, 178; mind-independent reality and, 181; nature and, 177, 188; ontological nonsense and, 120, 121
Pinker, Steven, 102–103
placement problem, 20
Plato, 2, 3, 6, 144, 158, 167, 236n121; on absolute being, 238n130; distinction between name and predicate, 239n137; history of the copula and, 239n139; knowledge understood by, 166; *Sophist,* 3, 144; *Theaetetus,* 6, 144, 166; on true belief and knowledge, 63
Platonism, 63
Plotinus, 158
poetry, 128–129, 130, 134
point of view, 223n1, 229n46
polyads, 72
Popper, Karl, 221n4
Porphyry, 241n151
postmodern theory, 75, 136, 233n88
Pound, Ezra, 128
predicates, 46, 68, 239n137, 239n139

presentation, modes of, 35, 41, 116, 158; linguistic, 55; logico-mathematical, 55; subjective, 42; visual, 55
Price, Huw, 257n109
Priest, Graham, 72, 240n146
propaganda, 3, 48, 196, 210, 214–217; critical diagnoses of modern society and, 212; as inevitable feature of complex systems, 212; practical subjectivity and, 148; as social formation of practical negativity, 211; value judgment and, 47, 212
proper names, 44, 52, 237n129, 255n98; decomposition of propositions and, 51; descriptive content and, 128; predicates and, 46, 68
properties, 46, 49, 59; non-determining, 74; of objects, 10, 14, 53, 61, 74; ontological, 74; of propositions, 4; realism about sense and, 11
propositions, 8, 44, 54, 71; decomposition of, 51, 58; propositional thinking, 8, 102; truth and falsity as properties of, 4; unity and disunity of, 153
psychoanalysis, 157, 173
psychologism, 33–34, 62
psychology, 8, 102, 235n107
public sphere, 3, 217; fallibility and, 216; ideology and, 211; transformed by science and engineering, 209
Putnam, Hilary, 15, 50, 224n12
Pythagoras, 236n121

qualia debate, 186
quantum mechanics, 79, 91, 92, 242n164, 263n54
Quine, Willard V. O., 129, 242n167, 256–257n103

Ramsey, Frank, 131
randomness, 92
rational reconstruction, 145, 259n7
realism, 31, 54, 125, 230n56; ancestrality and, 230n61; "conscious realism" of Hoffman, 56, 57; epistemological thesis of, 31; fictionalism as form of, 178–183; naive, 76, 77; neutral, 230n49; ontological thesis of, 31; plural, 30; reality and, 76; in social ontology, 208

INDEX

reality, 11, 31, 66; basic reality, 181, 263n60; confusing quality of, 114, 117; consciousness associated with, 85; as field-like, 36; fos and, 43; hypercomplexity of, 218; intentional, 45; knowability of, 31, 88, 225n15; language and, 44; mathematical structure of, 93; mind-independent, 19, 39, 50, 94, 135, 138, 143, 151; non-linguistic, 45, 46, 48, 69; no-world-view and, 75–80; obscured by consciousness, 55; ontological nonsense and, 87, 122; partially hidden from perceptual system, 121; presentation of, 12; propositional thought and, 83, 136; representation of, 10, 68; self-disclosure and, 28; sense in constitution of, 5, 25; senseless parts of, 20; singular (unified), 80, 241–242n157; temporal unfolding of, 140; as thickness of being, 226n19; thought and, 19; as whole of objective senses, 28; as world "out there," 75

reality, objective, 57; mind as interface and, 37, 38; objectivity of thought and, 53; perception and, 55; spatiotemporality and, 56; subjective representation and, 61

redshifts, 42

reference, 22, 44, 51, 136, 243n173; brute, 128; language and, 53; nonsense and, 189; object as reference point, 116, 129; points of view and, 229n46; postmodern critique of, 233n88; reference-dependence, 39, 232n79; reference magnet, 59; role in FOS, 113; self-reference, 9, 48, 158; sense detached from, 135; sense–reference distinction, 45, 55, 61, 109, 113, 115, 237n129

reference relation, 49, 51, 52

regress problems, 49

relativity, ontological, 121–122, 131

representation, modes of, 25, 68, 79, 229n46

representations (*Vorstellungen*), Fregean, 13, 53, 63

Retrieving Realism (Dreyfus and Taylor), 14

Rickles, Dean, 48–49, 50, 51

Rorty, Richard, 76, 136, 233n90

Rosenberg, Alexander, 245–246n9

Russell, Bertrand, 153

Ryle, Gilbert, 84, 113

Sartre, Jean-Paul, 127

scalars, 67

Scanlon, Thomas M., 266n94

Schelling, Friedrich Wilhelm Joseph, 112

Schopenhauer, Arthur, 107, 133, 251n55, 258n120

Schrödinger, Erwin, 242n164

Schrödinger equation, 71

science, 2, 84, 164, 195; cognitive, 102, 142; deep methodology of, 182; fictionalism and, 183; natural sciences, 90, 120, 176, 246n9; scientific method, 95

Searle, John R., 135, 255n98

self-consciousness, 8, 9, 32, 34, 96; false consciousness as failure in, 212; field confusions and, 101; infallible, 111–112; ordinary, 196; paradox of, 157–165; as pure subjectivity, 112; as self- determination, 197–198

self-knowledge, 11, 32, 139, 144, 145; scientific, 164; skepticism and, 151, 260n18; subjectivity and, 156

semantics, 45, 81–82, 159

sense: consciousness and, 53–57, 101; in constitution of reality, 5; no-world-view and, 73–75; objective and subjective, 29–37; objective realm of, 28; as ontological concept, 68, 123; overlap with nonsense, 178; as part of nature, 190; reference and, 55, 115; restriction of, 66–67; sense–reference distinction, 109; unified realm of, 21

sense, realism about, 8, 11, 14, 16, 115, 228n36; Cartesian split and, 50; flat ontology and, 28; FOS and, 21; idealism and, 112; language and, 192; nonsense and, 87; radical ontological pluralism and, 75; senseless parts of reality and, 20; subjective idealism as, 236n121

sense, realm of, 11, 13, 24, 25, 48, 58, 79; accessing of, 27; coherence of, 28; difficulty of conceptualizing, 64; dualism and, 22; knowledge claims and, 66; language and, 45; nature as part of, 20; no-world-view and, 67; objective, 47; ontological nonsense and, 75, 128; propositional thought and, 80; singular fos

INDEX

and, 72; subjective–objective interface and, 43; subjectivity and, 175; subject's position in, 26; thinker's thinking and, 63; unified, 21

"Sense and Reference" (Frege), 239n138

sense-dependence, 39, 50, 232n79

sense modality, 11–12

senses, 10–11; connection of subjective and objective, 37, 40; consciousness and, 22; as furnishing functions, 101; Husserl's conception of, 20; natural-scientific, 18; as part of reality, 18, 226n19; propositional, 81; reality of, 17; totality of, 28

senses, as modes of presentation, 10, 12, 18, 43, 189; Frege and, 11, 15, 56; Husserl and, 56; mind's accessing of, 25, 27; misleading appearance of, 14; non-conscious, 13; realism about sense and, 25; subject and object of reference relation and, 49

Seth, Anil, 98–99

set theory, 65

Severino, Emmanuele, 245n4

Sextus Empiricus, 168

skepticism, 7, 8, 88, 219, 250n47; return of, 76–77; self-knowledge and, 151, 260n18

social media, 3, 210, 216

spatiotemporality (space-time), 21, 91; laws of nature and, 87; objective reality and, 56; reality of senses and, 17; structures of observable universe and, 55; unfolding of consciousness in, 106

Speculative Realism, 232n80

Spielmann, Carla Franciska, 224n8

Spinoza, Baruch, 91, 115

Stanley, Jason, 211

subjective senses, 11, 12, 33; consciousness and, 42; defined, 11, 29; as distorting presence in reality, 40; indexicality and, 232n71; notion of objective realm of sense and, 28. *See also* subject–object relation, interface of

subjectivity, 6, 13, 17, 27, 32, 141; absolute, 146; animality and, 223n13; as distorting presence in reality, 48; embedded in realm of sense, 47; fallibilism and infallibilism in relation to, 157; fallibility and, 148–175; integration into non-mental

reality, 174; linguistically grounded, 123; nature and, 174–193; nonsense and, 85, 86, 218; objectivity achieved on basis of, 35; paradox of self-consciousness and, 158; as part of reality, 77; practical, 148, 194–200, 201, 202, 204; public sphere and, 216; social networks and, 200; subjectivity assumption, 6, 10, 149, 165, 174, 194; thinking and, 64; totality and, 134

subjectivity, theory of, 11, 19, 148, 149, 155; epistemology and, 165; fallibilistic, 7; false thought and, 4; norm of truth and, 201; as site of confusion, 9; subject's position in realm of sense, 26

subject–object relation, interface of, 15, 17, 29, 38, 224–225n12; as reciprocal sense-dependence, 50; scientific evidence and, 42

subjects, 15, 20; Heidegger's *Dasein* concept, 127; as legitimate part of reality, 16; mental life of, 63; nonsense as ontological signature of, 136–140; non-subjective environment of, 37; position in realm of sense, 26; sense modalities as part of, 32

Tarskian tradition, 154

Taylor, Charles, 14, 29, 30

temporality (time), 26, 85, 91, 245n4; entropy and arrow of time, 257n109; ontological time, 130; philosophy of time, 230n49; reality and, 140

Theaetetus (Plato), 6, 144, 166

thinkables, 27, 36, 64

thought, 12; being and, 2, 19, 23; concepts of thinking, 62; decomposition of, 58–59, 235n109; embodied thinker and, 12, 32, 36, 42; fact and action in relation to, 147; false, 1, 3, 4, 5, 6, 16; grasping of, 37; non-linguistic, 21; non-propositional, 81; objective, 18, 19; objectivity of, 6; propositional, 136; subjective, 13, 16; thinking and thinkers, 57–66; thinking as sense modality, 37, 49; thinking itself, 19; true and false objects designated by, 44

Tononi, Giulio, 98

topic-neutrality, 191, 193

totalities, 227n29

INDEX

Tractatus Logico-Philosophicus (Wittgenstein), 68, 85, 91, 136, 137
transcendental worry, 70
transparency conjecture, 164
Travis, Charles, 77, 122, 252–253n62
true thoughts, 16, 60, 139, 172, 237n127; facts and, 144; mistakes and, 175; Plato's pigeon simile and, 15; sharing of knowledge and, 147; thinker as knower and, 63
truth, 1, 4, 45, 80, 183, 210; bullshit discourse and, 211; correctness distinguished from, 81, 83, 243n169; fact as, 154; metatruths, 81; non-propositional, 82; objectivity and, 222n10; post-truth, 196, 216; propositional, 4, 59, 81, 113; theoretical subjectivity and, 201; truth-apt thought and discourse, 88, 128, 228n36
truth values, 51, 69, 239n138, 253n62; propositional, 59; thoughts as proper names of, 44

uncertainty principle, 92
understanding, 49, 50, 60
unintelligibility, 125, 131
universe, as material-energetic system, 90
unknowns, 40, 224n5, 230n60
unobservables, 46

Vaihinger, Hans, 179
van der Schaar, Maria, 228n42
van Inwagen, Peter, 245n2
vector fields, 17, 67
veridicality, 14, 47
Vienna Circle, 84
visual perspectives, literal, 43, 47
Voosholz, Jan, 229n45

Wigner, Eugen, 103
William IX, Count of Poitiers and Duke of Aquitaine, 129
Williamson, Timothy, 238n131
Wittgenstein, Ludwig, 8, 68, 78, 122, 124; language and, 113–114, 128, 135; nonsense research and, 84; poetic thinking and, 129; propositions of, 137; on subjectivity, 136–137
Wolf, Susan, 194
world, the, 15, 23, 31, 39, 44, 145; as absolute whole, 66; as aesthetic phenomenon, 134; as all-encompassing field, 91; conscious realism and, 56; existence of, 73, 82, 83, 132; field confusions and, 90; mind excluded from, 53; non-existence as a whole, 75; as an object, 30; point of view and, 229n46; reality as, 17, 20; subject's "life-world," 227n29; as totality in propositional terms, 137
Wright, Crispin, 31, 227n24
wrong, being, 1, 9, 114, 115, 143; agnotology (theory of ignorance) and, 4; change and temporality associated with, 85; consciousness and, 8, 42; distance from reality and, 175; ethics and, 205, 206–207; finite quality of knowledge and, 139; FOS and, 5; impossibility of absolute falsity, 138; manifold modes of, 3, 32, 209, 217; modes of, 142; nonsense and, 88, 136; practical negativity and, 209; subjectivity assumption and, 6; subjectivity tied to, 141. *See also* fallibility

Zeno, paradoxes of, 160